Human Rights in Latin America

Pennsylvania Studies in Human Rights
Bert B. Lockwood, Jr., Series Editor
A complete list of books in the series is available from the publisher.

Human Rights in Latin America

A Politics of Terror and Hope

Sonia Cardenas

PENN

University of Pennsylvania Press
Philadelphia

Published by
University of Pennsylvania Press
Philadelphia, Pennsylvania 19104-4112

Printed in the United States of America on acid-free paper
10   9   8   7   6   5   4   3   2   1

Library of Congress Cataloging-in-Publication Data
Cardenas, Sonia.
Human rights in Latin America: a politics of terror and hope / Sonia Cardenas.
p.   cm. — (Pennsylvania studies in human rights)
Includes bibliographical references and index.
ISBN 978-0-8122-4197-6 (alk. paper)
1. Human rights—Latin America. 2. Political persecution—Latin America.
3. Government accoutability—Latin America. I. Title.
JC599.L3C368   2009
323.098—dc22   2009008427

For Andy and our children,
Alex and Samantha

Contents

Preface   ix

Introduction: Terror and Hope   1

PART I. VIOLATING RIGHTS

Chapter 1: A Regional Survey   21

Chapter 2: Explaining Violations   52

PART II. PROMOTING REFORM

Chapter 3: Global Governance   83

Chapter 4: Transnational Networks   102

Chapter 5: Human Rights Change   132

PART III. SECURING JUSTICE

Chapter 6: Accountability Versus Impunity   159

Chapter 7: Never Again?   187

Appendix 1: American Convention on Human Rights, Part I   209

Appendix 2: Human Rights Treaties: Regional Ratifiers   223

Appendix 3: Human Development Indicators   227

Appendix 4: Select Internship Opportunities   231

Appendix 5: Suggested Assignments for Instructors   235

Index   239

Preface

This project was entirely unforeseen. I had finished my first book, which included lengthy case studies of human rights in Chile and Argentina. That was a long and sinuous affair, with its origins in a dissertation begun over a decade earlier. With that behind me, I had no immediate plans to pursue another project on Latin America. It was nothing about the region per se. It was just that my research on human rights was much more global in scope.

Despite my broad interests, I regularly teach a course titled The Politics of Human Rights in Latin America. That too is an accident. Weeks after accepting a new position, I was in India conducting human rights research, when I received an urgent message from my soon-to-be department chair: they needed me to teach a human rights course on Latin America. Caught off guard, I raced against a flickering Internet connection and reluctantly agreed to teach the course.

Like the writing of this book, the course turned out to be immensely rewarding. I worked to capture the things that had originally moved and excited me about the subject—troubled me into the late hours of the night. My technique in the classroom was to combine political science insights with images and stories of human rights in Latin America. Rather than lecture from afar, I sat with the students in a circle. The students, numbering about twenty, were noticeably responsive; and, I confess, the process energized me more than I might have imagined.

One challenge I had was in assigning readings, especially when I first taught the course in 2002. Regularly assembling a thick course reader, I wished someone would write a general text, one appealing to introductory human rights courses as well as regional surveys. Before long, I decided to write the book myself. *Human Rights in Latin America* follows my course outline, which served as a launching pad for the project, and draws on my own research as well as that of countless others. Fortunately, an increasing number of specialized books and films address many of the issues raised here, complementing the text; they are mentioned at the end of each chapter, and their creators have my gratitude for inspiring solidarity and setting high standards.

Tied so closely to my course, *Human Rights in Latin America* inevitably reflects my experiences with students. Their reactions, questions, and confusion have contributed fundamentally to this book. While there are too many students to thank individually, almost all of them—through their engagement or skepticism or even boredom and hostility—challenged me to sharpen my thinking and writing. Two additional students, Emily Costello and Danielle Harsip, served as my research assistants while I wrote the first draft of the book. Their enthusiasm was infectious, and I tried to keep them in mind as an important audience for the book as I struggled to set the right tone.

Most books depend on broader institutional support, and this one is no exception. The editorial team at the University of Pennsylvania Press were outstanding, and the book is better as a result of their intervention. I am especially indebted to my editor, Peter Agree, who encouraged me to pursue the project and is always a pleasure to work with. The anonymous reviewers made excellent suggestions, forcing me to be both comprehensive and accessible; and I am very grateful for their insights. Thanks are also due of course to Bert Lockwood, the series editor. While Getty Images and the United Nations permitted me to use their photographs, a generous grant from the Dean of Faculty's office at Trinity College proved invaluable for completing the project on schedule and as I had envisioned it; I am very appreciative.

In my first book, I used the full names of the victims of abuse when possible. Too often, however, I treated them as mere numbers and tragic factors in my analysis, perhaps understandable for a social scientist trying to make sense of human rights. As their stories have remained with me, I tried to give them a fuller voice in this venue. That said, one of my goals in the book is to demonstrate that human rights can be studied systematically, as a complex set of issues, *and* from a perspective that takes narratives of suffering and courage seriously.

My own beacons of hope—Alexander and Samantha—have infused this book with a sense of urgency. Watching them grow rapidly in a world where terror abounds for so many, I wanted to record for them a message of hope (tinged with realism). This meant I had to work at record speed, sometimes watching an energetic toddler and a new infant out of the corner of my eye. My parents stepped in at crucial moments, for which I am thankful. As always, Andy kept me grounded, with his singular steadfastness and humor, encouraging me to pursue yet another project while reminding me of the few things in life that really matter.

Introduction: Terror and Hope

In October 1992, when I was 19 years old, I was kidnapped at the entrance to La Cantuta University. . . . When I was completely naked, they gave me an injection in the left arm. I felt dizzy but despite that, I could feel the terrible pain. They did the same thing the next day. I would have rather died than that. They weren't human beings.

—Testimony of Magdalena Montesa to Peru's Truth and Reconciliation Commission; pardoned in 1998 after spending six years in prison, falsely accused of terrorism

Fernando, my brother, used to discuss a lot with me. In the tough times, he did not want to leave. . . . Fernando felt happy there, with his political activity in his neighborhood and psychology and political theory studies. He spoke softly, unlike me. . . . My mother dedicated most of her life to looking for him. She still wears the white handkerchief with his name. In the intimate moments of life at home, a disappearance acquires its real meaning. There is an empty chair, with no clear explanation.

—Marcelo Brodsky, commenting on his brother's disappearance in Argentina in 1979

Survivors of torture and captivity often describe their experience as a seemingly impossible mix of terror and hope: agonizing fear and pain, combined with an ardent wish for a better day. Studying human rights issues also entails an uncomfortable blend of terror and hope: terror at witnessing the betrayal of other human beings, a restrained hope for greater justice. As observers, we can be simultaneously drawn to and repelled by human rights accounts. Stories of terror expose the darkest side of humanity while evoking empathy for the victims; given a different set of conditions, any one of us could fall prey to human rights abuse. Stories of hope inspire confidence in the ability of human beings to overcome horrific obstacles, even as we wonder whether we could muster similar courage in comparably terrifying circumstances.

Latin America is fertile ground for exploring the twin themes of terror and hope that underlie the study of human rights. Four factors, in particular, make the region a productive arena for studying human rights issues: an inordinately high level of abuse, powerful human rights organizations, impressive efforts to promote truth and accountability, and a checkered history with the United States.

- In the span of only a few decades, the region experienced an enormous share of egregious abuses and terror. These have led to hundreds of thousands of deaths; clandestine detention centers, where people of all ages and walks of life have been tortured; and the disappearance of countless individuals, some of whose bodies have never been found.

- During the same period, the region has also seen the formation of thousands of vibrant and courageous human rights organizations, whose members have dared to protest even during the height of repression. Today, activists and nonactivists alike continue to fight against impunity, or the idea that those who commit human rights abuses will not be punished. To this end, some of the first systematic attempts in the world to pursue truth and justice for past human rights abuses have taken place in the region.

- Truth commissions and human rights trials have been facilitated in part by the Inter-American human rights system, the developing world's most extensive regional system of institutions to promote human rights. A network of treaties, a body of experts who investigate and monitor abuse, and a regional court all offer forums for human rights victims and their advocates. While imperfect, the region's human rights mechanisms are setting important precedents around the world.

- Finally, no discussion of Latin America can ignore the region's geographic position. As a southern neighbor of the United States, the region has always served as an important testing ground for human rights considerations in U.S. foreign policy. And whether one is critical or supportive of U.S. policies, the role of this powerful country has to be factored into most discussions of human rights in world affairs.

We will grapple with all these issues in this book, which joins a broad range of research and testimony to understand three central concerns: *the origins of abuse, the sources of reform*, and *the challenge of accountability*. These issues together reveal the human rights story in Latin America and the political themes running through it. Our goal is to fuse real-world issues with political analysis to understand why human rights conditions vary so widely, serving both to terrorize and to liberate people.

What Is at Stake?

Human rights violations and impunity are an ongoing reality in Latin America. A recent annual report by Amnesty International observed that "Respect for human rights remained an illusion for many as governments across the Americas failed to comply with their commitments to uphold fundamental human rights."[1] Amnesty International documents that at the outset of the twenty-first century, torture, disappearances, extrajudicial executions, and ill treatment persist throughout the region, alongside systematic violence against women; attacks on human rights defenders; and an endemic poverty that disproportionately harms society's most vulnerable members, including children and indigenous groups. Even if the "geography" of political violence has shifted over time or the overall magnitude of abuse has declined in recent decades, as subsequent chapters show, oppression still is a way of life for many of the region's people. Despite the progress associated with truth commissions and legal trials, the vast majority of human rights violators continue to walk the streets of Latin America, often in close proximity to their victims.

This book takes these human rights violations as its point of departure. These abuses are more than historically significant or intellectually interesting. The ongoing pervasiveness of some rights violations makes them a pressing matter: at stake are the lives and welfare of individual human beings who are confronted daily by systems of oppression and perpetrators of abuse. Perhaps this is why the subject of human rights continues to evoke such intense controversies, as different groups struggle to define the limits of acceptability for past and present behavior. From a policy perspective, moreover, devising effective human rights strategies—whether by governments, international organizations, or activist groups—may require a more accurate assessment of the roots of abuse. Without knowing why violations occur, stopping or preventing them can prove elusive. Taking human rights violations seriously also requires listening carefully to the voices of victims, some of which are presented in these pages. When these voices are silenced, it is all too tempting to overlook key questions, or to forget what really is at stake.

Human rights norms are defined in this book as *standards for how to treat human beings*. This is a deliberately minimalist, simple definition. Since human rights are standards, or rules about the way things *should* be, they exist even when they are not protected. In other words, having a right is not the same thing as enjoying a right. An analogy from domestic law illustrates this fundamental claim. The law stipulates that people should stop at red lights; everyone has a right not to be hit and injured by people who run red lights. Just because people do not always obey this standard does not mean that it does not exist. Likewise, I have a right not to be tortured. If I am tortured, my right is being violated; but it does not change the fact that I still have this right. Consequently, others can act on my behalf to assure that my right not to be tortured is protected.

Human rights are also *entitlements*, or things that any human being can hypothetically claim simply by virtue of being alive. When different human rights come into conflict with one another, an international legal consensus exists as to which rights should never be suspended; these protect individuals from slavery, torture, and extrajudicial executions. From a broader philosophical perspective, some experts claim that the most important human rights are those needed to assure a life of basic human decency, including rights to subsistence (i.e., basic food, shelter, health care) and physical security.[2]

For specifics about which standards constitute human rights, the principal international human rights documents can be consulted. Three of these documents, in particular, are at the core of global standards: the 1948 Universal Declaration of Human Rights (UDHR), the International Covenant on Civil and Political Rights, and the International Covenant on Economic, Social, and Cultural Rights. Together, these three accords comprise the International Bill of Human Rights. All other human rights treaties, whether international or regional, are more or less offshoots and elaborations of the standards enshrined in the UDHR (Table 1) and the two international human rights covenants.

Table 1.
Standards in the Universal Declaration of Human Rights (1948)

Everyone is entitled to all the rights and freedoms set forth in this Declaration, without distinction of any kind, such as race, colour, sex, language, religion, political or other opinion, national or social origin, property, birth or other status (Article 2)

Right to life, liberty, and security of person	Right to education
Freedom from slavery or servitude	Right to a nationality
Freedom from torture or cruel, inhuman, and degrading treatment or punishment	Right to marry and found a family
Right to be recognized before the law	Right to own property
Freedom from arbitrary arrest, detention, or exile	Freedom of thought, conscience, and religion
Right to a fair and public hearing by an independent and impartial tribunal	Freedom of opinion and expression
Right to be presumed innocent until proved guilty	Freedom of peaceful assembly and association
Freedom from ex post facto punishments	Right to participate in government, including in periodic and genuinely free elections
Freedom from arbitrary interference with privacy, family, home, or correspondence and from attacks on one's honor or reputation	Right to social security . . . "indispensable for . . . dignity"
Freedom of movement	Right to work; equal pay for equal work; just renumeration; and right to form and join trade unions
Right to seek and enjoy asylum from political persecution	Right to participate freely in the cultural life of the community; protection of intellectual property
Right to a standard of living adequate for health and well-being	

Nothing in this Declaration may be interpreted as implying for any State, group or person any right to engage in any activity or to perform any act aimed at the destruction of any of the rights and freedoms set forth herein (Article 30)

What is at stake in studying human rights in Latin America, therefore, are the rights enumerated in the major human rights documents, including the American Convention on Human Rights (1969). Approaching these standards critically requires confronting competing visions of how human beings should be treated. Are some people in some circumstances not subject to all of the rights enumerated in the Universal Declaration of Human Rights? If so, who gets to determine the exceptions, and according to what criteria? Alternatively, are *all* human beings entitled to certain rights, and if so, which ones? These are some of the difficult questions that any student of human rights must tackle.

Latin America and the Evolution of International Human Rights Norms

Contemporary observers tend to equate the story of human rights in Latin America with the region's relatively recent authoritarian past. The subject immediately evokes images of military coups, disappearances, death squads, and bloody civil wars. Accordingly, Latin America's relationship vis-à-vis international human rights norms is depicted as a one-way street; human rights norms are treated as external to the region, significant only insofar as governments comply with them or not. While this characterization is understandable, rooted in the region's recent violent history, it remains vastly incomplete and misleading.

Latin America has contributed uniquely to the evolution of international human rights norms. These influences may not be widely known, but their legacy is nonetheless fundamental. Three historical developments deserve particular consideration: (1) philosophically, current notions of human equality and the rights of indigenous people are rooted in Bartolomé de las Casas's influence during the sixteenth century; (2) institutionally, national constitutions across the region, beginning with Mexico's revolutionary 1917 constitution, catapulted economic and social rights onto the world stage; and (3) politically, Latin Americans played a crucial role in developments of the 1940s, helping to place human rights norms on the global agenda and to craft key international legal documents.

Bartolomé de las Casas

A Spanish friar during the sixteenth-century conquest of the Americas, Bartolomé de las Casas left an indelible imprint on contemporary notions of human rights. Las Casas is interesting partly because he was not always and fully committed to human equality. A participant in the Conquest, he experienced firsthand the slaughter, enslavement, and mistreatment of indigenous groups. This led him to advocate vigorously, impressively ahead of his time, for the equal treatment of indigenous groups. In a sense, he was the region's first human rights advocate, writing extensively about the plight of the Indians. Remarkably, he deemed Indians equal to other human beings, drawing on their capacity to reason. He traveled the region widely, despite the physical impediments and dangers of the period, spreading his message. And he argued passionately before the royal court in Spain for the liberation of all Indians, a step that he put into practice by freeing his own servants.

Las Casas's positions vis-à-vis human rights, however, were imperfect and inconsistent, which has made him somewhat controversial today. For example, the Spanish cleric's opposition to slavery did not extend initially

---

UP CLOSE: BARTOLOMÉ DE LAS CASAS, SIXTEENTH-CENTURY ADVOCATE

". . . the entire human race is one; all men are alike with respect to their creation and the things of nature, and none is born already taught. And so we all have the need, from the beginning, to be guided and helped by those who have been born earlier" (*Apologetic History*, Chapter 48)

". . . by what right or justice do you hold these Indians in such cruel and horrible servitude? On what authority have you waged such detestable wars against these peoples, who dwelt quietly and peacefully on their own land? Wars in which you have destroyed such infinite numbers of them by homicides and slaughters never before heard of? Why do you keep them so oppressed and exhausted, without giving them enough to eat or curing them of the sicknesses they incur from the excessive labor you give them, and they die, or rather, you kill them, in order to extract and acquire gold every day?" (*History of the Indies*, Book III)

Source: For a basic selection of Bartolomé de las Casas's writings, see *Witness: Writings of Bartolomé de las Casas*, ed. George Sanderlin (Maryknoll, N.Y.: Orbis, 1992).

to Africans, a position he adjusted only in his old age. Nor did he oppose the use of repression, including torture, against heretics in Spain.

Despite these serious problems, Las Casas's writings and work were critical in advancing notions of human equality, as applied to the Indians in Spanish America. Scholars recently have observed, therefore, that while he cannot fairly be credited with developing the idea of *human* rights per se (that is, rights held by individuals), Las Casas was one of the first people in history to advance the idea of *group* rights.[3] He was also the first archbishop of Chiapas, the predominantly indigenous region in southern Mexico that has attracted global attention in recent decades with the massacre of peasants and the rise of the Zapatista movement, which we will revisit later. The leading human rights organization in the heart of Chiapas, a way station for activists from around the world, still carries the sixteenth-century advocate's name: Fray Bartolomé de las Casas Center for Human Rights.

Pathbreaking National Constitutions

The region has also been essential in elevating the profile of economic and social rights, especially through its national constitutions. As independence came to most countries of the region in the nineteenth century, newly formed postcolonial governments turned to European Enlightenment thinking, the French Declaration on the Rights of Man and Citizen, and to a relatively lesser degree the U.S. constitutional model of rights.[4] Most of the region's constitutions therefore incorporated notions of individual rights and liberties apart from the state (following its northern neighbor) alongside an emphasis on equality and citizen duties (borrowing from continental Europe). Simón Bolívar, the talented Venezuelan general who helped liberate five South American countries and draft some of the region's constitutions, embodied this hybrid constitutional approach to rights: he upheld rights to liberty, equality, and private property; condemned slavery as a "shameless violation of human dignity"; and promoted active government involvement in securing rights.[5] This model shaped constitution after constitution in the region for over a century.

Whereas Latin American countries during the first century of independence incorporated civil rights and duties drawn from various constitutional traditions, in the beginning of the twentieth century the region broke new ground by promoting economic and social rights. The introduction of economic and social rights into Mexico's revolutionary constitution of 1917 (still in effect today) was a watershed for constitutional development around the world. For the first time, labor rights and fair working conditions were emphasized in a national constitution, setting the stage for including them in new constitutions throughout the region and beyond. While the Mexican constitution also called for the expropriation and redistribution of property—quintessentially socialist concepts—its contribution to human rights standards should not be ignored. By incorporating economic and social rights alongside civil and political rights, Latin American constitutions played a key role in legitimating *both* sets of rights.

The region's national constitutions were therefore pathbreaking. Following in the tradition of Bartolomé de las Casas and indigenous influences, they acknowledged the importance of group rights beyond individual rights. The region's early constitutions were also innovative in fusing notions of rights *and* duties, which in turn influenced constitutions across the developing world. Likewise, the Mexican constitution built on these developments to highlight the role of previously overlooked economic and social rights that numerous countries in and out of the region then incorporated into their own constitutions. Just as Latin America's early constitutions imported and combined foreign constitutional insights, they also played a crucial role in advancing new human rights ideas: the importance of groups like minorities and indigenous people; the complementary nature of rights and duties; and the fundamental significance of economic and social rights, beyond traditional civil and political rights.

Between Bartolomé de las Casas and the emergence of national constitutions, there were three centuries of colonial rule. What happened of relevance during this period, between the conquest of the Americas in the 1500s and independence in the 1800s? This period of colonialism did not make a positive impact on the evolution of international human rights norms. Rather, in the human rights story, colonialism is more closely tied to a long trail of abuse throughout the region (Chapter 1). While human rights violations in the second half of the twentieth century could trace their historical roots to colonialism, they would ironically be challenged by a set of internationally recognized norms that Latin Americans themselves helped draft after World War II.

Leadership at the United Nations

The origins of the contemporary international human rights system are commonly traced to the Universal Declaration of Human Rights in April

1948. Far less is known, however, about the contribution of Latin American states to this key moment in the history of human rights. Perhaps most dramatically, the American Declaration of the Rights and Duties of Man came into existence a full six months before the UDHR. Four years earlier, at a regional conference in Mexico City in 1944, the need for such an international declaration was already discussed. And in 1946, six Latin American countries were joined by the United States to support collective intervention on behalf of democracy and human rights. Even if individual states had ulterior motives for promoting universal human rights, the region's proposals were unique and significant in global terms. One scholar has gone as far as to suggest that "Latin American diplomats, documents, and traditions had such a profound influence upon both the decision to include human rights protection among the purposes of the UN, and the content of the Universal Declaration, that it is fair to refer to Latin America as the forgotten crucible of the universal human rights idea."[6]

The most direct influence that Latin American countries had on international human rights norms was in drafting the UN Charter and, subsequently, the UDHR. As early as 1938, the Inter-American Conference (predecessor to the Organization of American States, the OAS) adopted a "Declaration in Defense of Human Rights." At the end of World War II, at the April 1945 San Francisco meeting charged with completing the UN Charter, Latin America had the largest bloc of countries present at the meeting. Representatives of twenty countries from the region pushed for human rights to play a more prominent role in the charter. In addition to establishing the promotion and protection of human rights as central goals of the postwar international architecture, the UN Charter established a human rights commission charged with drafting formal international human rights norms. Eleanor Roosevelt headed this eighteen-person commission, which also included three delegates from Latin American countries (Chile, Uruguay, and Panama). In attempting to reconcile cultural and other differences, the Commission called for a proposed bill of rights. Significantly, the models submitted by Chile and Panama quickly became the dominant ones considered; and Chile's proposal became the basis of the 1948 American Declaration on the Rights and Duties of Man.

Part of the appeal of the Latin American proposals was that they resonated globally, beyond Western societies. The proposals attempted to identify similarities in human rights norms across a broad range of cultures and polities. Thus, Latin America's proposal regarding economic, social, and cultural rights made its way quite directly into the first draft of the Universal Declaration. Once the first draft was complete, the UN Human Rights Commission created a three-person subcommittee to finalize the human rights declaration, one of whose members was Chilean Hernán Santa Cruz—a passionate advocate of the international importance of economic and social rights.

In a crucial fall 1948 meeting before a fifty-eight-person UN body, leading up to the final General Assembly vote on the UDHR, Latin American delegates made essential contributions. Perhaps most notably, the Dominican Republic's representative got the preamble amended to ascribe human rights to both men and women. Other representatives from the region were responsible for the Declaration's references to the needs of family, protection from arbitrary exile, and the right to legal remedy for human rights violations.

Figure 1. UN General Assembly committee meeting under the chairmanship of Hernán Santa Cruz of Chile, 3 October 1949. UN/DPI Photo.

All told, Latin American countries played a much more consequential role in the development of international human rights norms than is commonly assumed. In addition to the historical influences sketched above, the region has contributed pivotally in recent years to international human rights law. It has been most influential in codifying specific civil and political rights, especially norms about disappearance and the right to democracy. With disappearances featuring prominently in the region's violations between the 1960s and the 1980s, the first treaty addressing freedom from disappearances entered into force in Latin America in 1996.[7] Perhaps more far-reaching is the Inter-American Democratic Charter of 2001, the first international instrument focused on a human right to democracy. For all the violence that has characterized the region, Latin American countries have long contributed in uniquely important, if largely forgotten, ways to the evolution of international human rights standards. As Amnesty International's 2008 annual report (*State of the World's Human Rights*) recognizes, "If human rights are today at the heart of the UN project, it is in large part thanks to the efforts of Latin American countries."[8]

Studying Human Rights in Latin America

This book sets out to explore human rights dynamics in a particular region. The goal is to offer a concise and comprehensive introduction to human rights, as applied to Latin America. The book is therefore intended for students of human rights and of Latin America; no specialized knowledge of the region is required. It synthesizes much of the existing research, while outlining a broad range of concrete cases and issues. The book is also intended as a resource guide, suggesting related readings, complementary films, and useful Internet Websites. Active engagement with material beyond this book—through film images, dramatic firsthand accounts, and organizations' pragmatically designed Websites—is essential. Each chapter also contains boxed items, zeroing in on a particular issue or providing firsthand testimony to complement the main text.

If human rights can be studied from a variety of perspectives, what does it mean to study the "politics" of human rights? Political analysis often emphasizes the role of power in structuring relations of governance. Political analysis is therefore relevant to human rights issues in at least three ways. First, the state is integral to any discussion of human rights, just as it is a central actor in world politics. States, according to international human rights law, are responsible both for not violating human rights and for protecting citizens whose rights are violated (even if the perpetrators are private actors). In practice, moreover, states continue to be the principal violators of human rights. Second, politics can be essential to the study of human rights because change and reform always entail struggles, often between the state and society. These struggles are fundamentally political in nature, as groups vie to define the limits of each other's appropriate behavior. Third, international political factors are crucial for understanding domestic human rights change. International actors (whether states, international organizations, or international nongovernmental organizations) apply pressures on states to comply with human rights norms and, under more sinister circumstances, themselves contribute to repression. The international political context is thus essential for understanding human rights practices. Politics and human rights go hand in hand.

For pragmatists and advocates concerned with improving human conditions in the region, relying on political insights is useful only if it clarifies more than it obscures the issues and only if it suggests concrete avenues for change. As we think critically about human rights concerns, we should therefore keep in mind these twin practical goals (i.e., the clarification of complex issues and the formulation of hands-on advice for activists and policymakers). Although firsthand and journalistic accounts often make for a good read, they do not necessarily offer systematic tools and methods for understanding human rights. At the same time, theoretically informed analysis can sometimes be divorced from on-the-ground practicalities, or "real-world" dynamics. Despite the challenges of fusing academic insights with human rights realities, we should remain open to alternative ways of studying human rights—precisely because the stakes are so high.

For the purposes of this book, Latin America is comprised of the thirty-three countries (other than the United States and Canada) that are members of the Organization of American States. Countries in this geographic region share broad commonalities, including experiences with conquest and colonialism as well as a complicated history with the United States. At the same time, just as the region's landscape is starkly diverse—from Mexico's arid deserts to jungle forests in Central America and polar caps in southern Chile—countries in the region show enormous diversity in wealth, social composition, and political trajectories (see Appendix 3). And perhaps no other region's human rights story has changed so markedly over time, allowing us to witness dramatic and far-reaching changes that have not always occurred elsewhere.

While the word "terror" immediately evokes images of the world after September 11, 2001, the region's history reminds us that terror and the politics of fear are longstanding—though not necessarily permanent—practices. Non-state actors are not the only ones who use terror as a political weapon; states terrorize populations when they systematically deprive them of their basic human rights. To better understand how people in the region have been terrorized, Chapter 1 surveys past and ongoing human rights abuses, while Chapter 2 presents a framework for explaining human rights violations. The second part of the book turns to the politics of hope. Accordingly, Chapters 3, 4, and 5 examine why human rights reforms sometimes occur; the focus is on the role of global and regional institutions as well as transnational networks of activists and their allies. The final part engages broader questions of justice. Chapter 6 explores struggles over accountability and impunity, including truth commissions and the Pinochet case, while Chapter 7 takes stock of institutional reforms as well as the current global "wars" on drugs and terrorism, the rise of populism in the region, and some of the key challenges that lie ahead. Human rights abuses will not disappear from Latin America or from anywhere else, but rising awareness and activism can improve individual lives and occasionally lead to dramatic reform.

Questions and Debate

1. What are the dominant stereotypes about human rights in Latin America?
2. What are the advantages and disadvantages of a minimalist definition of human rights?
3. Are you surprised by any of the rights advanced in the Universal Declaration of Human Rights (Table 1)? Compare this document with the Inter-American Convention on Human Rights (Appendix 1).
4. What, if anything, do you find most interesting about the region's contributions to international human rights norms?
5. Is it better to study regions on their own, compare them with other areas of the world, or use a different category of analysis altogether (e.g., individual countries)?

References

Additional Reading

Marjorie Agosín, ed., *Writing Toward Hope: The Literature of Human Rights in Latin America* (New Haven, Conn.: Yale University Press, 2006). Anthology of the best-known fiction, plays, and poems addressing various human rights themes in the region.

John Charles Chasteen, *Born in Blood and Fire: A Concise History of Latin America*, 2nd ed. (New York: Norton, 2005). Concise and highly accessible history of Latin America, tracing the impact of conquest and colonization on contemporary dynamics.

Andrew Clapham, *Human Rights: A Very Short Introduction* (Cambridge: Cambridge University Press, 2007). Brief but comprehensive introduction to the study of human rights.

Edward Cleary, *Mobilizing for Human Rights in Latin America* (Bloomfield, Conn.: Kumarian Press, 2007). Places contemporary human rights movements in the context of the region's unique contributions historically. Follow-up to Cleary's *The Struggle for Human Rights in Latin America* (New York: Praeger, 1997).

Jack Donnelly, *International Human Rights*, 3rd ed. (Boulder, Colo.: Westview Press, 2006) and David P. Forsythe, *Human Rights in International Relations*, 2nd ed. (Cambridge: Cambridge University Press, 2006). Two of the principal introductory human rights textbooks.

Human Rights Quarterly. The leading interdisciplinary journal focused on human rights issues, often addressing regional topics.

Michael Goodhart, ed., *Human Rights: Politics and Practice* (London: Oxford University Press, 2009). Thorough, up-to-date textbook, examining a broad range of human rights issues.

Micheline Ishay, *The History of Human Rights: From Ancient Times to the Globalization Era* (Berkeley: University of California Press, 2004). Broad introductory survey of the historical evolution of human rights norms, of interest to any student of human rights.

Todd Landman, *Studying Human Rights* (New York: Routledge 2006). Concise introduction to social science approaches to human rights problems.

Beatriz Manz, *Paradise in Ashes: A Guatemalan Journey of Courage, Terror, and Hope* (Berkeley: University of California Press, 2005). Cultural anthropologist's engaging account of the extermination and rebuilding of one village in the Guatamalan highlands, exemplifying the twin themes of terror and hope.

Filmography

Innocent Voices (2004). Feature film depicting the war in El Salvador through the eyes of an eleven-year-old boy who must decide whether to enlist in the army or join the guerrillas. 120 minutes.

Welcome to Colombia (2003). Filmmaker traverses the wartorn country, giving voice to paramilitary groups, government officials, guerrilla fighters, and ordinary people wanting peace. 65 minutes.

The World Is Watching (1988). Behind-the-scenes look at a major American network's news coverage of the U.S. role in Nicaragua in the 1980s, suggesting that foreign news stories are best approached with a healthy dose of skepticism. 59 minutes.

Americas in Transition (1982). Fast-paced account of politics in Chile, El Salvador, Guatemala, and Nicaragua in the 1970s and early 1980s, including the role of the United States. 29 minutes.

Guatemala: Personal Testimonies (1982). Mayan Indians who survived massacres speak. 20 minutes.

Useful Websites

University of Minnesota Human Rights Library. One of the world's most extensive online collections of human rights material, including regional resources. http://www1.umn.edu/humanrts/.

Inter-American Institute of Human Rights. Created in 1980, the IIHR is the region's leading teaching, research, and documentation center for human rights—a wealth of information by themes and countries, much of it in Spanish. http://www.iidh.ed.cr/.

Latin American Network Information Center (LANIC). Mammoth Website addressing virtually every topic imaginable on Latin America; includes regional and country-specific resources for human rights, and direct links to the region's newspapers and other media outlets. http://lanic.utexas.edu/.

Derechos. Internet-based international organization providing information about human rights issues around the world, with extensive resources specific to Latin America. http://www.derechos.org.

Political Database of the Americas. Easy-to-navigate database with access to basic political data (e.g., constitutions, elections, civil society organizations) for individual Latin American countries. http://www.georgetown.edu/pdba/english.html.

Notes

Epigraphs: Amnesty International, *Peru: The Truth and Reconciliation Commission—A First Step Towards a Country Without Injustice* (London: Amnesty International, August 2004), http://www.amnesty.org/en/library/info/AMR46/003/2004; Marcelo Brodsky, "Life and Death in Argentina," *The Independent* (31 March 2004).

[1] Amnesty International, *Amnesty International Report 2005: The State of the World's Human Rights* (New York: Amnesty International, 2005).

[2] For the latter claim, see especially Henry Shue, *Basic Rights: Subsistence, Affluence, and U.S. Foreign Policy* (Princeton, N.J.: Princeton University Press, 1996).

[3] William J. Talbott, *Which Rights Should Be Universal?* (Oxford: Oxford University Press, 2005), chap. 4.

[4] This section draws on Paolo Carozzo, "From Conquest to Constitutions: Retrieving a Latin American Tradition of the Idea of Human Rights," *Human Rights Quarterly* 25, 2 (May 2003): 281–313.

[5] Carozzo, "From Conquest to Constitutions," 301.

[6] Discussion of the UDHR in this section is based on Mary Ann Glendon, "The Forgotten Crucible: The Latin American Influence on the Universal Human Rights Idea," *Harvard Human Rights Journal* 16 (Spring 2003): 27.

[7] The International Convention for the Protection of All Persons from Enforced Disappearances had not yet entered into force as of mid-2009.

[8] Amnesty International, *Amnesty International Report 2008: The State of the World's Human Rights* (London: Amnesty International, 2008), 11.

PART I

Violating Rights

1

A Regional Survey

*It was August 4, 1976, at four o'clock in the afternoon, when
[Doctor] Carlos Godoy Lagarrigue, aged 39, left the San Bernardo
Hospital by car. He had just finished his daily ward round and
was as usual on his way to his outpatient clinic in La Granja. . . .
He never arrived. Somewhere along the way, he vanished and has
not been seen or heard of since. His wife and children waited at
home that evening, and continued to wait for years and years.*

—A friend recalling the disappearance of
a young doctor in Chile; testimony to the Chilean National
Commission on Truth and Reconciliation

Understanding why people are tortured or disappeared requires, at a
minimum, stepping back and getting up close—stepping back to
identify key facts and trends, getting up close to hear personal experiences of abuse. In this sense, description is a first step to prevention. Any
attempt to explain and prevent human rights violations must be based on
an accurate understanding of past and ongoing abuses. Which rights have
been violated in the region? How have these abuses changed over time?
Are there significant cross-national differences? How does Latin America
compare to other world regions? This chapter examines these questions,
by presenting both quantitative trends and qualitative "snapshots" of
particular episodes of abuse. It also provides eyewitness accounts of the
human toll these violations have taken, showing a side of the story that
numbers and figures can never entirely capture.

Types of Violation

Most people tend to think of violations when they think of human rights: torture, summary executions, genocide, arbitrary incarceration. There is indeed something captivating about human rights abuse, perhaps evoking deep-seated fears of pain and powerlessness. In general, human rights violations consist of noncompliance with internationally recognized human rights norms. While there are as many types of violations as there are human rights, this book focuses mostly on a particular set of civil-political rights known as physical (or personal) integrity rights. These rights involve bodily harm, usually but not exclusively at the hands of state officials, and consist of four key rights: freedom from torture, extrajudicial executions, disappearances, and political imprisonment. These violations also go by more common terms like repression and coercion.

This book emphasizes these violations because these are the abuses that have most elicited attention and shaped policy debates vis-à-vis Latin America. Not surprisingly, most of the research and testimonies on human rights focus precisely on these abuses. While violations of economic and social rights can be equally important, both ethically and pragmatically, we focus in this chapter and the next on those egregious violations that have come under the heaviest scrutiny.

That said, there is increasing consensus that all human rights are *interdependent*. Even if a hierarchy of human rights exists, the view is that Cold War debates over the primacy of civil-political versus economic-social rights are nonproductive and largely moot. All types of human rights are interdependent and necessary for human dignity, regardless of ongoing controversies over specific rights (e.g., debates over the importance of the right to a paid holiday). In view of this interdependence, issues like poverty and other economic-social inequalities are discussed in this book whenever possible alongside physical integrity rights.

International human rights treaties have defined physical integrity rights. For example, the Convention against Torture and other Cruel, Inhuman or Degrading Treatment or Punishment (1984) defines torture as

> any act by which severe pain or suffering, whether physical or mental, is intentionally inflicted on a person for such purposes as obtaining from him or a third person information or a confession, punishing him for an act he or a third person has committed or is

suspected of having committed, or intimidating or coercing him or a third person, or for any reason based on discrimination of any kind, when such pain or suffering is inflicted by or at the instigation of or with the consent or acquiescence of a public official or other person acting in an official capacity. It does not include pain or suffering arising only from, inherent in or incidental to lawful sanctions. (Article 1)

In practice, some of the most common forms of physical torture include electric shock, bodily suspension, beatings, food and water deprivation, forced ingestion of chemicals, and sexual violence. Psychological torture includes threats of violence (often directed at loved ones), solitary confinement, forced observance of torture or killing (including of children and spouses), sham executions, and intense sleep deprivation. All these abuses have been prevalent in Latin America.

According to the Inter-American Convention on Forced Disappearance of Persons (1996), a disappearance is

the act of depriving a person or persons of his or their freedom, in whatever way, perpetrated by agents of the state or by persons or groups of persons acting with the authorization, support, or acquiescence of the state, followed by an absence of information or a refusal to acknowledge that deprivation of freedom or to give information on the whereabouts of that person, thereby impeding his or her recourse to the applicable legal remedies and procedural guarantees. (Article 2)

Various human rights treaties also define extrajudicial executions and political imprisonment. In general, extrajudicial executions refer to killings committed by governments outside of legal boundaries. Murders by paramilitary groups directly supported or instigated by governments fall into this category as well. The identity of the victim does not matter as long as the death is the result of excessive or illegal use of force by state agents. Political imprisonment is in turn the incarceration of people because of their identity, including their religion, ethnicity, race, sexual orientation, or political beliefs.

There are different approaches to measuring these rights violations. On the one hand, we can count the number of human rights abuses (or "events"). Some truth commissions, for example, have followed this "events-based" approach in an attempt to reveal the overall magnitude of a situation. While this approach is ideal in many ways, bringing us closest to the truth, the practice of quantifying abuses is often fraught with guesswork or necessarily limited to a select number of years or cases—particularly in places where people who have been "disappeared" have never been found, or where the location of unmarked graves remains undisclosed.

On the other hand, for those who study systematically the causes of human rights abuse, it is important to collect measures for as many years and countries as possible. Since an events-based approach is not always feasible, scholars have opted for measurements that assess the overall *level* of abuse. Like other attempts at quantification, this "standards-based" approach can be imperfect. For example, one of the leading measures of personal integrity violations employs a three-point scale, reflecting the extent to which violations are frequent (more than 50 incidents reported in a given year), occasional (fewer than 50), or rare. While this kind of measurement is somewhat arbitrary and unable to differentiate between 100 cases of torture and 10,000, experts tend to view these measurements as relatively reliable. At the very least, they permit a general comparison of violations across countries and over time.

Historical Context: Colonial Legacies and State Formation

If human rights violations are closely related to states as political actors, these violations can only be understood by examining the historical context in which states form. In Europe, for example, states were forged out of a great deal of violence and coercion. In the developing world, the context in which states were formed is inextricable from the process of colonialism. This is certainly true in Latin America, where today's human rights violations can be traced historically to the experience of colonial rule, which left an enduring mark on the region's states. Attention to this historical context does not exonerate individuals today for their role in committing human rights violations; it merely helps to explain one aspect of a deeply complex phenomenon.

Contrary to popular images, colonialism itself was not particularly violent in Latin America. After the horror of the conquest, which took over 65 million lives (approximately ten times the number of victims in the Holocaust), European colonizers set out to control primarily through "consent" rather than brute force. This required empowering local allies, promoting sentiments of inferiority, and transplanting cultural traditions like religion and patriarchy. In short, colonialism thrived on ideological domination, an essential component of any repressive system.

When struggles for independence spread throughout the region in the early nineteenth century, states adopted the language of liberation and resistance (emblazoned in their constitutions and sometimes linked to the abolition of slavery), but they remained chained to the legacy of colonialism. As one observer notes, "unfinished revolutions" marked the era of state formation.[1] Colonial domination shaped subsequent repression by leaving at least two important legacies: ideological systems of subjugation and economic disarray.

If new states governed themselves without the shackles of colonialism, they nonetheless inherited the idea that men were superior to women and that race was tied to privilege; thus, indigenous people and those of African descent, especially women, were automatically at the bottom of the social ladder. On the economic front, colonialism left in its wake a system marked by extreme rural-urban disparity, with marginalized locations relying on noncompetitive subsistence economies that privileged landowners over peasants. Overreliance on goods like cocoa, sugarcane, and mining has continued to cripple the region's economies over a century later.

These legacies—ideological and economic—translated into what would become a familiar pattern of political instability. As liberal governments came to power, paying lip service to the ideals of equality, they quickly had to confront economically harsh circumstances. Governments in the region also inherited a particular kind of state: weak in terms of its administrative and revenue-extracting apparatuses, while overly strong in terms of the coercive apparatus. The latter was itself partly the result of lengthy wars for independence, which in some cases lasted over two decades, as colonial rulers fought hard to retain their grip on power.

In short, the region's new rulers faced a situation of economic hardship, weak states, strong armies, and a substantial gap between norms of equality and the reality of social discrimination. Political life was subject to few democratic checks, as patronage politics, corruption, and *caudillo* rule (with legendary strongmen at the helm of power) became commonplace. The stage was set for new elites to rely on the use of force to maintain order and stability, unleashing a vicious cycle of repression whose impact would be felt into the current millennium.

Trends and Cross-National Dynamics

Before we can attempt to explain why human rights are violated in Latin America, we need to understand the patterns of abuse that have characterized the region. These patterns have varied across countries and over time, as identified below. Due to the limited availability of quantitative data, most of the discussion focuses on rights violations after 1980; subsequent case studies nonetheless survey earlier periods.

Differences in abuse over time. Since the 1980s, torture has been the most common type of personal integrity violation in Latin America, followed by extrajudicial killings, political imprisonment, and disappearances—in that order.[2] It should also be noted that in the last quarter century, torture has been twice as common as political imprisonment, despite its strong global prohibition. Figure 2 illustrates these broad differences. Over time, moreover, these dynamics have shifted somewhat. Disappearances, in particular, have abated steadily, declining sixfold since the 1980s. In contrast, torture is still frequent (more than 50 cases per year) in almost half the region's countries.

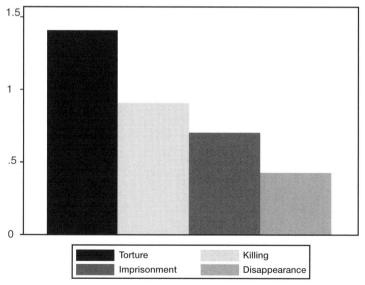

FIGURE 2. Human rights violations in Latin America: types and level of abuse, 1981–2006. Data from Cingranelli-Richards (CIRI) Human Rights Dataset (http://www.humanrightsdata.org). See note 2, p. 51 for levels of violation.

Subregional differences. State repression across Latin America seemed to sweep over the continent at the end of the twentieth century in three successive waves. Roughly speaking, these waves of repression occurred in distinct subregions. Human rights violations were most prominent in the 1970s in the South American countries of Argentina, Chile, Uruguay, and Paraguay, as well as Brazil in the first half of the decade. The 1980s were the decade in which Central American regimes like those in Guatemala and El Salvador captured the world's attention with brutal civil wars and egregious human rights abuses. The 1990s and the turn of the millennium shifted the locus of abuse more distinctly to Andean countries, especially Colombia, where a war on drugs was at the epicenter of widespread abuses. Human rights violations certainly occurred in other countries as well, but these subregional waves of repression remain noteworthy.[3]

Cross-national differences. Looking more closely at individual countries within the region (Table 2), a few trends are apparent. One group of countries has experienced high levels of human rights violations since the 1980s: Colombia, Haiti, Mexico, and Peru. While human rights conditions in countries like Chile, El Salvador, Honduras, Nicaragua, and Uruguay have improved in recent years, the human rights climate has deteriorated in both Brazil and Venezuela. In terms of specific violations, the practice of disappearances has declined substantially throughout the region, with a few exceptions like Haiti. Most countries have also reduced their use of political imprisonment since 2000, except for Argentina and Brazil, where the practice has risen. In general, it is noteworthy that, despite improvements over time, moderate to high levels of human rights violations persist in virtually all of the region's countries.

The region in global perspective. How do these trends compare to human rights violations outside the region? In general, Latin American countries have had higher than average levels of human rights violations since 1980. Before 2000, the level of abuse in Latin America was among the worst in the developing world; since 2000, however, it has shown the greatest overall improvement in human rights conditions, although abuses still are commonplace. These trends refer to the frequency with which personal integrity rights have been violated, not the number of people killed in political violence. In terms of specific abuses, Latin America now has

Table 2. Level of Human Rights Violations:
Select Latin American Countries, Post-1980

Country	1980s	1990s	Post-2000
Argentina	Medium	Medium	Medium
Bolivia	Medium	Medium	Medium
Brazil	Medium	High	High
Chile	High	Medium	Medium
Colombia	High	High	High
Cuba	High	High	Medium
El Salvador	High	Medium	Medium
Guatemala	High	High	Medium
Haiti	High	High	High
Honduras	High	Medium	Medium*
Mexico	High	High	High
Nicaragua	High	Medium	Medium
Peru	High	High	High
Uruguay	Medium	Medium	Low
Venezuela	Medium	High	High

Human rights violations refer to a composite of four physical integrity rights: freedom from torture, forced disappearance, extrajudicial execution, and political imprisonment.
Source: adapted from CIRI Human Rights Data Project, http://ciri.binghamton.edu/index.asp; data cover 2000–2006. *Before the 2009 coup.

among the world's lowest rates of disappearance, although a few decades ago it had the highest. Nor is the region entirely unique when it comes to torture: as elsewhere in the world, torture has been the region's most common physical integrity violation.

Snapshots of Repression

The human rights violations that have enveloped Latin America cannot be recounted easily. Countless human rights organizations, truth commissions, and journalists have recorded hundreds of thousands of stories of abuse, as told by victims, relatives, and witnesses. This section offers a glimpse into some of these accounts, as well as a basic chronology of dominant trends in the region's contemporary history. It is not intended as a comprehensive survey of the region's human rights abuses; readers are directed to the Reference section at the end of each chapter for additional sources. More recent developments, including issues of impunity and the current war on terror, are also discussed in later chapters.

Chilean Executions in the National Stadium

On 11 September 1973—which may be called the first 9/11—Chile's democratically elected president Salvador Allende was ousted from office, in a violent coup led by General Augusto Pinochet. Until then, Chile was widely considered to have the region's longest-standing democracy. After bombing the presidential palace and assuming the reins of power, Chile's military and police forces quickly took control of the population and dramatically overturned a tradition of not intervening in politics. Nowhere was this surreal scene played out more vividly than in the country's National Stadium, usually reserved for soccer matches like the 1962 World Cup. Days after the coup, the stadium was turned into a massive detention center, holding 40,000 prisoners. With music blaring from loudspeakers to block out victims' screams, detainees were tortured and killed in the locker rooms and interior of the stadium while others awaited their fate in the main quad.

FIGURE 3. Chilean man crossing the street in Santiago in 1973, during the September 11 military coup. AFP/Getty Images.

Nineteen days after the coup, as the horrors of the National Stadium continued, Pinochet appointed General Sergio Arellano Stark as his official delegate and charged him with traveling the country to assure that the same policies being implemented in the capital city of Santiago were applied throughout the country. Thus Arellano Stark along with ten army officers boarded a Puma helicopter on September 30, 1973, and systematically traversed the country; in just three weeks they left almost 100 political prisoners dead, most of whom were taken out and shot at night. Their trip became known as the "caravan of death." As one witness described the delegation, "It seems to me that one of the reasons for the mission was to set a drastic precedent in order to terrorize the presumed willingness of the Chilean people to fight back. But without a doubt, it was also intended to instill fear and terror among the commanders. To prevent any military personnel, down to [the] lowest ranking officers, from taking a false step: this could happen to you!"[4]

Throughout Pinochet's rule, human rights violations spiked twice. The most concentrated volume of human rights violations occurred in the immediate aftermath of the coup, as illustrated above, although a relatively high level of abuse continued until 1976 under the leadership of Chile's intelligence service—the Directorate for National Intelligence (DINA). A resurgence in political violence occurred in the mid-1980s, when state agents killed scores of people. Between these prominent episodes of abuse, a steady stream of violence characterized the full course of Pinochet's regime (1973–90). This regime of terror was based on a policy of indiscriminate killings, clandestine detention centers, and the systematic torture of opponents.

UP CLOSE: WITNESS TO ATROCITIES

"He was 18 and was studying at the Liceo Industrial. He was on an outing when they arrested and killed him."

"They allowed my brother-in-law and me to dig up about twenty graves. Finally we came across one whose build was like my husband's but he had no arms and legs. We buried him to put my in-laws at ease. I'm sure we buried someone else."

"They shot him on the road near our house. I heard the shots, and I came out and found his body. They yelled at me to go bury the dog that had just been killed. That dog was my only son. They gave me three hours to bury him and get out of town. I had to wrap him in a blanket, get an oxcart, and leave him in the cemetery."

"He was useful to society. Why should they eliminate him? He was good in sports and at chess."

"They hung him from a crane. He was in such bad shape as we were returning to the cell, that we wrapped him up, and helped him down the narrow staircase. He was very much beaten up and traumatized. When no one was looking, he threw himself over into the bottom of a hatchway. He couldn't endure one more day of torture."

"I had searched for him so much. I went down to the beach to cry, and there he was, all swollen with bullet wounds. They had pulled out his teeth."

"They brought my son to my cell, unconscious and all bruised from torture."

"I took them where my son was because they promised me that they would treat him well. I wanted to save the younger ones from abuse. They killed him just the same."

"While they were raping me, my husband was screaming at them to let me go."

"When they took my father, they took my husband and me as well. I was raped by a whole group that was guarding me. I never told my husband. That was fifteen years ago."

"I got married on August 5. By October 5, I was a widow. Why did they deprive me of my chance to be happy with my husband?"

"I was six months pregnant when they killed my husband. My little baby was never born; I couldn't hold it back."

"They arrested them because they didn't have their identification cards. They were minors and weren't politically active. After all, they were practically illiterate. And they shot them to death."

Source: Chilean National Commission on Truth and Reconciliation, *Report of the Chilean National Commission on Truth and Reconciliation*, (Notre Dame, Ind.: University of Notre Dame Press with Center for Human Rights, Notre Dame Law School, 1991), Part III, Chapter 4.

Argentina's Dirty War

The period between 1976 and 1983 has come to be known as Argentina's dirty war, a term now ascribed to other repressive regimes. A military junta took power in 1976 through a coup, quickly proceeding to suspend basic rights and repress anyone remotely considered a threat to national security. Using a complex system of clandestine detention centers, death squads proceeded to "disappear" and detain people from all walks of life. In the next four years, at least 20,000 people were killed or disappeared (their bodies often washing ashore in river beds or on the Uruguayan coast), with thousands more tortured. While the most intense period of violations occurred in the first two years of military rule, cases of egregious abuse persisted throughout the dirty war.

Historically, Argentina had already known its share of violence and military rule before the 1976 coup. A military coup in 1955, for example, led to more than 3,000 deaths. The 1976 coup itself had been preceded by about twenty other coups during the century. The repression launched during the dirty war also had a more immediate precursor, as clandestine detention facilities were used in 1974 and 1975 to detain suspected opponents. Death squads, including the infamous Triple A (Argentine Anticommunist Alliance) also confronted armed leftists (e.g., the Montoneros) after 1970. Groups on both sides of the ideological spectrum clashed in an increasingly polarized conflict.

All of this occurred in the aftermath of a military regime that had installed itself in Argentina in 1966, adopting the national security rationale of its Brazilian neighbor. By 1969, student and labor groups, which had been particularly strong in the country's modern history, mobilized and protested visibly against repressive conditions. The most symbolic event in this regard was the *cordobazo* of 1969, as young people and workers took to the streets in the heartland province of Córdoba and the military proceeded to crush social protest. Even during a brief interlude of civilian rule in the early 1970s, the military lay the foundations for complete control. Indeed, Juan Perón, who had had been Argentina's president after World War II (famously married to Evita), returned from exile in Spain and was reelected president in 1973; he died a year later, and was succeeded by his third wife and vice president, Isabel Perón. All the while, the military continued to detain and torture dissidents under the cover of national security.

Argentina's dirty war illustrates dramatically the full reach of a repressive state apparatus. An extension of the physical abuse inflicted on victims was an explicit attempt to dehumanize the population, a goal partly achieved through the use of language. To this end, an entire linguistic system of categorizing people as enemies was devised. This included labeling torture devices casually; for instance, an electric cattle prod, popular in torture sessions, was called "Carolina." In neighboring Uruguay, a system of labeling was similarly created, as people were assigned one of three letters (A, B, or C) depending on their potential for engaging in "subversive" activities, with dire consequences to follow; subversives were defined broadly to include students volunteering in poor neighborhoods or studying psychology. The language of war, with all of its ramifications, was deployed alongside physical repression. Argentina's dirty war therefore exemplifies a common tendency in political repression: words are a crucial if overlooked form of terror, used to dehumanize opponents, sanitize repression, desensitize abusers, and engender unimaginable fear.

UP CLOSE: "THE NIGHT OF THE PENCILS"

"The night of 16 September is sadly remembered in La Plata as the 'Night of the Pencils.' That night the following people were seized from their homes by the Security Forces and they are still on the list of the disappeared: Horacio Angel Ungaro (file No. 4205), Daniel Alberto Rasero (file No. 4205), Francisco López Muntaner (file No. 5479), María Claudia Falcone (file No. 2800), Victor Treviño (file No. 4018), Claudio de Acha (file No. 148), María Clara Ciocchini (file No. 1178). They formed part of a group of sixteen people, aged between fourteen and eighteen, who had taken part in a campaign in favour of school subsidies. Each of them was taken from their homes. The Buenos Aires Provincial Police had decided to punish everyone who had participated in the pro-school subsidy campaign, because the Armed Forces considered it to be 'subversion in the schoolroom.' Three of the youngsters were freed. According to the inquiries carried out by this Commission, and witnesses' accounts in the Commission's possession, the young people seized were killed after undergoing the most horrible tortures in different secret detention centers."

*   *   *

The "night of the pencils" illustrates how children can be the targets of human rights violations. In Argentina alone, about 1 percent of disappearances during the dirty war were of children under age 10; over 10 percent of those disappeared were teenagers, while over half of all disappearances involved young people in their twenties. In addition to being killed, parents were often abducted in front of their children; kidnapped children, in turn, were sometimes adopted by members of the military. Other children were simply born in captivity, prone to a range of neuro-psychological problems. Still others were held at the same detention facilities as their parents, where they all were tortured.

Today, children across Latin America—from the Caribbean to the Central American countries of Honduras and El Salvador to the slums of Colombia and Brazil—suffer human rights abuses in other ways. About 40 million *street children* (almost the size of the entire Hispanic population in the United States, and more than the population of California) live in Latin America. Police and death squads have often targeted these vulnerable members of society for abuse, just as private actors smuggle them into human and sexual trafficking. For example, in Guatemala City, about 2,000 children are made to work in 600 brothels; in Brazil, approximately half a million girls work as prostitutes, many of them sent to gold-mining areas in the Amazon. Moreover, in direct violation of several international human rights treaties, children in the region do not have their basic needs met, suffering from very low life expectancy and poor overall well-being.

Sources: CONADEP, *Nunca Más: The Report of the Argentine National Commission for the Disappeared* (New York: Farrar Straus Giroux, 1986), 236–37. Data on child trafficking from Alison Phinney for Women, Health and Development Program, Pan American Health Organization, "Trafficking of Women and Children for Sexual Exploitation in the Americas," 11 May 2005.

Extermination in the Guatemalan Highlands

Unlike many of the abuses under South America's dictatorships, the gravest abuses in Central American countries like Guatemala occurred in the 1980s. In contrast to the Southern Cone (consisting of Argentina, Chile, Uruguay, and Brazil), most of Guatemala's population lived in non-urban areas; and the majority was indigenous, mainly Mayan Indians.

Furthermore, despite the fact that Guatemala's population was smaller than Chile's (see Appendix 3, Table 1), the number of people killed in political violence was substantially higher, between 150,000 to 300,000 deaths. Another unique feature of human rights violations in Guatemala was their concentration in rural areas, where people's livelihood was specifically targeted. Entire villages were essentially turned into rural concentration camps, intended to set an example for others. And a scorched earth policy, more akin to Cambodia's killing fields than the Americas, resulted in burned tracts of land on which people lived and relied for food and income. Civilians were also forced into patrol systems, so that at any moment the state's arm could reach as deeply as possible into the dense jungles of Guatemala's highlands and terrorize the population.

FIGURE 4. Family members in a Guatemalan village carry the remains of relatives killed by the military in a massacre in the 1980s. Cesar Perez/AFP/Getty Images.

Guatemala's travails did not begin, of course, in the 1980s. A military coup in 1954, enmeshed in Cold War politics and now recognized as having been inspired by the CIA, overthrew democratically elected Jacobo Arbenz, whose policies were viewed as friendly to the Left and hurtful of U.S. business interests. With the military intervening in politics, the same social tensions and volatility that gripped other countries in the 1960s were present in Guatemala, leading to episodes of political violence and repression of indigenous people, culminating in a thirty-six-year civil war that lasted from 1960 to 1996.

After fighting the state in the 1970s, a lull in hostilities allowed armed rebel groups to flee from the urban center to Mayan communities in the western highlands. The state responded with widespread repression, targeting a broader popular movement. This intensified further in the 1980s, when absolute military rule was implemented. Under the brief leadership of General Efraín Ríos Montt, repression spiked in 1982, resulting in 18,000 deaths that year alone. Given the difficulties of isolating armed opponents who had fled to the jungle highlands, the state oversaw a policy of extermination, eliminating entire villages on sight. The objective was to destroy any potential threats to national security, whether from armed dissidents or communist sympathizers, while pacifying those who remained alive.

Peru's Shining Path

In contrast to other countries in the region in which guerrilla insurgents have been relatively small and targeted mostly the state, Peru's human rights violations have been linked closely—though not exclusively—to the Shining Path (Sendero Luminoso). The group is a Maoist, communist organization, which formed in the 1960s. Though initially it was tied to student activism, in the 1980s it embarked on a militant path of violence, launched from its stronghold in the Andean highlands and targeting the population-at-large.

Unlike Uruguay's Tupamaros—a small, urban group that committed Robin Hood-like acts against the state—the Shining Path's members were largely rural in origin and included indigenous peasants. More importantly, they killed indiscriminately, including peasants and other civilians. Their extremism, which rejected participation in the political system, also led Senderistas to oppose human rights per se, which they considered a bourgeois and imperialist concept.

Although the Shining Path committed more human rights abuses than the Peruvian state in the 1980s and 1990s, the latter's role in killing and torturing thousands of people should not be forgotten. According to the country's Truth and Reconciliation Commission in 2003, the Shining Path was responsible for killing over 22,000 people while government forces executed about 7,000 people; at least an additional 46,000 people remain unaccounted for. President Alberto Fujimori moved in the 1990s to counter the guerrilla movement by arming peasants, though militarizing the conflict only served to worsen overall conditions. Colombian drug traffickers and right-wing paramilitary groups also have heightened the violence in Peru and served to raise the level of fear. The state capitalized on the role of the Shining Path by staging atrocities and then blaming the insurgents. In more recent years, the group has lost considerable strength and thousands of its members have been detained in dismal conditions—including 14,000 feet high in the Andes mountains at below-zero temperatures—conditions that, ironically, violate basic human rights.

UP CLOSE: THE EL MOZOTE MASSACRE

"On 10 December 1981, in the village of El Mozote in the Department of Morazán, units of the Atlacatl Battalion detained, without resistance, all the men, women and children who were in the place. The following day, 11 December, after spending the night locked in their homes, they were deliberately and systematically executed in groups. First, the men were tortured and executed, then the women were executed and, lastly, the children, in the place where they had been locked up. The number of victims identified was over 200. The figure is higher if other unidentified victims are taken into account. . . .

"In the course of Operación Rescate [Operation Rescue], massacres of civilians also occurred in the following places: 11 December, more than 20 people in La Joya canton; 12 December, some 30 people in the village of La Ranchería; the same day, by units of the Atlacatl Battalion, the inhabitants of the village of Los Toriles; and 13 December, the inhabitants of the village of Jocote Amarillo and Cerro Pando canton. More than 500 identified victims perished at El Mozote and in the other villages. Many other victims have not been identified. . . . In the case of El Mozote, the accounts were fully corroborated by the results of the 1992 exhumation of the remains. Despite the public complaints of a massacre and the ease with which they could have been verified, the Salvadoran authorities did not order an investigation and consistently denied that the massacre had taken place."

Source: United Nations Truth Commission Report on El Salvador, *From Madness to Hope: The 12-Year War in El Salvador* (New York: United Nations, 1993), Part IV, Section C., No. 1.

Brazilian Death Squads

As Latin America's largest country, Brazil has had its share of human rights abuses. The military forcibly ousted the civilian government in 1964, initiating a period of widespread repression and military rule lasting two decades. Brazil was one of the region's first countries to adopt a national security doctrine, which called for suppressing political dissent to assure domestic stability. The 1960s thus saw egregious human rights violations, including disappearances, extrajudicial executions, and systematic torture (like the *pau de arara*, or parrot's perch, a form of torture that the Brazilian military perfected—a person is suspended upside down from a tube, with hands and ankles tied together, while being beaten).

Human rights violations were particularly intense until 1974, when the regime permitted some political and economic liberalization, a period commonly referred to as the *abertura* (opening). The next decade saw regular human rights abuses, including severe censorship and suppression of labor unrest. In 1980, for example, about 1,000 people were killed in the context of labor struggles.[5]

Even after the return of civilian rule in 1985, human rights abuses persisted in Brazil. Two disturbing trends are especially evident in this large country, whose urban centers are widely perceived to be dangerous. First, death squads have been prevalent in Brazil, often targeting street children and other urban poor living in *favelas* (shanty towns) as well as landless peasants in rural areas. (The latter include those resisting the encroachment of multinational corporations into the country's jungles, one such resister being the renowned labor activist Chico Mendes, who was assassinated in 1988). Second, human rights abuses in Brazil have been characterized by a notoriously high degree of institutionalized violence, especially by the police and in the prison system. Police respond regularly to altercations among people living in urban slums with unrestrained abuse, often leading to torture and summary killing. The country's prisons, moreover, are among the most overcrowded, dangerous, and dismal in the world; and they include minors as detainees. Problems in the prison system are exemplified by the 1992 Carandiru massacre, in which military police killed more than one hundred prisoners, an event that attracted global attention and became the subject of an acclaimed film.

FIGURE 5. Street children in Brazil pursued by death squads in the 1990s. John Chiasson/Liaison/Getty Images.

Colombia's Drug War

Some of the world's worst human rights violations are currently occurring in Colombia, which represents the region's most dangerous conflict zone. The drug war has certainly been central to political violence in the country, but the context of human rights abuses is also much broader. Beginning in the late 1940s, a civil war essentially ensued in the country, pitting conservatives against liberals in violent street clashes. The result was a period in Colombia's history known as La Violencia, in which approximately 250,000 people died between 1949 and 1962. The 1960s saw familiar social upheaval and polarization, including the formation of the now-notorious Revolutionary Armed Forces of Colombia (Fuerzas Armadas Revolucionarias de Colombia, FARC) and the National Liberation Army (Ejército de Liberación Nacional, ELN). As drug lords gained prominence in the 1980s, they entered into sporadic conflict with insurgents and supported death squads to combat them. While over time some of the insurgents have crossed the line into drug trafficking, others have moved to protect peasants—in exchange for a "fee"—from government attempts to eradicate their coca crops.

Peasants who depend on coca for their livelihood have been caught in the crossfire of drug traffickers, guerrilla insurgents, paramilitary groups, and state efforts to fight the U.S.-financed war on drugs. Since the late 1990s, in particular, several paramilitary forces joined in creating the United Self-Defense Forces of Colombia (Autodefensas Unidas de Colombia, AUC), which has been accused by human rights organizations of committing massive abuses in the struggle to eliminate guerrilla forces. The numbers of victims are staggering, with over 50,000 people killed since the mid-1980s, and thousands of kidnappings committed by all sides of the conflict. The nexus between an already challenging state-insurgency struggle and the drug trade, which promotes peasants' dependency on coca growing while criminalizing their activity and placing them squarely in the middle of the violence, has translated into an exorbitant level of abuse.

Mexico in the Spotlight

In an unprecedented move, Mexico's government completed a draft report in early 2006 detailing human rights abuses committed by the state between 1964 and 1982. The report documents the country's "dirty war," calling it by that name. The toll amounted to hundreds of murders and disappearances as well as thousands of cases of torture and illegal detention. In addition to daily abuse of human rights, Mexico has been mired since then in a system of heavy corruption, overseen by militarized police forces that have enjoyed substantial autonomy and impunity. The country has had three prominent episodes of abuse, attracting varying degrees of global attention: a student massacre in Mexico City in 1968; the conflict in Chiapas in the mid-1990s; and the recent rise in murders and disappearances of women, especially in Ciudad Juárez.

Known as the Tlatelolco massacre, this signal instance of state repression occurred in October 1968, the same year when the Olympics were held in Mexico City. Like students elsewhere, those in Mexico's capital city had been engaging in peaceful protest. When an unarmed demonstration of 15,000 of them gathered in a public square in the district of Tlatelolco, the military and police moved in and began firing indiscriminately on the crowd and beating bystanders. By the end, hundreds of dead bodies lay piled on the streets. Despite the draw of the Olympics, international attention to the events of Tlatelolco was minimal.

The Zapatistas, or the Zapatista Army of National Liberation (Ejército Zapatista de Liberación Nacional, EZLN) in Chiapas went public on 1 January 1994, the same day the North American Free Trade Agreement) (NAFTA) went into effect. The timing was no coincidence. Taking their name from a guerrilla leader during Mexico's revolution in 1910 who fought for indigenous land rights, the group called for basic reforms, separation from Mexico, and resistance to globalization. Initially, the Zapatistas' use of arms led to a few direct clashes with the government, but otherwise the group's masked members deployed nonviolent means of protest, including marches and an extensive campaign on the Internet that some have dubbed the first global "cyberwar."

Subcomandante Marcos has been the group's articulate and educated spokesperson. The enigmatic figure is believed to be a former university professor from Mexico City who was influenced deeply by the 1968 massacre. Regardless of his actual identity, he has been able to transform successfully the needs of Mexico's indigenous poor people into a compelling global script. (Marcos, now called Delegate Zero, has also toured Mexico on a motorcycle trip that recalls Che Guevera.) Individuals opposed to globalization, and other activists from around the world have responded to the charismatic figure, traveling in solidarity to the Mexican jungle to attend large-scale meetings.

The Mexican state, for its part, responded initially to the Zapatistas with violence, as the military moved in to suppress the group and killed hundreds of people in the process. On other occasions, the armed forces and police stood by and did nothing while paramilitary groups carried out vicious attacks: in the Acteal massacre of December 1997, forty-five indigenous people (including women and children) were killed savagely while attending a pacifist meeting in a village church.

Even before the outbreak in Chiapas, young women had started disappearing in the border town of Ciudad Juárez. Many of these women worked for *maquiladora* factories, which populate the town. *Maquiladoras* are essentially assembly plants used by multinational corporations—in a global economy, production increasingly occurs in multiple stages and different countries. Over time, the number of women who have disappeared or been murdered has risen into the hundreds, just as the incidence has spread to other parts of the country. Not only do the killings continue, but the official response has been dismal. Critics tend to blame the media for making a mountain out of a molehill, and they suggest that the women were involved in illicit sexual activities that explain the incidents and exonerate the state. In fact, a corrupt police force has refused to investigate the killings, and punishment has been virtually nonexistent. Failure on the part of the state has led to the formation of transnational linkages between members of civil society in and out of Mexico (see Chapter 4).

Turmoil in Haiti

Another ongoing hotspot, the small Caribbean country of Haiti has experienced monumental turmoil on the human rights front. The poorest country in the Western hemisphere and the world's poorest non-African country, with three-quarters of the mostly black population living in extreme poverty, Haiti has a long history of instability and military rule. It was ruled brutally for almost thirty years by the Duvalier family, first father and then son (François "Papa Doc" beginning in 1957; Jean-Claude—also known as "Baby Doc"—from 1971 to 1986). During this period, hundreds of Haitians expressed their discontent at the level of violence, repression, and poverty by attempting to leave the country in small boats, at great risk to their lives. A brief glimmer of hope came in 1990, when Catholic priest Jean-Bertrand Aristide won a UN-monitored election, only to be overthrown in a military coup one year later. The level of violence immediately escalated, as the state moved to suppress all

UP CLOSE: TWENTY-FIRST-CENTURY FEMICIDE

It began in the early 1990s in Juárez, Mexico, a border city, where hundreds of women were murdered after being raped and tortured. It spread to Guatemala, where the first five years of the millennium saw more than 2,000 women killed in similar circumstances. The murders have diffused throughout Mexico and Guatemala and are now occurring in many Latin American countries (most notably, Bolivia, Peru, and Colombia, as well as Honduras and El Salvador). Human rights organizations like Amnesty International have identified a modus operandi: the torture, mutilation, and dumping of the bodies of young and mostly poor women.

This new form of femicide—violence specifically targeting women—is highly political: some of the killings have been traced to state agents like members of the police force but, much more commonly, public authorities throughout the region have shown little inclination to investigate, let alone hold anyone accountable, for these abuses. On occasions when people have been arrested, the evidence has been flimsy or confessions have been coerced. Subsequent chapters address the question of why femicide is on the rise in the Americas and how women around the world are resisting this disturbing trend.

Source: Kent Paterson, "Femicide on the Rise in Latin America," Americas Program Report, Center for International Policy, Washington, D.C., 8 March 2006.

Pink crosses throughout the border town of Ciudad Juárez, Mexico, mark where the bodies of young murdered women have been found. Alfredo Estrella/AFP/Getty Images.

potential opposition with the help of death squads and by resorting to systematic torture and killing. Given the refugee problem confronting the United States, it pushed to reinstate Aristide in 1994. He ruled until 1996 and was reelected president in 2001.

Haiti illustrates how even the good intentions of a leader can get caught in a spiral of violence. Aristide had initially been popular due to the social justice reforms that he advocated and that resonated with the people; he had also dismantled the army, responsible for many human rights abuses. After taking office, however, economic discontent and political mismanagement embroiled Aristide in rumors of electoral manipulation and corruption, as well as accusations of some human rights abuse. Regardless of the validity of these charges, Aristide failed to prosecute human rights violators and did not always meet U.S. economic demands that may have been the condition of his return to power. In this context, in which the rule of law was extremely weak, vigilante justice moved to fill the void; and a wave of revenge killings and lynchings swept the country. With opposition to the status quo mounting, alongside a climate of intense violence, rebel groups composed of former soldiers marched into the capital in March 2004 and—with the support of the United States and the former colonial power France—overthrew Aristide. Paradoxically, human rights violations were central to the coup's rationale.

Body Counting: Ethics, Politics, and Law

Focusing on the number of human rights victims (Table 3) is sometimes essential for political and legal reasons. Politically, international pressure is more likely to mobilize around cases of widespread and egregious human rights violations. While a high number of victims is clearly not sufficient to mobilize international pressure (note the sluggish response to the atrocities in Rwanda and Darfur), a high magnitude of violations is more likely to elicit international attention. Legally, moreover, knowing the extent of violations is crucial for securing justice. The likelihood that individual

Table 3. Human Rights Victims Killed:
Selected Data from Latin America

Country (years)	Estimated number of victims (median)
Colombia (1949–62)	250,000
Guatemala (1966–96)	150,000
El Salvador (1979–92)	75,000
Nicaragua (1978–90)	70,000
Colombia (1984–2007)	50,000
Peru (1982–97)	30,000
Chile (1973–87)	28,000
Argentina (1976–80)	20,000
Haiti (2004–7)	2,000
Honduras (1970–90)	1,000
Brazil (1980)	1,000
Jamaica (1980)	1,000
Mexico (1994–97)	1,000

Source: Monty G. Marshall, "Major Episodes of Political Violence," Center for Systemic Peace, University of Maryland, http://members.aol.com/cspmgm/warlist.htm.

perpetrators will be held accountable certainly can rise with the number of victims. A high number of victims, in contrast to a few isolated incidents, helps establish a pattern of abuse. A high level of abuse also makes it more likely that a state and its leaders can be held responsible for human rights violations. For survivors of abuse and their relatives, extensive documentation and evidence can have a cathartic effect by exposing hidden truths.

Despite the advantages of counting victims, students of human rights should be aware of a few caveats. First, numbers are only useful if they are accurate, and often they are not. This is why many human rights researchers and international nongovernmental organizations (INGOs) who compare violations across countries and over time prefer to examine the level of abuse rather than the number of violations. Errors in reporting can take various forms, including underreporting by governments and their foreign allies, double-counting victims when data is drawn from different local sources, or even exaggeration by political opponents. Not surprisingly, government figures often vary wildly from those reported by human rights nongovernmental organizations (NGOs). This requires examining as many sources as possible and being aware that "low" and "high" estimates of repression can exist.

Second, in addition to reflecting measurement errors, human rights data can be very difficult to interpret since victims' willingness to come forward and report abuses may itself reflect the extent of violations. Thus, the number of violations may be deceptive. A low level of violations, for example, could indicate a climate of terror in which victims are fearful to report human rights crimes. Conversely, data indicating a higher level of violations may only mean that reporting is relatively better, not that abuse is objectively rising. This constitutes an "information paradox": more data about violations may reflect improved reporting rather than a rise in abuse; less data could be evidence of poor reporting rather than a low level of violations. Attention to the broader climate facilitating the reporting of human rights violations is therefore essential for interpreting human rights data.

Third, understanding changes in human rights violations requires differentiating among different types of abuse. A reduction in disappearances, for instance, may not correspond to a decline of torture. Using abuses selectively to generalize about a country's overall human rights conditions should therefore be avoided. Similarly, if numbers of violation are compared cross-nationally, victims should be counted as a percentage of a country's overall population. Note the case of Uruguay in the 1970s. The number of political prisoners in Uruguay would not have appeared that significant when compared to its Southern Cone neighbors; in fact, however, Uruguay had the highest per capita incidence of political imprisonment in the world. Examining violations within Uruguay, it would be entirely misleading to interpret that the country had no major human rights violations simply because virtually no people were killed or disappeared, given the high incidence of other abuses like political imprisonment.

Finally, on an ethical level, thinking about human rights victims in numerical terms can be vexing. On the one hand, even one victim of torture or disappearance can be one too many. While the indeterminacy of human rights data requires speaking of a range of casualty figures, this can seem an ethically futile exercise. A cautious observer refers to a range of 9,000 to 40,000 *desaparecidos* in Argentina, a sensible precaution to take from the perspective of data analysis. But is the give-and-take of 31,000 human lives really inconsequential? On the other hand, some argue that the number of victims may matter in holding violators accountable. Is there a difference between killing a few dozen people versus 40,000? Should the number of victims, relative to the overall size of the population, matter legally? The answers to these questions are highly debated, but one thing is certain. Playing the numbers game with human rights violations requires settling on a threshold: determining how many victims it will take before a legal or political response is triggered.

Quantifying the number of human rights victims is necessary politically and legally, even if it is more challenging than it may seem. Focusing too much on numbers can nonetheless have a numbing and detaching effect, as figures are tossed about without consideration for the moral magnitude of what is at stake—the pain and suffering of individual flesh-and-blood human beings. Ethically, casualty figures may be a necessary evil, worthwhile as long as they illuminate the human lives attached to them.

Questions and Debate

1. Does a hierarchy of human rights exist? Which human rights norms should be at the top of the list? What criteria should be used to determine this?
2. According to the author, how do colonial legacies and state formation contribute to contemporary human rights violations? Do you agree?

3. Which trends in human rights violations described by the author do you find most interesting or surprising, and why? What would you guess explains those trends?

4. Is it possible to measure human rights violations? Desirable? What role, if any, do political factors play in quantifying human rights abuses?

References

Additional Reading (including memoirs and testimonials)

Cristina Aldini, Liliana Gardella, and Munu Actis, eds., *That Inferno: Conversations of Five Women Survivors of an Argentine Torture Camp* (Nashville, Tenn.: Vanderbilt University Press, 2006). First-hand recollections by former female torture victims.

Luz Arce, *Inferno: A Story of Terror and Survival in Chile*, trans. Stacey Alba Skar (Madison: University of Wisconsin Press, 2004). Memoir by a Chilean female torture survivor, turned collaborator, who testified against the regime under democracy.

Patrick Ball, Paul Kobrak, and Herbert F. Spirer, *State Violence in Guatemala, 1960–1996: A Quantitative Reflection* (Washington, D.C.: American Association for the Advancement of Science, 1999). Thorough overview of human rights violations in Guatemala, with an emphasis on quantifying abuses, http://shr.aaas.org/guatemala/ciidh/qr/english/.

Carlos Basombrío Iglesias. "Sendero Luminoso and Human Rights: A Perverse Logic that Captured the Country," in *Shining and Other Paths: War and Society in Peru, 1980–1995*, ed. Steve J. Stern (Durham, N.C.: Duke University Press, 1998). Essay exploring the complex links between Peru's Shining Path and human rights.

Beverly Bell, *Walking on Fire: Haitian Women's Stories of Survival and Resistance* (Ithaca, N.Y.: Cornell University Press, 2001). Moving narratives by a diverse group of Haitian women who recount their experiences in defying abuse.

Herbert Braun, *Our Guerrillas, Our Sidewalks: A Journey into the Violence of Colombia*, 2nd ed. (Lanham, Md.: Rowman & Littlefield, 2003). Riveting true account of the political kidnapping of an American businessman in Colombia.

Alison Brysk, "The Politics of Measurement: Counting the Disappeared in Argentina," *Human Rights Quarterly* 16, 4 (November 1994): 676–92. Illustrates the challenges of measuring human rights abuses.

Marguerite Feitlowitz, *A Lexicon of Terror: Argentina and the Legacies of Torture* (London: Oxford University Press, 1998). Fascinating, accessible account (based largely on testimonials) of the abuse of language and the distortion of reality by the Argentine state, showing how words and symbols can be turned into tools of repression.

Gabriel García Márquez, *Clandestine in Chile* (New York: Holt, 1987). The famous writer retells the daring story of the filmmaker and his six-person crew who shot *Inside Pinochet's Prison* shortly after the 1973 coup. (See filmography section below.)

Francisco Goldman, *The Art of Political Murder: Who Killed the Bishop?* (New York: Grove Press, 2007). Highly acclaimed and gripping account of the murder of Bishop Juan Gerardi, a Guatemalan human rights leader.

Subcomandante Marcos, *Our Word Is Our Weapon* (New York: Seven Stories Press, 2002). Collection of this internationally influential persona's writings on behalf of Mexico's indigenous peoples.

Alicia Partnoy, *The Little School: Tales of Disappearance and Survival in Argentina* (Pittsburgh: Cleiss Press, 1998). One woman's brief and moving recollections of her time in a clandestine prison—"the little school"—in 1970s Argentina.

Patricia Politzer, *Fear in Chile: Lives Under Pinochet* (1989; New York: New Press, 2001). Journalist's interviews with both supporters and opponents of Pinochet, revealing widespread abuse and fear in Chile.

Elena Poniatowska, *Massacre in Mexico* (Columbia: University of Missouri Press, 1992). This well-known writer reports on the brutal killing of more than 300 student protestors just before the 1968 Olympics in Mexico City.

Teresa Rodriguez, Diana Montané, and Lisa Pulitzer, *The Daughters of Juárez: A True Story of Serial Murder South of the Border* New York: Atria Books, 2007). Gripping investigative account of the femicide in Juárez.

Jacobo Timerman, *Prisoner Without a Name, Cell Without a Number* (1979; Madison: University of Wisconsin Press, 2002). Newspaper editor's internationally influential testimony about his capture and torture in Argentina; also offers a glimpse into anti-Semitism during the dirty war.

Alberto Ulloa Bornemann, *Surviving Mexico's Dirty War: A Political Prisoner's Memoir* (Philadelphia: Temple University Press, 2007). First book-length testimony from a political prisoner in Mexico.

Horacio Verbitsky, *The Flight: Confessions of an Argentine Dirty Warrior* (1996; New York: New Press, 2005). Written by one of Argentina's leading journalists, the book exposes one government official's confession and chronicles abuses during the dirty war.

Daniel Wilkinson, *Silence on the Mountain: Stories of Terror, Betrayal, and Forgetting in Guatemala* (Durham, N.C.: Duke University Press, 2002). Engaging account of Guatemala's civil war, told largely through travel narratives and countless personal interviews.

Filmography

Feature Films

City of Men (2007). Follow-up to *City of God*, depicting young men's lives in a violent slum in Brazil. 110 minutes.

Chronicle of an Escape (2006). Young men kidnapped, detained, and tortured in 1970s Argentina plan an escape. 103 minutes.

Machuca (2005). Story of two schoolboys before and after the 1973 coup in Chile, against the backdrop of the country's political turmoil. 121 minutes.

Imagining Argentina (2004). Based on a well-regarded novel of the same title, a woman is disappeared in 1970s Argentina and her husband sets out to find her; incorporating the genre of "magical realism." 108 minutes.

Carandiru (2003). The lives of the prisoners in this massive Brazilian penitentiary and the 1992 massacre that attracted the world's attention. 148 minutes.

City of God (2003). Graphic images of life in a notorious slum in Rio de Janeiro, as captured by a young man aspiring to be a photographer; award-winning film. 130 minutes.

The Silence of Neto (1994). Life in 1950s Guatemala, through a boy's coming-of-age story and against the backdrop of Cold War politics. 106 minutes.

Golpes a mi puerta (*Knocks at My Door*) (1993). Kidnapping of two Catholic nuns in Latin America by the military. 106 minutes.

Rojo Amanecer (1989). One Mexican family's experience during the government's brutal suppression of the 1968 student uprising. 96 minutes.

La noche de los lapíces (*Night of the Pencils*) (1986). Disappearance in 1976 of ten Argentine teenagers who had called for lower bus fares. 101 minutes.

El Norte (1983). Two Mayan siblings, whose parents are disappeared in Guatemala, set out on a perilous journey to Los Angeles. 139 minutes.

Missing (1982). Critically acclaimed drama about a father searching for his son, who has disappeared in a Latin American country. 122 minutes.

Documentaries

Our Disappeared (2008). Highly regarded personal account of a disappearance in Argentina, placed in its broader context. 99 minutes.

La Sierra (2005). Vivid documentary tracking one year in the lives of three young people in a violent Medellín *barrio* in Colombia, alternating between armed street battles and domestic life. 84 minutes.

Aristide and the Endless Revolution (2005). Detailed account of Aristide's removal from power in Haiti and the U.S. role. 84 minutes.

Memoria del saqueo (*Social Genocide*) (2004). Documentary recounting Argentina's 1976 coup that launched the dirty war. 120 minutes.

Scars of Memory (2002). Oral testimonials by survivors of the 1932 massacre in El Salvador. 53 minutes.

Pinochet's Children (2002). Award-winning documentary showing how three young people's lives unfolded under Pinochet's regime. 83 minutes.

National Stadium (2001). Based on eyewitness testimony, this documentary details the detention of more than 12,000 people in Chile's National Stadium during two months in 1973. 90 minutes.

Alonso's Dream (2000). Impact of paramilitary and Zapatista violence on the daily lives of Mayan peasants. 71 minutes.

Chiapas: Landscape After Battle (1999). Examines the conflict between the indigenous population of Chiapas and the Mexican government. 60 minutes.

Human Rights in Haiti (1999). Covers the violent history of human rights in this Caribbean country. 56 minutes.

Mexico: Dead or Alive (1996). Mexican political refugee returns to his country to examine the relationship between politics and human rights violations. 53 minutes.

The Burning Season (1994). Award-winning story of Brazilian rubber tapper Chico Mendes, confronting the government and developers. 123 minutes.

If the Mango Tree Could Speak (1993). Ten children's perceptions of the wars in Guatemala and El Salvador. 58 minutes.

Rigoberta Menchú: Broken Silence (1992). Discussion with the 1992 Nobel Peace Prize winner about the lack of human rights enjoyed by Guatemala's indigenous people. 25 minutes.

Inside Pinochet's Prison (1974). Film crew secretly captures live footage inside Chilean prison camps after the 1973 military coup. 30 minutes.

Useful Websites

Amnesty International. For up-to-date, country-specific information on human rights violations across the region, refer to Amnesty's annual report. The Website is easy to navigate, and it includes special reports and regional topics. www.amnesty.org.

CIRI Human Rights Database (Cingranelli-Richards). A breakthrough and easy-to-use tool for students of human rights, providing quantitative measurements for a large number of human rights practices since 1980; regional data can be isolated. http://ciri.binghamton.edu/.

Human Development Reports. Broad range of relevant statistics offered by United Nations Development Programme; interactive, highly searchable database by region. http://hdr.undp.org/statistics/.

Notes

Epigraph: *Report of the Chilean National Commission on Truth and Reconciliation*, 2 vols. (Notre Dame, Ind.: University of Notre Dame Press, 1993), Part III, Chapter 2, http://www.usip.org/library/tc/doc/reports/chile/chile_1993_toc. html.

[1] John Charles Chasteen, *Born in Blood and Fire: A Concise History of Latin America* (New York: Norton, 2001), chap. 3.

[2] Data from Cingranelli-Richards (CIRI) Human Rights Dataset, used for Figure 1 and Table 2, reflect the extent to which the level of violations is high (over 50 incidents, a score of 2), medium (under 50 incidents, a score of 1), or rare (a score of 0). The CIRI scale, which assigns 0 to high and 2 to rare, is inverted here.

[3] Kathryn Sikkink discusses similar subregional trends in Sikkink, *Mixed Signals: U.S. Human Rights Policy and Latin America* (Ithaca, N.Y.: Cornell University Press, 2004).

[4] Olagier Benaventes Bustos, Talca Regiment, cited in Jorge Escalante Hidalgo, *La Misión era matar: el juicio a la caravana Pinochet-Arellano* (Santiago: LOM, 2000); trans. from Memoria y justicia, a Website devoted to Chilean legal cases against Pinochet, http://www.memoriayjusticia.cl/english/en_focus-caravan. html.

[5] "Major Episodes of Political Violence, 1946–2006," http://members.aol.com/ cspmgm/warlist.htm.

2

Explaining Violations

Human rights violations do not just happen. They reflect particular choices made by specific individuals. Despite their frequency, both in Latin America and around the world, these choices can appear quite puzzling. It is not altogether clear why human rights abuses are even committed, especially in the face of intense international and domestic scrutiny. What is it that leads certain individuals to inflict unimaginable pain and suffering on others? Why do neighbors and former classmates torture and sexually abuse people they used to run into at their local grocer? How do people decide to mutilate bodies or throw them from helicopters into the sea? While this book cannot offer any definitive answers to these difficult questions, it summarizes the leading explanations for human rights violations and lets readers judge the merits—and limits—of existing research.

The Conventional Wisdom

Attempting to explain why rights are violated is a crucial endeavor. Assumptions about rights violations shape the actions taken by advocates, policymakers, scholars, and citizen-voters. Indeed, any effort to improve human rights conditions is guided, at least implicitly, by assumptions about why rights are violated. Before turning to explanations from the social sciences, it is therefore necessary to consider conventional responses to the question "why are human rights violated?" Three views are particularly popular, informing many people's assumptions about the roots of abuse.

The animosity assumption. "They can't get along." This view ascribes violations to a natural and longstanding (if not primordial) hatred among people who appear to be different. Such hatred thrives on categorizing people into mutually exclusive categories: communists and noncommunists; indigenous peoples or Afro-descendants and those of European ancestry; rich and poor; homosexuals and straight people; immigrants and citizens; terrorists and nonterrorists. When people are divided into "in-groups" and "out-groups," the stage is set for mistreatment and abuse.

The animosity assumption, often held by apologists for violating rights, generally implies that violations will occur as long as competing groups interact. Accordingly, governments may portray human rights abuses as necessary responses to social or ethnic conflict. They may blame, in particular, minority groups who engage in militant activism, accusing them of triggering broader hostilities. Some variants of this argument advocate separating groups of people (such as indigenous groups) or making them get along (forced assimilation of refugees, for example). Those who buy into this perspective often excuse human rights violations, seeing them as natural responses to conflicting social identities.[1]

The "evil" assumption. "Human beings are evil." According to this view, human rights are violated because people are inherently evil. A witness to Chile's truth commission expressed this popular sentiment: "It's frightening to think that you are as human as they are. Where could such evil come from?"[2] When confronted with disturbing images of human rights abuse, it is tempting to distance ourselves from atrocities by attributing them to evil in others. This perspective is sometimes related to a "natural rights" view, especially one assuming that rights are divine (or god-given) in origin. If human rights are sacred, literally, then violations are more likely to be seen as arising from evil. Even those who do not approach human rights religiously may think of human rights work in good-versus-evil terms, with human rights taking on the traits of a secular religion and abuses necessarily reflecting evil.

Taken one step further, the assumption is that human rights violations will vary in intensity depending on the degree to which individual perpetrators are evil. This implies that notorious dictators like Chile's Pinochet or Cuba's Castro were especially perverse, sadistic, and diabolical. Broader structural conditions are insignificant, compared to individual malevolence. Focusing on the intrinsically evil nature of human beings is a highly pessimistic view, since it holds that evil—and therefore human rights violations—can never be entirely eradicated.[3]

The cultural assumption. "It's their culture." Of the three conventional assumptions, this may be the most relevant for human rights in Latin America. Rather than focusing on the traits of individuals or particular groups, this view emphasizes broader cultural characteristics. It assumes that societies share overall traits, which make human rights violations more or less likely. Examples of this include assuming that Latin American culture is prone to violence and that the abuse of women reflects a society where *machismo* is commonplace. Like most stereotypes, cultural explanations of human rights can seem appealing due to their simplicity.

Cultural stereotypes explain human rights practices largely in terms of values, attitudes, and traditions. For instance, some observers believe that Latin America has a distinctive "Latin political culture"—including an engrained tradition of authoritarianism and corruption—that inhibits democracy, development, and respect for human rights.[4] Some have extended this argument, warning about the dangers of Hispanic immigration to the United States; the fear is that Latino culture (which purportedly does not value individual rights, for example) threatens prevailing Anglo-Protestant values.[5]

Proponents of a cultural perspective tend to focus on what they perceive to be the root cause of the region's contemporary problems. Consequently, they are not interested in why cultural patterns have emerged historically, how many Latin Americans actually share these traits, or what else might explain human rights abuses. Whereas a "strong" version of this assumption would not expect cultural norms to change much, a "weaker" version might support resocialization efforts, or attempts to gradually replace "backward" cultural norms.

These three positions adopt a static and homogeneous view of social groups, individuals, and regions respectively. On the face of it, they may seem persuasive. They are, after all, virtually impossible to disprove, since support for them is evident only *after* violations have occurred. What they cannot account for, however, is the enormous diversity within social groups, among individuals, and throughout a region. And if social animosity, human evil, and cultural traits are relatively unchanging characteristics, why do human rights abuses break out during some periods more than others? As long as these basic questions remain unanswered, we need to explore alternative explanations.

Insights from Social Science

Human rights research offers various leads to explain why violations occur in a world where rights abuses are expressly outlawed. Social science explanations tend to emphasize two types of argument: decision-making approaches and ideological ones. Decision-making approaches assume that leaders are rational actors who essentially undertake cost-benefit calculations when choosing whether or not to violate human rights. Accordingly, scholars have found evidence that certain factors increase the benefits of violating human rights: war, poverty, the absence of democracy, and domestic threats to a regime. Where these factors are present, states are more likely to violate internationally recognized human rights. Ideological factors, by contrast, focus on the broader, nonmaterial context that makes violations acceptable. Researchers note for example the role of anticommunism, national security doctrines, racism and sexism, economic ideologies, and patriarchy. Not surprisingly, scholars increasingly recognize that both decision making and ideology may be necessary for explaining violations.

The German philosopher Hannah Arendt, commenting on the Adolf Eichmann trial, famously referred to the "banality of evil": not the banality of the Holocaust, but the commonplace nature of the individuals responsible for executing it. Perpetrators of human rights abuse, she suggested, are no more evil than anyone else; they are simply unthinking individuals operating in an environment that encourages violence. The factors identified in social science research represent in some ways the structural conditions that push and shove seemingly ordinary people to commit or condone atrocious acts.

Decision-Making Factors

Of all the factors known to increase the likelihood that human rights violations will occur, *war* is among the strongest. Statistical studies have shown that the incidence of war is highly correlated with the onset of human rights abuses. This has been found to be true even when other potential variables are taken into account (i.e., controlled for using statistical programs).

This is not all that surprising. Both international and civil wars involve the use of force against enemies. The stakes are high in war, and exceptional times often lead both state and non-state actors who have taken up arms to act outside the strictures of international human rights law. Even before the twentieth-century rise of international human rights norms, wars fought over independence, border demarcations, or natural resources in Latin America and elsewhere have involved the repression of civilians. This is precisely why international humanitarian laws, as enshrined in the Geneva Conventions and implemented by the International Committee of the Red Cross exist, to set guidelines for humane conduct during war.

In the Latin American context, the role of war seems to be highly relevant, if incomplete. Countries that have had full-blown armed conflicts in recent decades—El Salvador, Guatemala, Colombia, and Peru—have also seen an inordinately high level of human rights violations. Interestingly, moreover, even when countries were not technically at war, leaders across the region have often used the *language* of war (metaphorically) to justify the suspension of human rights. Yet despite the obvious significance of war, it is also true that egregious human rights violations often occur outside the context of war. Chile and Argentina were notorious human rights violators in the 1970s, for example, in the absence of civil or international war. A much fuller exploration of other factors is clearly required.

While *poverty* can be an indicator that economic and social rights are being abused, it can also be a *cause* of other human rights violations. Researchers have found that higher levels of poverty, in particular, are associated with greater violations of physical integrity such as torture and disappearances. This too may seem not all that surprising. When countries are poor, governments seeking to maintain stability (and retain power) may respond to intractable social demands with repression and violence.

Certainly, there is something at least partly compelling about this argument. The countries that perhaps most people associate with egregious human rights violations tend to be relatively poor. This is true of Latin American countries like Haiti and Guatemala, which are among the region's poorest. Some critics caution, however, that focusing on poverty alone obscures more important questions, such as why countries are poor in the first place and why human rights violations are not identical across poor countries. Perhaps this is why statistical studies have shown that although poverty is associated with personal integrity violations, the association is not a particularly strong one. Honduras, for example, is relatively poor in the region, and while it has certainly experienced violations, these are not comparable in scope to those of Haiti or Guatemala. The effects of poverty may therefore be more indirect, as governments in poor countries face higher demands that they cannot meet. How governments respond to poverty, nonetheless, still begs for an answer.

Not surprisingly, a much stronger relationship is known to exist between the *lack of democracy* and human rights violations. It is almost a truism to say that nondemocracies are more likely to violate human rights norms. Several explanations exist for this. Democracy is a type of regime, or domestic institution, which reflects a particular configuration of state-society interaction and a specific set of norms. Democracies are structured so that in principle societal interests are represented; the assumption is that most people will not support widespread repression. Democracies also tend to resolve conflicts peacefully or legally. In contrast, in less democratic regimes, societal opposition to human rights violations will not be voiced as openly, let alone shape government decision making, since leaders are not beholden to a popular constituency. In nondemocratic regimes, only the most powerful members of society, including the coercive apparatus and economic elites, have access to decision makers. A vicious cycle ensues, as the institutions of governance block social opposition but privilege powerful actors who support coercion as a way of maintaining their own standing.

Two caveats are in order. First, some scholars emphasize that democracy is a matter of degree, since all regimes are "more" or "less" democratic. This implies that human rights violations can occur under any type of regime, including established democracies; after all, human rights abuses persist even after transitions to democracy, and violations can exist in longstanding democracies. Human rights abuses are therefore a matter of degree, so that less democratic regimes will engage in relatively more human rights violations (e.g., the number of victims will tend to be much greater or the abuses more egregious).

The second caveat is that the process of democratization itself can be fraught with instability. As states democratize, members and allies of the former regime attempt to retain control while competing sets of norms may collide. Whether international actors should impose democratization is therefore subject to much dispute. A democratic transition does not necessarily signal full human rights protection, as human rights abuses can continue and accountability mechanisms remain weak. These nuances aside, the degree of democracy may provide a missing link between poverty and human rights violations. It offers a political-institutional explanation for why human rights violations vary across similarly developed countries.

If the above factors indirectly influence decision makers' calculations about violating human rights, *security threats* directly alter a leader's assessment of the costs and benefits of initiating repression. Security threats occur when a group poses an apparent challenge to national survival or identity. In practice, many scholars have interpreted this to mean armed attacks against a state, whether by other states or by non-state actors. Others have focused attention on broader perceived threats, including the role of domestic protests. While government responses to protests may depend on the overall political context, security threats involving the use of armed force tend to elicit violent reactions on the part of many if not most states. Since states are partly defined by their monopoly over the legitimate use of force in a given territory, as German sociologist Max Weber first contended, it is unsurprising that leaders would seek to defend this basic attribute of the modern state. Most leaders will calculate that when national security is at stake, it pays to violate personal security.

The evidence throughout Latin America strongly supports the claim that security threats are tied to human rights violations. Many spikes in human rights violations have occurred in the aftermath of guerrilla attacks or public appearances by armed groups. For example, General Ríos Montt of Guatemala launched a savage campaign in 1982, following the public resurgence of armed insurgents the previous year. The notorious violations that occurred in Argentina in the 1970s were partly responses to the apparent threat posed by extremist groups like the Montoneros and the ERP (Popular Revolutionary Army). In Chile, interestingly, human rights violations reignited in the early 1980s, just as armed groups resurfaced and domestic protests intensified significantly, although abuses had been declining. In the 1990s, the Mexican government did not hesitate to respond to the rise of Zapatista rebels with widespread repression, just as Peru's Shining Path provoked the fury of the state apparatus. Violence and abuse in Colombia has also partly mirrored the dynamics of armed guerrilla groups. Acknowledging that a link exists between armed groups and human rights violations, however, is not the same as justifying the use of force by any particular actor or exonerating state violence as reactive.

Even when groups are mostly unarmed, governments may treat opponents—especially those who take to the streets to protest—as security threats. In many of the region's countries, for example, indigenous groups are viewed as threats, especially in the context of the U.S.-sponsored "global war on terror" and the "war on drugs." Attempts by indigenous groups to mobilize for greater rights and the return of their territory have been met with systematic violence. Relying on antiterrorist laws, governments detain indigenous activists without due process and for extensive periods of time. Police also restrict the freedom of movement of indigenous communities, displacing them from their homes or forcing them to remain within the confines of a particular area. Police brutality during peaceful demonstrations has even resulted in the death and detention of indigenous minors. Ricardo Díaz, an indigenous representative of the strongest opposition party in Bolivia, describes the dynamics: "It's true that indigenous peoples are a threat, from the point of view of the political and economic powers-that-be. They see us as terrorists, but we aren't, because our struggle is open, legal and legitimate."[6] Other protesters have also been abused. For example, police responded with violence to poor people rioting in Haiti—where 80 percent of the population lives on less than two dollars per day—after soaring global prices in summer 2008

Figure 6. Police confront Haitians protesting food shortages in front of Presidential Palace in Port-au-Prince in mid-2004. Scott Olson/Getty Images.

made basic food staples unaffordable.[7] When groups publicly oppose the existing political order, authorities are more likely to label them security threats and violate their basic human rights.

Yet not everyone is convinced that the relationship between security threats and human rights violations is straightforward. One critique is the age-old chicken-and-egg question: rather than security threats leading to violations, people may protest and take up arms against the state largely in response to violation of their rights. Even if social protest is partly a response to human rights abuses, security threats very often trigger new rights violations. Likewise, arguments that emphasize security threats disturb some people because they sound too much like the arguments made by abusive governments: "we had to do it." It is true that security threats rarely threaten a state objectively, since armed groups tend to be much smaller than states and can be controlled through standard avenues of law enforcement. The reasons for this are discussed below, suggesting the importance of the ideological context in defining what constitutes a threat in the first place. All told, security threats are the excuse that governments use most often to rationalize, to themselves and others, violence against society.

The research reviewed so far shows how decision makers face certain material conditions (war, poverty, the lack of democracy, security threats) that make violating human rights relatively desirable. These conditions, more precisely, put at risk two fundamental and related goals that most leaders share: to reduce instability and retain power. When these goals are threatened, states are likely to violate human rights norms. What remains unclear is why engaging in repression is deemed an *appropriate* response to domestic instability. The choice to violate human rights can be particularly perplexing since other viable responses often exist, and violations can elicit global opprobrium. This is where the role of ideology enters the picture.

Ideologies and Repression

If domestic instability triggers human rights violations, it may well be because of *exclusionary ideologies*. Exclusionary ideologies are systems of belief that justify the use of violence or discrimination against certain people or under specific situations; these ideologies exclude people from basic human rights protections. Examples of exclusionary ideologies that underlie human rights abuses include anticommunism, racism, bigotry, sexism, national security doctrine, neoliberal economic orthodoxy, impunity, and "the war on terror." These ideologies serve to label categories of people as "outsiders" or enemies; from there, the slippery slope to dehumanization follows easily. In some cases, discussed below, exclusionary ideologies are institutionalized, so that their transmission occurs through regular channels like the professional training of security forces. In other cases, their influence is much more diffuse and subtle, though perhaps no less powerful.

The most obvious exclusionary ideologies that have shaped human rights events in the region relate to *anticommunism* and national security. Much has been written elsewhere about the ideological struggle that characterized the Cold War, a world divided largely into two blocs, each upheld by a superpower. Latin America, of course, was not the only battleground during the Cold War, but in the closest region to the United States the stakes were deemed high on all sides. Particularly after the Cuban Revolution in 1959, the United States moved even more aggressively to root out communist influence in the region. Similar dynamics, propelled by the Sandinista takeover of Nicaragua in 1980, help explain the Reagan administration's interventions in the region. Miniature cold wars played out within individual countries, as groups on the right and left of the political spectrum confronted one another, sometimes in armed conflict.

Closely related to anticommunism, the *doctrine of national security* was developed and transmitted throughout the region during the Cold War. National Security Doctrine (NSD) was a virulent ideology developed in the United States in the 1950s that defined a state's security in terms of containing communism. Any person suspected of potentially supporting or sympathizing with leftist ideas was to be eradicated from society. This goal was considered so valuable that any means could be used to assure a society free of communist interference. Personal security could be sacrificed for national security. In practice, these ideas were transmitted mostly through military training, so that members of a country's security forces learned repressive means to respond to the threat of domestic insurgents or "subversives." Political opponents were redefined as vital threats to national security. They were labeled enemies, in an internal war where freedom, Western civilization, and Christian values were pitted against a totalitarian, non-Western, and atheistic communist future. In this manner, national security ideology defined enemies and legitimated human rights violations in the name of a higher national ethos.

Despite international pressures to create national security states during the Cold War, especially in response to armed insurgents, it would be a mistake to overlook the fact that national security ideology resonated with certain intellectual strains and historical experiences in Latin America. Latin American constitutions had always left the door open for the suspension of personal rights during times of exceptional threat to the homeland. And just as Enlightenment ideas about the importance of rights influenced early state formation in the region, the dominant Catholicism underlying colonialism promoted notions of an organic state, whose health depended on the integrity of the nation. In this context, it is not surprising that state leaders late in the twentieth century described political opponents as "cancers" to be extirpated from the body politic. Historically, as Chapter 1 suggests, the protracted nature of independence in Latin America had forged militaries who came to view themselves as key actors guaranteeing domestic political stability and order. National security ideology was transmitted through military training in the context of the Cold War, but the idea resonated strongly with the region's basic legal frameworks and the historical experience of its armed forces.

In recent years national security ideology has translated most directly into *antiterrorism*, or the idea that terrorist threats must be destroyed at all costs. Antiterrorism was a corollary of earlier national security doctrines that targeted insurgents and guerrilla movements. Then and now, in and out of Latin America, the overriding notion is that the rights of suspected terrorists should be suspended. The label "terrorist" is significant, denoting a person who is an enemy of the nation-state, and therefore a threat to national security and identity. This labeling has important implications for antiterrorism as an ideology. First, antiterrorism necessitates a climate of exceptionalism; that is, given the potentially high risks for national security, governments must be permitted to break existing laws, including human rights. Arbitrary detentions, harsh interrogations, and even torture are fair game. Second, and closely related, antiterrorism calls for proactive measures. Rather than merely responding to concrete terrorist threats, precautionary measures like preventive detention (i.e., arresting people for what they might do, often accompanied by indefinite periods of detention without appropriate recourse to legal counsel) are required. Third, antiterrorism is naturally expansive, continually broadening its definition of who constitutes an enemy. Thus, antiterrorism laws across the region, modeling themselves partly on the U.S. Patriot Act, were used after 9/11 to arrest a broad segment of people, including shantytown dwellers, human rights activists, street vendors, and indigenous people—in the same way that during the Cold War students, psychiatrists, social justice workers, and acquaintances of suspected terrorists were disappeared. While Latin America has not been the most prominent battleground in the U.S.-led war on terror, as discussed at greater length in Chapter 7, antiterrorist ideology has been tied since 9/11 to human rights violations in the region.

Economic ideology also shapes human rights violations. In particular, neoliberal economic ideas exerted their most visible influence in the 1990s, though their reach extended back to the 1970s and continue to this day under the umbrella of globalization. These ideas originated in the United States among economists and were supported by professional counterparts in Latin America and elsewhere. They motivated international financial institutions like the World Bank and International Monetary Fund (IMF), and they propelled the interests of both multinational corporations in the region and local business groups.

Substantively, neoliberal economic ideology typically has called for a package of policies that include privatization, heavy foreign investment, export-oriented growth, and free trade. Governments are simultaneously to cut back on social subsidies and public support for social services. The problem is that these cuts, along with rising prices and unemployment, often produce social discontent. Particularly in countries with relatively well-organized labor movements, such as Argentina, or exceedingly high levels of poverty, like Haiti, this discontent is likely to produce public riots, strikes, and other contentious demands on the state to curb its economic policies.

Consequently, for neoliberalism to succeed, it requires domestic stability and social quiescence as a country undergoes painful short-term cuts in anticipation of longer-term economic growth. In this manner, economic ideology fuses with national security doctrine, as security forces assure domestic stability by way of human rights abuses if necessary. The picture is complicated by the fact that members of the military often become implicated in the disproportionate wealth befalling some members of society at the expense of others, making them personally vested in perpetuating violence.

Perhaps more fundamentally, *racism and other discriminatory ideologies* make human rights violations possible. Whenever ideas define some human beings as inferior to or less equal than others, the stage is set for suspending rights. Racist ideas focus on perceived differences among people. The arbitrariness of determining who belongs to a race is amply evident in Latin America, where intermarriage has obscured the boundaries between African and European descent.

Yet racism is endemic across Latin America, as it is in many parts of the world. Racist ideas trace their roots partly to Spanish colonialism, which created power disparities and served to disenfranchise indigenous people and descendants of African slaves, groups that to this day represent most of the region's minorities. *Mestizos*, those descended from European ancestry and therefore generally lighter in skin tone, often reinforce historical power asymmetries by perpetuating ideas about the natural inferiority of minorities. Since minorities also tend to be poorer, less educated, and therefore not as powerful as *mestizos*, breaking out of the cycle of racism has proved difficult. Racism also factors into human rights violations targeting indigenous people, such as the genocide perpetuated against Mayan peasants in Guatemala during the 1980s.

Other discriminatory ideas show that, even in the absence of security threats, some groups are perceived to threaten national identity. This helps to explain why women, homosexuals, and ethnic or religious minorities can be targets of abuse. In practice, these underprivileged groups suffer systemic and legally sanctioned discrimination, including grave violations of basic economic and social rights. They may have their activities criminalized (e.g., same-sex relations are illegal in the Caribbean and Central America); enjoy limited access to public services like health care and legal institutions (e.g., indigenous people have limited access to health services and, consequently, higher rates of HIV/AIDS and maternal mortality); or be deprived of basic rights (e.g., in the Dominican Republic, Guatemala, and Peru, some ethnic groups are denied proper birth certificates, de facto excluding them from key services).[8] When human rights violations occur, exclusionary ideologies assure that there is little if any public outrage or mobilization. Deeply entrenched in social relations, exclusionary ideologies can be exceedingly difficult to change.

The case of women's rights illustrates these tensions. While some countries and municipalities have passed laws regarding violence against women, and the region has seen women rise to positions of power (including the presidency), discrimination against women is built into many of the region's legal systems. For instance, the right to choose an abortion is illegal—under any circumstances—in Chile, El Salvador, Honduras, and Nicaragua.[9] Additionally, in some countries, laws stipulate that husbands have primary control over decision making, while women can marry at a younger age and face more legal barriers to remarrying.[10] Legal discrimination is certainly not universal, but it perpetuates ideologies of discrimination that exclude people from basic rights to equality on the basis of gender. The problem also manifests itself within the private sphere, as domestic violence often goes unpunished. For example, according to the World Bank, one woman is killed every nine days in Uruguay—a country with a strong human rights record—as a result of domestic violence.[11] These abuses, inadequately punished by the state, signal the presence of exclusionary ideologies that lead to serious abuse.

While exclusionary ideologies are never entirely responsible for human rights violations, and the treatment of the region's minorities has improved, their role should not be overlooked. When minorities are targeted in large number, the role of race and other discriminatory ideologies should be examined alongside related socioeconomic and political factors. At the same time, the political status of minorities across Latin America certainly has improved since the 1990s, as is evident in the extension of land and cultural rights in Colombia and Venezuela and in the rise of indigenous political parties in Bolivia and Ecuador. The surprising victory of Evo Morales, an indigenous activist who became Bolivia's president in 2005, further illustrates these transformations. Despite these improvements, experts contend that social discrimination and exclusion remain serious problems throughout the region.

Finally, an ideology of *impunity* (the belief that perpetrators of human rights violations will not be punished) can lead to human rights violations. Ideas about impunity can shape decision making, as leaders discount the risks of violating human rights. In fact, leaders will often violate human rights precisely to avoid responsibility for other violations. This explains, for example, the targeting of human rights activists, a pervasive problem throughout Latin America. From the perspective of those violating human rights, beliefs about impunity (discussed in Chapter 6) make violations possible—sometimes even necessary.

The Role of the United States

Latin American politics cannot be understood apart from the region's complex historical relationship with its massive and powerful neighbor to the north, the United States. The United States has played over time the role of both friend and foe of human rights in the region. Indeed, single administrations have followed seemingly contradictory policies of promoting internationally recognized norms while aiding and abetting human rights violators. This chapter focuses on the darker side of U.S. human rights policies in Latin America, while Chapter 4 examines U.S. efforts to promote human rights reform in the region.

How exactly has the United States contributed to human rights violations in the region? One systematic way of responding to this question is to consider the U.S. role vis-à-vis the roots of abuse: war, poverty, lack of democracy, security threats, and exclusionary ideologies. The history of U.S. involvement in Latin America is beyond the scope of this book, but the evidence—from the Central American regimes of Guatemala and El Salvador during the Cold War to the current war in Colombia— amply shows that the United States has taken sides in the region's conflicts, often allying itself with authoritarian states against insurgents. The evidence is also clear that the United States has encouraged, to varying degrees, the overthrow of democratically elected governments it has found threatening. The Guatemalan coup of 1954, the overthrow of Salvador Allende in Chile in 1973, and a more recent possible coup attempt against Venezuela's Hugo Chávez in 2004, all feature among the prominent examples.

The United States, according to some accounts, has also exacerbated poverty across the region through its support of harmful policies by the World Bank, the IMF, and multinational corporations, as well as in its bilateral trade relations with individual countries. Not all of these actions are deliberate attempts to undermine human rights per se. For example, the United States has initiated coca eradication programs in the Andes to pursue the drug war. Widespread aerial fumigation of coca fields, however, has had the unintended consequence of destroying other crops that represent the only source of livelihood for poor peasants; and it has compromised the health of local residents. Likewise, multiple endeavors to modernize the region's economies by exploiting natural resources— whether in the banana plantations of the Caribbean or deep in the Amazonian jungle—have had detrimental consequences on local power relations, the state of the environment, and the health of peasants and indigenous people.

It is no exaggeration to say that U.S. policies have been harmful to human rights abroad. Certainly, the United States and its allies do not always set out to commit human rights abuses. In fact, they have often taken steps to improve human rights conditions, ameliorate poverty, and promote conflict resolution in the region (Chapter 4). Yet insofar as U.S. policies contribute to destabilizing democratically elected regimes, militarizing conflicts (by providing local allies with arms, for example), and exacerbating endemic poverty in the region, they undoubtedly contribute to human rights abuses.

Direct evidence of U.S. complicity in the region's rights abuses does exist. Recently declassified documents reveal example after example of U.S. leaders explicitly giving authoritarian despots in the region a "green light" for committing abuses, often at the same time that the United States was publicly applying pressure on these regimes. In a document declassified in 2004, for instance, Henry Kissinger is quoted as saying to Argentina's generals in 1976: "If there are things that have to be done, you should do them quickly."[12] Likewise, we now know that the United States directly assisted Operation Condor, a regional network of intelligence agencies that coordinated repression across borders.

UP CLOSE: OPERATION CONDOR

In a secret meeting held in Santiago, Chile, in November 1975, the intelligence and security services of five South American countries—Argentina, Bolivia, Chile, Paraguay, and Uruguay—agreed to set up a regional network of repression; Brazil soon joined in the endeavor. Orchestrated by Chile's notorious intelligence service (DINA), military and police forces in the region pooled their resources and exchanged information to detain, torture, and kill alleged subversives. In addition to conducting operations across one another's borders, Operation Condor reached as far as France, Spain, Italy, Portugal, and the United States (where two people were assassinated in 1976 by a car bomb in downtown Washington, D.C.). While not directly involved in Operation Condor, the governments of Peru, Colombia, and Venezuela also filtered intelligence to the Southern Cone regimes.

Records of this transnational repressive network emerged in 1992, when a Paraguayan judge discovered the "terror archives" in a suburban police station of Asunción. The gruesome details of the network were revealed: Operation Condor had been responsible for 50,000 deaths, 30,000 disappearances, and 400,000 detentions. The

Operation ceased to exist formally in 1983, when Argentina's dirty war ended, although transnational cooperation among intelligence services and some killings continued into the 1980s.

Recently declassified U.S. State Department documents suggest that the United States may have been a silent partner behind Operation Condor. In a 1978 cable, the U.S. ambassador in Paraguay referred to a "U.S. communications installation in the Panama Canal Zone" (Condor-Tel) used to coordinate information exchange by the intelligence chiefs running Operation Condor. Other declassified documents reveal that U.S. agencies (including the CIA, FBI, and Defense and State Departments) knew about and approved of Condor's existence.

The case of Jorge Isaac Fuentes Alarcón, a Chilean sociologist, illustrates this collusion. In mid-1975 Paraguayan police detained Fuentes Alarcón as he crossed the border from Argentina. An FBI agent in Buenos Aires purportedly notified the Chilean military of his arrest and revealed the names and addresses of U.S. residents Fuentes Alarcón had mentioned during interrogation. He was then handed over to Chilean police, transferred to a detention facility, subsequently tortured, and permanently disappeared.

Sources: For access to 16,000 relevant documents declassified by the United States in 2000, see National Security Archive, Chile Documentation Project, http://www.gwu.edu/~nsarchiv/news/20001113/. The case of Fuentes Alarcón is from Chilean National Commission on Truth and Reconciliation, *Report of the Chilean National Commission on Truth and Reconciliation* (Notre Dame, Ind.: University of Notre Dame Press with Center for Human Rights, Notre Dame Law School, 1991), Part III, Chapter 2.

A recent study documents carefully how Latin American leaders in the 1970s and 1980s perceived the "mixed signals" that the United States was sending as direct permission and encouragement to violate human rights.[13] Thus, Guatemala's violations spiked to genocidal proportions in 1981–82, despite the fact that U.S. pressure appeared to be quite high. Under the influence of the Kirkpatrick Doctrine—named after the U.S. representative to the United Nations, who claimed that the United States should maintain friendly relations with right-wing authoritarian regimes even if they violated human rights, but oppose left-wing totalitarian regimes—the Reagan administration in its first term repeatedly assured authoritarian regimes that they could repress leftist insurgents. The region's militaries happily obliged, while indiscriminate abuse led to suffering among large segments of the region's people. Onlookers felt betrayed by the hypocrisy of a superpower that claimed to promote human rights.

Ideologies undoubtedly play a role in explaining U.S. support for repression and other policies that have undermined human rights. Anticommunism, national security doctrines, neoliberal economic ideas, and antiterrorism can motivate people to support human rights abuses as temporary exceptions required by a seemingly unique set of circumstances. During the Cold War, for example, the belief prevailed that any challenge to the status quo carried the risk of communist infiltration and therefore necessitated widespread repression. Yet ideas influential enough to shape policies do not just float freely between individuals. They tend to get transmitted through regularized institutional channels and mechanisms. According to some influential human rights scholars, the puzzle of why so many human rights abuses were clustered in the decades between the 1960s and 1980s in Latin America is precisely because this period saw a generation of military professionals who had been indoctrinated after World War II to accept national security ideology.

The School of the Americas

Training in national security ideology, with all it implied for human rights, took place at the School of the Americas (SOA), where the U.S. government trained Latin American militaries. Indeed, perhaps no image conveys more starkly the negative effects of the United States on human rights in the region than the controversial SOA. Opened in 1946, the school has trained more than 60,000 members of the region's security forces in basic military skills, counterinsurgency tactics, and the use of antinarcotics tools. Many of its trainees have gone on to join the annals of the region's most notorious rights violators, including leaders of Argentina's dirty war; one of the commanders of the El Mozote massacre; the founder of Honduras's most infamous death squad, Battalion 3-16; a slew of violent coup leaders; and the instigator behind the assassination of El Salvador's Archbishop Oscar Romero.

A couple of issues are worth clarifying. First, despite the notoriety of

FIGURE 7. Critics of the School of the Americas demonstrate in front of U.S. Justice Department in Washington, D.C., in 2005. Alex Wong/Getty Images.

some of its graduates, most of the students training at the SOA are low-level members of the military, whose classes last from one week to four months; the elite officer-training program is one year. Second, the SOA is but one of approximately 150 facilities that the United States uses to train members of foreign militaries. Some of these schools, including the Inter-American Defense College in Washington, D.C., also offer courses in Spanish geared to officers from the region.[14]

Since its creation, the SOA has passed through four distinct phases: a formative period (1946–58), followed by periods of consolidation (1959–83), expansion (1984–95), and defensive reform (after 1996). During the early, formative years the SOA was called the Latin American Ground School and (after 1949) the U.S. Caribbean School; it was housed in the Panama Canal Zone. True to its name and location, about half the almost 8,000 students during this period were from Central American countries.

The Cuban Revolution in 1959 and Fidel Castro's rise to power were crucial to U.S. policy in the region and the ascendance of the School's popularity. Thoroughly restructured and renamed the SOA in 1963, the institution's primary mission was to train the region's militaries to fight communism under the banner of national security. Attendance at the

SOA virtually doubled in the 1960s. By the 1970s, the SOA was catering heavily to students belonging to repressive militaries, especially Chile's armed forces.

While SOA practices in the 1980s were largely consistent with previous decades, the institution moved to Fort Benning, Georgia, in 1984 when the Panama Canal reverted to Panama. The move proved to be highly consequential, as part of the SOA mission expanded: buying students' allegiance by exposing them to the American way of life. Professional socialization acquired a more openly cultural component, playing off the race, class, and nationality divisions among the region's students. With George Bush at the helm in the early 1990s, training during this period also extended to countering the drug war in the Andes. Most of the students during this period were from El Salvador's military, itself involved in a gruesome civil war.

Securely ensconced within its fenced compound, the SOA came under intense criticism and scrutiny after 1996, leading it to undertake defensive reforms. In 1996, the discovery of teaching manuals supporting the use of physical coercion led activists and concerned citizens to question and expose the School's involvement in the region. In 1999, as public debate intensified, funding for the SOA was almost eliminated. This culminated in a brief closure of the SOA and its reopening in 2001 under a new name: the Western Hemisphere Institute for Security Cooperation. Additionally, in response to intense pressure, the new Institute (which critics continue calling the SOA) has incorporated human rights rhetoric and content into its courses. All trainees are required to take dozens of hours of human rights instruction, though critics assert that attention to human rights remains one-sided, superficial, and subject to cynicism.

Coinciding with the new global "war on terror," the institute has shifted its mission to accommodate emerging security threats, including the "war on drugs." (The links between this new mission and previous efforts to combat subversives is discussed in Chapter 7.) While over half of all students in recent years have been from Andean countries, notably Colombia, a few countries in the region have moved to resist the Institute and U.S. hegemony. Surprisingly, since 2006, a few countries have refused to send their military or police forces to the Institute, including Venezuela, Argentina, Costa Rica, and most recently, Bolivia in 2008. Some critics predict that it is only a matter of time until the Institute is closed, even if it eventually resurfaces in a different form.

UP CLOSE: THE TORTURE MANUALS

"While we do not stress the use of coercive techniques, we do want to make you aware of them and the proper way to use them.

"The 'questioning' room is the battlefield upon which the questioner and the subject meet. However, the 'questioner' has the advantage in that he has total control over the subject and his environment.

"Tapes can be edited and spliced, with effective results, if the tampering can be kept hidden.

"Throughout his detention, subject must be convinced that his 'questioner' controls his ultimate destiny, and that his absolute cooperation is essential for survival.

"[The questioner] is able to manipulate the subject's environment, to create unpleasant or intolerable situations, to disrupt patterns of time, space, and sensory perception.

"The number of variations in technique is limited only by the experience and imagination of the 'questioner.'

"The purpose of all coercive techniques is to induce psychological regression in the subject by bringing a superior outside force to bear on his will to resist. Regression is basically a loss of autonomy, a reversion to an earlier behavioral level.

"For centuries 'questioners' have employed various methods of inducing physical weakness: prolonged constraint; prolonged exertion; extremes of heat, cold, or moisture; and deprivation of food or sleep.

"There is a profound moral objection to applying duress beyond the point of irreversible psychological damage, such as occurs during brainwashing. . . . Aside from this extreme, we will not judge the validity of other ethical arguments.

"If a subject refuses to comply once a threat has been made, it must be carried out.

"Some subjects actually enjoy pain and withhold information they might otherwise have divulged in order to be punished.

"There are a few non-coercive techniques which can be used to induce regression, but to a lesser degree than can be obtained with coercive techniques.

"A psychiatrist should be present if severe techniques are to be employed, to insure full reversal later."

Source: Central Intelligence Agency, *Human Resource Exploitation Manual* (1983), used in several Latin American countries by CIA and Green Beret trainers in 1983–87, National Security Archive Website (http://www.gwu.edu/~nsarchiv/).

Frameworks for Understanding State Terror

Human rights abuses in Latin America reveal the importance of both decision-making and ideological factors for understanding state terror. While each of the factors identified in this chapter enhances the likelihood that human rights will be violated, none absolves any human rights violator from responsibility; repressors tend to know that what they are doing is illegal internationally. Still, structural conditions do help to explain why human rights violations can be so prevalent even when they are internationally prohibited.

Identifying individual factors that contribute to rights violations is not the same as offering a more general explanation of why states inflict horrible abuse on human beings. This requires combining the various contributing factors into an overall account of human rights violations— specifying how different factors explain distinct aspects of the *decision* to act abusively. Taking this analytical step is crucial. For example, if democracy is significant for understanding human rights violations (and large-scale statistical studies, as well as commonsense observations, tell us that it is), then why do egregious abuses persist even under democratically elected regimes like those in Colombia or Mexico? A broader theory can help clarify questions such as these.

Figure 8 offers one explanatory framework for understanding state terror. According to this depiction, exclusionary ideologies are the starting point for explaining rights violations. Before leaders undertake cost-benefit calculations about the utility of engaging in repression, they must first deem repression appropriate. Deeply ingrained, institutionalized ideas define who counts as a full human being, entitled to state protection, and

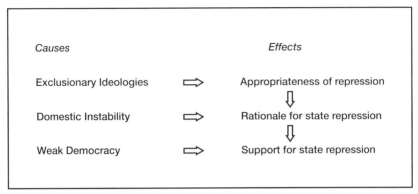

FIGURE 8. Why are human rights violated? A framework for explaining state terror.

who does not. Thus racism excludes people with certain characteristics who challenge the identity of powerful actors; anticommunism targets leftist sympathizers, seeking to protect the greater good, as well as the twin values of democracy and capitalism; national security doctrine vilifies any challenge to the status quo as a threat to the security of the nation and Western civilization; neoliberal economic ideology silences social protest in the name of long-term economic growth; and antiterrorism negates the rights of suspected terrorists to protect the security of a greater number of people. Anywhere that these ideologies are found, the possibility for human rights abuse exists.

The actual trigger for human rights violations comes in the form of domestic instability, which makes repression a desirable outcome, given the exclusionary ideologies already in place. Domestic instability can take various forms, including most of the decision-making factors discussed earlier in the chapter, namely war, poverty, and security threats. The more these factors are present, the greater the state's rationale for abusing human rights. From the perspective of state leaders, instability (especially prevalent in military and security crises) threatens their hold on power. Yet leaders have a variety of options other than repression for responding to domestic instability; they may co-opt challengers or cooperate with them, for instance. Just as exclusionary ideologies make repression viable, domestic instability makes them appear necessary. In justifying abuses, therefore, leaders will point to domestic instability as evidence of exceptional circumstances. This is why higher degrees of domestic instability are so often associated with greater human rights abuses.

Focusing on the broader role of domestic instability helps to explain some otherwise puzzling outcomes, including why human rights violations often occur in the absence of war and poverty. Linking domestic instability to exclusionary ideologies also accounts for why security threats of widely varying degrees nonetheless seem almost always to trigger a violent response from the state. Indeed, in virtually every case in Latin America, states whose leaders and their allies had adopted exclusionary ideologies responded to security threats with violence.

The final step in understanding human rights violations is democracy, a factor that many studies have found significant. Democracy helps to explain the support that state leaders will enjoy for pursuing repression. Exclusionary ideologies and domestic instability alone will produce human rights abuses, but the degree to which a country is democratic can help to explain the scope of repression. In relatively nondemocratic regimes, those who support violations tend to have more institutionalized access to decision-making, and the state's coercive apparatus enjoys substantial autonomy from public opinion.

In democracies, where some exclusionary ideologies always survive, leaders will also respond to serious domestic instability with repression. The key difference is that the consequences of their actions are much less certain for democratic leaders, due to electoral accountability, the lack of severe censorship, and the presence of legal opponents. This means that they will repress, but do so in ways that attempt to distance the state from blatant acts of violence. Consequently, in democratic regimes, repression may be farmed out to paramilitary groups (as evident in Colombia) or meted out to nondemocratic allies (e.g., the United States policy of rendition sends suspected terrorists to be interrogated by governments who may use torture).

According to this framework, moreover, explaining horrific acts like torture takes on new meaning. In contrast to the conventional wisdom, which asserts that states torture to extract valuable information and save countless lives, this explanation views torture as being ultimately rooted in an exclusionary ideology. Torture is no longer merely a response to security threats; it is appropriate only in the context of institutionalized ideas about national security. And while torture is practiced more routinely in nondemocratic regimes, according to this analysis, even democratic regimes facing domestic instability will resort to it.

Indeed, paying attention to both the ideas and material structures underpinning human rights violations turns popular views of torture on their head. Torture becomes a way of controlling society through fear more than a crude mechanism for extracting information. This interpretation, when combined with evidence that torture rarely yields accurate information—as confirmed by the CIA itself in their "torture manuals"—may be surprising (and less palatable) than the common view that torture is necessary for national security.

Attempting to "solve" or prevent a problem always requires understanding its causes. As common as this assumption is in almost all fields, the temptation to treat human rights differently can be overwhelming. People often gravitate to one of two polar views: they assume that human rights advocacy is sufficient, and then inevitably become disappointed, or they despair at the seeming impossibility of using policies to correct human wrongs. Insights from social science suggest that the structural conditions that make violations desirable and appropriate for political leaders must be targeted: war, poverty, the lack of democracy, security threats, and exclusionary ideologies. There are no shortcuts around this. As long as these factors exist, human rights abuses will persist.

Questions and Debate

1. To what extent, in your view, are conventional explanations about human rights violations accurate?
2. Is ideology actually important for understanding human rights violations, or is it just an after-the-fact excuse? Discuss both sides of this issue.
3. How persuasive do you find insights from social science to explain human rights abuses? Which aspects do you find most and least compelling?
4. What concrete implications flow from the framework presented in Figure 8? For governments? Human rights advocates? The informed public?

References

Additional Reading

Elvia Alvarado, *Don't Be Afraid, Gringo: A Honduran Woman Speaks from Her Heart* (New York: HarperCollins, 1987). First-hand account, told by a Honduran woman, of poverty and violence in Honduras, including the U.S. role in that country.

Sabine C. Carey and Steven C. Poe, eds., *Understanding Human Rights Violations: New Systematic Studies* (Aldershot: Ashgate, 2004). One of the few book-length attempts to explain human rights violations; provides a solid state-of-the-art introduction.

Mark Danner, *The Massacre at El Mozote* (New York: Vintage, 1994). Award-winning journalist's analysis of why this village massacre occurred in El Salvador and the role of the United States.

Christian Davenport, *State Repression and the Domestic Democratic Peace* (Cambridge: Cambridge University Press, 2007). Sophisticated account of when and how democracies engage in state repression.

Christian Davenport, Hank Johnston, and Carol Mueller, eds., *Repression and Mobilization* (Minneapolis: University of Minnesota Press, 2005). Insights into how domestic threats make physical integrity violations more likely.

John Dinges, *The Condor Years: How Pinochet and His Allies Brought Terrorism to Three Continents* (New York: New Press, 2004). Journalistic, detailed account of Operation Condor.

Lesley Gill, *The School of the Americas: Military Training and Political Violence in the Americas* (Durham, N.C.: Duke University Press, 2004). Highly readable comprehensive account of the ins and outs of the School of the Americas.

Peter Kornbluh, *The Pinochet File: A Declassified Dossier on Atrocity and Accountability* (Washington, D.C.: National Security Archive Book, 2003). A reproduction of previously classified U.S. government documents, detailing human rights violations in Chile under Pinochet.

Cecilia Menjívar and Néstor Rodríguez, eds., *When States Kill: Latin America, the U.S., and Technologies of Terror* (Austin: University of Texas Press, 2005). Traces human rights violations in the region to technologies of terror, emphasizing the role of the United States.

Darius Rejali, *Torture and Democracy* (Princeton, N.J.: Princeton University Press, 2007). An award-winning book examining startling connections between democracies and the use of torture.

Jennifer Schirmer, *The Guatemalan Military Project: A Violence Called Democracy* (Philadelphia: University of Pennsylvania Press, 1998). An unusual opportunity to hear the views of military officials responsible for human rights abuses, drawing on extensive interviews.

Filmography

Between Midnight and the Rooster's Crow (2005). A multinational corporation in Ecuador, in collusion with the government, is responsible for environmental degradation and human rights violations. 66 minutes.

What Is It Worth? (2005). Brazilian film weaving together race relations during slavery with contemporary economic ideologies that perpetuate inequality. 110 minutes.

Condor: Axis of Evil (2003). Examines Operation Condor, based on interviews with both victims and perpetrators. 90 minutes.

Death Squadrons: The French School (2003). South American generals describe the torture and killing of victims during the dirty war, including the role of military training by French officers. 60 minutes.

Hidden in Plain Sight (2003). Different sides of the controversial debate over the School of the Americas. 71 minutes.

Tupamaros (1996). Members and former members of the Uruguayan urban guerrilla group recount the history of the movement. 50 minutes.

School of Assassins (1994) and *Father Roy: Inside the School of Assassins* (1997). Critical look at the School of the Americas, including activists and former graduates. 17 and 57 minutes respectively.

Maria's Story (1990). Documentary focusing on a female guerrilla fighter for the Farabundo Martí National Liberation Front in El Salvador; includes live combat footage. 53 minutes.

Fire in the Andes (1985). A look at the victims of political violence in Peru, as seen through the eyes of indigenous peasants and the relatives of a group of journalists murdered. 35 minutes.

Batalla de Chile (*The Battle of Chile*) (1976, 1978). Award-winning, three-part documentary focusing on Chilean political life before and after the 1973 coup, including the role of the United States. Part I, The Insurrection of the Bourgeoisie (96 minutes), Part II, The Coup d'État (88 minutes), and Part III, The Power of the People (78 minutes).

State of Siege (1973). Feature film set in Uruguay chronicling the interrogation of an American who is kidnapped; raises issues about the role of the United States in teaching torture techniques. 120 minutes.

Useful Websites

National Security Archive (George Washington University). A wide range of declassified documents relevant to human rights; special projects devoted to Chile, Colombia, Cuba, Guatemala, Honduras, and Mexico. http://www.gwu.edu/~nsarchiv/.

School of the Americas Watch. Critical, activist website with a wealth of information. http://www.soaw.org/new/.

Minorities at Risk. An impressive collection of qualitative and quantitative data on minority groups, searchable by region. http://www.cidcm.umd.edu/inscr/mar/data.asp.

International Relations Data Site (Paul Hensel). Access to hundreds of types of international data, including many of the factors discussed in this chapter. http://garnet.acns.fsu.edu/~phensel/data.html.

Notes

[1] This view is similar to "primordial" arguments about ethnic conflict, often held by governments and lay people. For the latter applied to Latin America, see Deborah J. Yashar, *Contesting Citizenship in Latin America: The Rise of Indigenous Movements* (Cambridge: Cambridge University Press, 2005), 9–11.

[2] *Report of the Chilean National Commission on Truth and Reconciliation*, 2 vols. (Notre Dame, Ind.: University of Notre Dame Press, 1993), Part III, Chapter 4.

[3] In *Radical Evil on Trial* (New Haven, Conn.: Yale University Press, 1996), Carlos Santiago Nino argues that people commit evil acts, but human rights prosecutions can help prevent future abuses.

[4] For example, Howard J. Wiarda, "The Struggle for Democracy and Human Rights in Latin America: Toward a New Conceptualization," in *The Continuing Struggle for Democracy in Latin America*, ed. Howard Wiarda (Boulder, Colo.: Westview Press, 1980). For a broader overview, see Hugo Fruhling, "Political Culture and Gross Human Rights Violations in Latin America," in *Human Rights in Cross-Cultural Perspectives: A Quest for Consensus*, ed. Abdullahi Ahmed An-Na'im (Philadelphia: University of Pennsylvania Press, 1995).

[5] Samuel P. Huntington, "The Hispanic Challenge," *Foreign Policy* (March/April 2004).

[6] Gustavo González, "'War on Terror' Has Latin American Indigenous People in Its Sights," *Inter Press Service*, 6 June 2005.

[7] See, for example, Marc Lacey, "After Protests, Haitian Leader Announces Rice Subsidies," *New York Times*, 13 April 2008.

[8] Amnesty International, *Amnesty International Report 2008: The State of the World's Human Rights* (New York: Amnesty International, 2007).

[9] As well as the Dominican Republic as this book went to press. Note that, in a break from other international human rights documents, Article 4 of the American Convention on Human Rights defines the right to life as beginning "from the moment of conception."

[10] See, for example, Human Rights Watch, "Women's Rights in Latin America and the Caribbean," http://www.hrw.org/women/overview-lac.html.

[11] World Bank, "Bank Supports Women's Fight Against Domestic Abuse," http://go.worldbank.org/LUII1BOGP0.

[12] Carlos Osorio and Kathleen Costar, eds., *National Security Archive Electronic Briefing Book 133*, http://www.gwu.edu/~nsarchiv/NSAEBB/NSAEBB133/index.htm.

[13] Kathryn Sikkink, *Mixed Signals: U.S. Human Rights Policy in Latin America* (Ithaca, N.Y.: Cornell University Press, 2004).

[14] See Lesley Gill, *The School of the Americas: Military Training and Political Violence in the Americas* (Durham, N.C.: Duke University Press, 2004).

PART II

Promoting Reform

3
Global Governance

When human rights violations occur, people need forums where they can go to demand justice. Domestic legal courts and political institutions, however, often fail to provide human rights accountability. Perpetrators go unpunished, victims are not compensated, and the truth remains untold. Fortunately, in situations where human rights victims or activists have exhausted all domestic remedies, they can turn to international and regional forums. Internationally, the UN system provides several interlocking mechanisms for upholding human rights. Regionally, the inter-American human rights system offers a range of possibilities for those seeking protection. Together, international and regional institutions act as a global safety net for human rights victims, giving them hope that justice will be served and violators will be held accountable.

The global system of human rights governance consists of specific international and regional institutions, including human rights *treaties*, *commissions*, and *courts*. These institutions create expectations about what constitutes human rights and what procedures should be followed when these rights are violated. Just as these institutions exist at the international level (under the umbrella of the United Nations), some regions have their own systems of human rights governance. In this regard, Latin America has one of the most developed region-wide mechanisms for regulating human rights. The inter-American human rights system is composed of numerous relevant treaties and institutions, including the American Convention on Human Rights; the Inter-American Commission on Human Rights; and the Inter-American Court of Human Rights. This chapter reviews these key institutions, along with prominent cases brought before Latin America's human rights bodies. The chapter also situates the inter-American human rights system in its broader global context, reviewing the role of UN mechanisms in the region, comparing the inter-American system with other regional mechanisms (in Europe and Africa), and examining the region vis-à-vis the nascent International Criminal Court. When states terrorize people, international and regional institutions can indeed step in on behalf of human rights victims.

UN Mechanisms

The United Nations is not a world government, but it is the foremost international intergovernmental body working to promote and protect human rights. As such, it applies human rights pressure on recalcitrant states, investigates situations of abuse, and provides concrete assistance to human rights victims. This complex organization has various mechanisms by which it carries out its human rights work. First, it has treaty- and non-treaty-based procedures, as detailed below, some of which have played a crucial role in Latin America. Second, specialized agencies of the United Nations work extensively on the rights of vulnerable groups, including refugees, children, and poor people. Third, UN peacekeeping missions in the region have integrated human rights issues into their mandates. In all of these cases, it is crucial to note that the United Nations is only as strong as its individual members states allow it to be.

One of the most basic acts a state can take internationally with regard to human rights is to ratify a treaty. In addition to defining standards, most human rights treaties create specific committees and procedures with which state parties must cooperate. For example, states that have ratified the International Covenant on Civil and Political Rights must submit regular reports to the Human Rights Committee, which monitors the treaty's implementation. The treaty also allows for inter-state complaints, so that one state can submit a complaint against another state alleging human rights abuses. The targeted state is then expected to cooperate with the Human Rights Committee, which investigates the allegations. Of course, parties to a treaty do not always comply with these requirements. They may fail to submit reports in a timely or accurate fashion, or they may otherwise refuse to cooperate with the Committee. Since international organizations tend not to have enforcement powers,

UN committees are limited in what they can do; but they do condemn state violators and can include their recommendations in public reports. While these pressures may seem weak, a large number of international and local actors draw on the work of these UN treaty bodies to mobilize even more intense pressure.

Beyond treaty-based procedures, the UN human rights system has other avenues for applying pressure. The Office of the High Commissioner for Human Rights, created in 1993, often plays a leading role. Its most important body is the Human Rights Council, which replaced the sixty-year-old Human Rights Commission in 2006. Victims and their representatives can submit complaints to this body, which considers them confidentially—under the premise that states are more likely to cooperate if they are not shamed publicly. Additionally, the new Council continues to have special procedures at its disposal, including special rapporteurs or working groups established to investigate a particular country or issue (e.g., disappearances, poverty, migrants, torture, violence against women). UN representatives can investigate conditions within a country (as long as the government grants it entry), prepare reports, and issue recommendations. The High Commissioner for Human Rights, the equivalent of the "Secretary General" in the human rights world, can also bring his or her public office to bear on state violators.

Special UN rapporteurs and working groups on human rights have played a crucial role in Latin America. In 1980, in response to the magnitude of disappearances during Argentina's dirty war, the United Nations created a special working group on disappearances. Consisting of five independent experts, the group has proven to be a valuable conduit between families of the disappeared and national governments around the world; its goal is to find those who have disappeared (or their remains), but not to establish responsibility per se. It has initiated tens of thousands of inquiries in the region, in some cases following up with in-country visits to investigate allegations more fully. While it has succeeded in solving only a relatively small number of disappearances, the working group has been most effective in calling attention to individual cases and challenging specific governments to provide information. Likewise, a special rapporteur for torture (created in 1985) has been very active in the region, transmitting urgent appeals to governments, visiting countries, and issuing an annual report with recommendations. Unlike most international mechanisms, individuals can approach the rapporteur even if they have not exhausted all domestic avenues; given the prevalence of torture in so many countries, this translates into a large volume of petitions and a heavy workload.

As with all international human rights bodies, UN groups can visit countries by invitation only—state sovereignty permits governments to control who enters their borders and what they do once there. This is a basic fact of the international system, producing mixed results. On the one hand, governments can orchestrate visits, sometimes going as far as to move prisoners or reconstruct entire areas of a detention facility. Governments can lie to foreign investigators, or refuse altogether to cooperate. On the other hand, the evidence suggests that states generally care about their international reputations; in an interdependent world, there is always a chance that trade or military relations might be linked to human rights performance. Consequently, governments will often concede to foreign demands for information and access, even as they try to manage the situation. The outcome may often be disappointing to foreign observers, but occasionally it will lead to significant improvements for the victims of abuse (e.g., a prisoner will be released, or the conditions of detention improved). In the context of atrocities, the power of such changes should not be underestimated.

More broadly, several UN programs and agencies work closely to protect human rights in Latin America. In particular, the UN High Commissioner for Refugees (UNHCR) has been an essential actor. Even at the height of human rights violations, UNHCR often has offices in a country and can assist refugees and internally displaced persons. Indeed, UNHCR saved thousands of people in the region during previous decades. Today, it is especially active in Colombia, which has one of the largest groups of internally displaced people anywhere in the world (about three million); UNHCR has over a dozen field offices in that country and is a staunch advocate for the rights of displaced persons. UNICEF, which works on behalf of children worldwide, has focused its efforts in Latin America on educating and protecting children against landmines, especially in Central America and Colombia. And the Pan American Health Organization (the regional arm of the World Health Organization) works at the intersection of health and human rights, calling attention to numerous issues, including health equity by race and poverty level, stigmas attached to HIV/AIDS patients, violence against women, and of course, the internationally recognized right to health. These organizations and others have broad access to countries in the midst of violence and abuse precisely because they are deemed to be largely humanitarian.

On the peacekeeping front, the region has seen a relatively small number of missions: a total of ten since the end of World War II, five of these in Haiti. The first UN peacekeeping mission to the region went to the Dominican Republic in the mid-1960s. Other forces were stationed in Central America, helping to assure regional stability during the 1990s. The one peacekeeping mission currently in existence (Haiti) illustrates broader challenges. Of the eighteen countries that have military troops stationed in Haiti, half of these are from Latin American countries; almost 10,000 peacekeepers are in the small Caribbean country. Their mandate is to stabilize Haiti through an extremely broad range of tasks, including election monitoring, police reform, de-arming of militias, public safety, rule-of-law promotion, and human rights monitoring. While trying to fulfill their vast mandate, UN peacekeepers in Haiti have received negative attention following allegations of sexual abuse, some involving minors. This sort of a problem is not unique to peacekeeping forces in Haiti. Peacekeepers have been mostly unable to stop the violence, amid routine gang violence, kidnappings, and lynchings. Despite efforts on behalf of peace and human rights, UN forces in Haiti reveal the limits of a military approach.

Observers of UN human rights bodies can grow frustrated and cynical at the apparent weakness of these institutions, which seem to be at the mercy of human rights violators. Yet in a world where states are so powerful, intergovernmental organizations like the United Nations are only as strong as their member states allow them to be. Since states remain the principal violators of human rights in the world, it is not all that surprising that they do not create strong institutions to regulate themselves. The key is to remember that UN pressure is only one part of a vast and interconnected transnational network (see Chapter 4), which uses a wide range of tools to pressure abusive states. Still, for human rights victims who may feel helpless, UN mechanisms—like the intervention of a special rapporteur or assistance by the UNHCR—can produce tangible results, if only by raising awareness of human rights abuses and demanding answers from state violators.

Latin America in Global Perspective

The inter-American human rights system, along with its European and African counterparts, constitutes one of the world's principal regional human rights systems.[1] All of these regional systems sit under an overarching international human rights system, including the United Nations and the International Criminal Court. Of all the regional human rights systems, Latin America's is the second oldest in the world and widely considered to be the second strongest, following the European system.

The inter-American human rights system differs from other parallel mechanisms in a few crucial ways:

First, some basic institutional structures vary: along with Europe, Latin America has the only functioning region-wide human rights court in the world (Africa has a court that is not yet fully operational); in contrast, the European system no longer has a Commission, only a full-time Court, a move designed in recent years to increase efficiency and emphasize the juridical nature of the system.

Second, unlike the European Court, the inter-American one does not accept cases directly from individual victims; instead, individuals are required to go through the Commission. This is of crucial significance, since it limits access to the Court and the number of cases considered.

Third, unlike other regional institutions, the Inter-American Commission on Human Rights (IACHR) is empowered to conduct onsite visits to countries where evidence exists of human rights violations. While states have to agree to allow the IACHR into the country, such visits can put governments on alert, generate publicity, and ultimately empower local activists.

Fourth, in contrast to Europe, most Latin American states do not automatically incorporate Court findings into their domestic legal systems. The result is that national courts and legislatures rely on the Inter-American Court's findings only sporadically, weakening the system of implementation and compliance.

Fifth, in terms of the volume of cases brought before these human rights bodies, the difference is phenomenal. Between 1979 and 2008, the Inter-American Court issued judgments on 192 cases, compared to more than 10,000 cases pending before the European Court in 2007 alone!

While the inter-American human rights system lags behind the European regime in terms of efficiency, access to victims, and compliance with Court rulings, it still remains relatively developed in global terms.

The Regional Human Rights System

Just as the international human rights system dates to the Universal Declaration of Human Rights, the inter-American system has its roots in the 1948 American Declaration on the Rights and Duties of Man. It was not, however, until 1959 that the IACHR was created. Initially much weaker than it is today, the IACHR was not authorized to investigate petitions until 1965. Four years later, in 1969, the American Convention on Human Rights was drafted. The convention entered into force in 1978, when the Inter-American Court of Human Rights also was formed.[2] With these central institutions in place, more specialized human rights treaties have been concluded since the 1980s (see Table 4). Together, these institutions and norms constitute the region's human rights system.

Table 4. Human Rights Treaties in Latin America

American Declaration on the Rights and Duties of Man (1948)

American Convention on Human Rights (1969)

Protocol of San Salvador: Economic, Social and Cultural Rights (1988)

Protocol to Abolish the Death Penalty (1990)

Cartagena Declaration on Refugees (1984)

Inter-American Convention to Prevent and Punish Torture (1985)

Inter-American Convention on Forced Disappearance of Persons (1996)

Inter-American Convention on the Prevention, Punishment, and Eradication of Violence against Women (1995)

Proposed American Declaration on the Rights of Indigenous Peoples (ongoing)

Inter-American Convention on the Elimination of All Forms of Discrimination against Persons with Disabilities (2001)

The Inter-American Commission of Human Rights

Headquartered in Washington, D.C., the IACHR is the official intergovernmental body charged with promoting human rights in the region. It is comprised of seven independent experts (not government representatives), appointed to four-year terms by the OAS General Assembly. The IACHR is charged primarily with investigating cases of human rights abuse by governments and reporting on human rights conditions in the region.

Investigations can be prompted by a petition. Petitions can in turn be submitted by an individual (either victim or third party) or by an interested organization. The IACHR can also launch an investigation on its own initiative, though investigations are usually sparked by reports from organizations and individuals. Interestingly, in cases where third parties approach the IACHR, they need not have the victim's consent. The Commission also publishes an annual report, detailing the cases it has examined in a given year and offering its views on the state of human rights in the Americas.

Petitions can be submitted against any member state of the OAS, regardless of whether it has ratified the American Convention on Human Rights. Petitions can also allege general human rights violations committed against a group of people. The following steps clarify the process by which the IACHR considers a human rights petition.

> *Step 1: Admissibility.* For the IACHR to deem a petition admissible, the petition must include specific information: location and date of the violation; name of the victim(s); name of any state official accused; detailed information of government involvement (whether direct or indirect), if possible; and a list of the human rights violated. Petitioners must also establish that they have exhausted all domestic legal remedies, a fairly standard requirement for any international human rights body. This implies that a petitioner has already pursued unsuccessfully all available domestic legal channels.
>
> *Step 2: Government response.* If a case is found admissible, the IACHR will request that the government in question respond to a petition within 90 days (extensions of up to 180 days are possible). Government responses must address the facts of a case and verify that domestic remedies have been exhausted. A government's failure to respond to the IACHR's request for information can be used to establish its guilt.
>
> *Step 3: Petitioner's comments.* If a government responds to the IACHR, the petitioner is given 30 days to comment on that response and/or submit additional material. In these comments, a petitioner can request that evidence be provided, an oral

hearing be held with witnesses, or an on-site investigation be conducted for general petitions.

Step 4: *Fact-finding and investigation.* The commission considers evidence, can hold a hearing, or even conduct an on-site investigation in the case of widespread abuses.

Step 5: Recommendations. The IACHR reaches a decision and forwards its recommendations to the government. For governments that have ratified the American Convention, the Commission is obligated to try and reach a "friendly settlement."

Step 6: Commission report. In cases where a friendly settlement is reached, the IACHR prepares a summary report that the OAS Secretary General publishes. When the parties do not reach a settlement, the IACHR writes a report detailing facts and recommendations. It then gives the parties three months in which to decide whether to submit the case to the Inter-American Court of Human Rights. At the conclusion of this period, the Commission issues a formal resolution along with a timetable for the government to undertake specific measures.

Step 7: Final judgment. When a state has both ratified the American Convention and accepted the optional jurisdiction of the Inter-American Court of Human Rights (discussed below), either the state or the Commission can refer the case to the Court. When this is not possible, the IACHR moves to issue a lengthy report with recommendations, including the possibility of monetary compensation. Unlike the Court's decision, however, the commission's recommendations are nonbinding.

Despite the intricate steps that need to be taken when a petition is submitted to the IACHR, the Commission is relatively active. Its caseload has increased substantially in recent years. Between 1997 and 2005, complaints to the IACHR more than tripled—from 435 to 1330. Many of its most prominent cases end up at the Inter-American Court of Human Rights, which can issue a pathbreaking decision. And in one of its most effective activities, the IACHR conducts on-site visits to trouble spots every year. In 2002, for example, the IACHR visited Ciudad Juárez and Mexico City to examine violence against women, issuing a widely circulated report the following year. Special rapporteurs address the rights of indigenous people, women, children, and human rights workers. Finally,

FIGURE 9. OAS general assembly meeting focuses on strengthening the Inter-American system of human rights. Teresita Chavarria/AFP/Getty Images.

the IACHR annual report serves as a valuable public and authoritative source of information on human rights conditions in the region.

UP CLOSE: THE BARRIOS ALTOS AND
LA CANTUTA MASSACRES (PERU)

On 3 November 1991, at 10:30 p.m., a group of people were having dinner in Barrios Altos, a neighborhood in Lima, Peru. Six masked men, driving cars with police sirens, burst into the party and fired machine guns (with silencers) indiscriminately into the crowd. Fifteen people died and four were seriously injured. A subsequent investigation revealed that the killers were members of a death squad; a leaked government document countered that the victims were subversives belonging to the Shining Path. Various attempts to investigate and prosecute those responsible for the massacre in Barrios Altos proceeded unsuccessfully. Then, in 1995, a general amnesty law exonerated all members of the military and security forces from being charged with human rights violations. Later that year, Peru's Supreme Court confirmed the importance of the amnesty law by shutting down the case permanently. In 1996, the case was taken to the IACHR by a human rights organization representing the relatives of victims. The IACHR referred the case to the Inter-American Court for Human Rights, which ruled in 2001 that *amnesty laws are illegal* and contravene basic international human rights obligations. The Court ruling had a ripple effect throughout the human rights world, marking the first time that an international court ruled explicitly against the use of national amnesties.

Eight months after the Barrios Altos massacre, violence struck again in Peru. Members of the Colina Group—a death squad—conducted a raid on La Cantuta University, considered a hotbed of radicalism and support for the Shining Path. On 18 July 1992, nine students and one professor were kidnapped and disappeared, never to be seen again. The case also found its way to the IACHR, after a nongovernmental organization submitted a petition in 1993. In 1999 the IACHR decided the case was admissible; but it was not until 2005 that the Commission found that the Peruvian government had violated basic human rights. In 2006, it referred the case to the Inter-American Court on Human Rights. In its final judgment of November 2006, the Court concurred with the Commission and awarded over $1.8 million in compensation to more than 40 people related to the victims of the massacre.

Sources: Inter-American Court of Human Rights, *Barrios Altos Case*, Judgment of 14 March 2001 (http://www.worldlii.org/int/cases/IACHR/2001/5.html); Inter-American Court of Human Rights, *Case of La Cantuta v. Peru*, Judgment of 29 November 2006 (http://www.corteidh.or.cr/docs/casos/articulos/seriec_162_ing.doc).

The Inter-American Court of Human Rights

Headquartered in San José, Costa Rica, the Inter-American Court of Human Rights is the main judicial body in the Americas for human rights. It was created in 1979, with the express purpose of upholding the American Convention on Human Rights. Like other international courts, it is empowered both to hear cases of rights violations (adjudicate disputes) and to issue legal opinions about specific provisions of the American Convention (advisory opinions).

UP CLOSE: THE *VELÁSQUEZ RODRÍGUEZ* CASE (HONDURAS)

Angel Manfredo Velásquez Rodríguez was a teacher and graduate student in Honduras. On 12 September 1982, he was disappeared in downtown Tegucigalpa by seven armed men, dressed in civilian clothes, who whisked him away in a white car with no license plates. He left a family behind, including three small children. After little progress within the Honduran legal system, the case was taken to the IACHR, which referred it to the Inter-American Court. Witnesses before the Court helped to establish that Velásquez Rodríguez had been abducted by state agents, held in a secret detention center before being tortured and killed, and that this case was one of many constituting a pattern of systematic human rights violations by the Honduran state. Consequently, in a landmark decision, the Court found that states have a dual obligation to desist from committing human rights violations *and* to protect individuals against their rights being violated. For the first time in international law, this case defined state obligations vis-à-vis human rights in positive terms: states must protect everyone under their rule from harm.

Source: Inter-American Court of Human Rights, *Case of Velásquez-Rodríguez v. Honduras*, Judgment of 29 July 1988 (Merits) (http://www.corteidh.or.cr/docs/casos/articulos/seriec_04_ing.doc).

The Court consists of seven judges, who must be from a member state of the OAS. The judges, who are elected by the OAS General Assembly, must meet the highest legal criteria and have superior ethical reputations. Judges serve for six-year terms, with the possibility of being reelected for one additional term. At any given moment, no two judges from the same country can sit on the Court. Judges, moreover, do not have to recuse themselves when hearing a case involving their own state, since—like all judges—they are expected to uphold the highest legal standards notwithstanding their personal commitments. From its inception, the Court has had one judge from the United States, Thomas Buergenthal, who served throughout the 1980s.

The Court can only hear cases involving a state that is party to the American Convention *and* that has accepted voluntarily the Court's jurisdiction. States can accept the Court's general jurisdiction (i.e., for any case that may arise) or on a case-by-case basis. While the notion that states

UP CLOSE: MEMORIES OF A JUDGE

"When I joined the Inter-American Court, much of the Western Hemisphere was still in the throes of massive human rights violations. In the Americas of that time, the Cold War permitted the military regimes and civilian dictators to torture and disappear anyone whom they labeled as subversives. Often, too, the mere public discussion of human rights could land a person in jail or worse. . . .

"In the 25 years since its establishment, the Court's docket of contentious cases has grown significantly, and, on the whole, states are complying with the Court's judgments. It is slowly but steadily gaining recognition in the region and successfully surmounting its initial growing pains. . . .

"That the message sometimes gets through even without massive public relations efforts was vividly demonstrated to me while I served on the United Nations Truth Commission for El Salvador. We were interviewing some *campesinos* in a small village where serious human rights violations had taken place during El Salvador's long civil war. One of the witnesses, an old farmer, reported on what had happened in his village. He concluded with the demand that the government comply fully with the 'Velásquez Rodríguez Law.' Our chairman responded, 'you mean the Velásquez Rodríguez Case?' 'Yes,' the old man replied, 'the law does away with impunity and makes governments pay for their human rights violations.' It will always remain a mystery for me how this farmer, living in that far away village in El Salvador, had heard about a judgment of the Inter-American Court sitting in San José, Costa Rica. But the fact that he heard of it suggests that sometimes news that inspires hope in people whose human rights are being violated has a way of getting through and giving them hope."

Source: Thomas Buergenthal, "Remembering the Early Years of the Inter-American Court of Human Rights," *New York University Journal of International Law and Politics* 37 (2005): 259–80.

get to decide when they will appear before the Court may sound bizarre, in a world of sovereign states these are fairly standard procedures in international law. Seventeen Latin American states have accepted the Court's general jurisdiction.[3]

Cases can be brought before the Court in one of two ways: (1) by state parties to the American Convention or (2) by the Inter-American Commission on Human Rights. It is important to note that the Court, like all international courts and reputable national ones, follows strict rules of procedure and requires a high threshold of evidence before it will issue a finding. This can entail listening carefully to witness testimony and consulting the views of experts. In cases of a negative judgment, the Court can require the state to compensate victims and undertake other remedial steps, although states do not always comply with Court decisions. The Court is nonetheless well regarded internationally and, as some of the Up Close entries in this chapter illustrate, it has issued landmark findings that have left their imprint far beyond Latin America.

Indeed, the Inter-American Court has established a reputation for upholding the rule of law regardless of political considerations. This is evident in the case of Lori Berenson, a New Yorker and former MIT student who has been imprisoned in Peru since 1995. Berenson was charged with assisting the Túpac Amaru Revolutionary Movement, a purported terrorist group; she is not scheduled for release until 2015. Though initially given a sham military trial and imprisoned in inhumane conditions, the Inter-American Court found that Berenson's subsequent 2001 trial was fair. While international supporters of Berenson called for her release, the Court focused its decision on the integrity of the legal proceedings. Amnesty International concurred. Legal standards weighed most heavily on the Court, despite the political backlash against upholding the imprisonment of a U.S. citizen considered by some to be a human rights activist.

The International Criminal Court

Complementing regional and national courts, the International Criminal Court (ICC) is the most impressive development in international law in the last half century and a cornerstone of today's international human rights system. The Court, which entered into force in 2002, is located in the Hague, Netherlands; more than 100 countries around the world have accepted its jurisdiction. This new court has oversight over three types of international crimes: crimes against humanity, war crimes, and genocide. Unlike the International Court of Justice (or World Court), which tries states, the ICC has jurisdiction over individuals. The Court's jurisdiction, moreover, extends only to crimes committed after a state has accepted the Court's competence; thus, the Court does not have jurisdiction over twentieth-century dictators. Furthermore, the ICC is expected to uphold the highest standards of due process and fairness in its deliberations.

Twenty-one Latin American and Caribbean states have ratified the Rome Statute, which created the ICC. These states, that is, have agreed to accept the ICC's jurisdiction. Those states in the region that, like the United States, have not accepted the Court's jurisdiction include Chile, El Salvador, and Suriname. Of the first eighteen judges elected to the ICC by state parties, four were Latin American (from Bolivia, Brazil, Costa Rica, and Trinidad and Tobago). The Costa Rican judge, Elizabeth Odio Benito, was also part of the first three-member presidency. Moreover, states parties elected Argentinean Luis Moreno-Ocampo, a world-renowned international legal expert, as the ICC's First Chief Prosecutor. Latin Americans therefore remain at the forefront of international legal developments.

On a more controversial front, the United States in its opposition to the ICC has entered into approximately 100 bilateral immunity agreements with countries around the world. Governments who sign these agreements consent not to transfer U.S. nationals indicted by the ICC. When pressuring states to sign these bilateral agreements, the United States has threatened to cut off military assistance. As of mid-2006, 13 countries in Latin America had signed such agreements with the United States, while another 14 countries had publicly opposed the agreements and suffered cuts in military aid.[4] For example, in 2004, Ecuador lost $7.6 million in assistance, Peru had $2.4 million cut, and Uruguay's aid was slashed by $1.4 million.

As the ICC develops, the role of Latin American states will be quite interesting to watch. So far, states in the region that have joined the United States to undermine the Court are relatively weak states or those fighting an internal conflict. What is striking, however, is that about half of the region's states—which the United States has long considered to be in its "backyard"—have resisted pressure to oppose the ICC, despite their close relations with and relative dependence on the hegemon to the north (see the list in note 4). Why? The answer is not self-evident, and it is likely implicated in these countries' broader international relations. (For example, countries with strong ties to large European countries may also have resisted signing bilateral immunity agreements with the United States.) Still, it is significant that even countries that continue to struggle domestically with issues of human rights accountability are unwilling to support immunity internationally.

Assessing Future Regional Cooperation

As the inter-American human rights system evolves over the years, it is likely to continue strengthening some of its mechanisms. One international legal expert referred in the late 1990s to this regional system as "no longer a unicorn, not yet an ox."[5] In comparative global terms, Latin American institutions indeed score somewhere between the effectiveness of the European and the African systems of protection. On the one hand, numerous specialized human rights agreements have been concluded, the IACHR's caseload continues to expand, and the Inter-American Court has issued landmark cases. Furthermore, the inter-American human rights system has increasingly turned its attention to newer issues, including the rights of vulnerable populations like children, indigenous people, and internally displaced persons; economic and social rights, including the right to health; and even the relationship between climate change and human rights. On the other hand, the efficiency of the overall system, its access to victims, and the lack of state compliance and domestic implementation represent major challenges to the current system.

Not only is the inter-American system younger than the European one, but the recent history of human rights abuses continues to restrict the effectiveness of a region-wide system of protection in the Americas. The legacy of years of authoritarian rule constrains the extent to which this regional system of protection can continue to improve. At some point, certain reforms will be necessary, including perhaps streamlining complaints and giving victims more direct access to regional institutions. At the domestic level, moreover, national laws have to be changed so that the findings of the Inter-American Court may be adopted automatically, leading to greater state compliance. Unfortunately, the climate of impunity that prevails in much of the region is likely to hamper regional reforms and domestic implementation.

Institutions, however, often change incrementally and in surprising ways. The last three decades have witnessed the gradual evolution of the international and inter-American human rights systems. Political transformation, namely, the turn toward democratization, has had an immense impact on the regional system's development. Transnational networks, the subject of the next chapter, have been at the forefront of these transformations, paving the way for greater human rights protection across the continent. The future of the inter-American human rights system will depend on the political climate within countries and broader international developments, alongside the power of transnational networks to promote concrete change. As international and regional human rights institutions evolve, victims of abuse will continue turning to them, hopeful that global governance can deliver a measure of justice.

Questions and Debate

1. What do you find most interesting about UN human rights mechanisms? About the inter-American human rights system?
2. To what extent do you think that a hegemonic power like the United States can influence regional human rights mechanisms? Which other factors might be significant?
3. What criteria could one use to judge the effectiveness of governmental human rights bodies, including UN mechanisms or the IAHCR?
4. Why would states like Chile not accept the ICC's jurisdiction? Alternatively, why would over a dozen states resist U.S. pressures to sign bilateral immunity agreements?

References

Additional Reading

Iain Guest, *Behind the Disappearances: Argentina's Dirty War Against Human Rights and the United Nations* (Philadelphia: University of Pennsylvania Press, 1990). Engaging and thorough account of UN human rights pressure against Argentina's dirty war regime.

David J. Harris and Stephen Livingstone, eds., *The Inter-American System of Human Rights* (London: Oxford University Press, 1998). Experts discuss the regional human rights regime from numerous angles.

Julie Mertus, *United Nations and Human Rights: A Guide for a New Era* (New York: Routledge, 2005). Comprehensive guide to understanding UN human rights machinery.

Jo M. Pasqualucci, *The Practice and Procedure of the Inter-American Court of Human Rights* (Cambridge: Cambridge University Press, 2003). Detailed examination of the regional court.

Dinah L. Shelton, "The Inter-American Human Rights System," in *Guide to International Human Rights Practice*, ed. Hurst Hannum, 4th ed. (Ards-ley, N.Y.: Transnational Publishers, 2004). Concise and thorough overview of regional human rights institutions.

Filmography

Raw footage from human rights NGOs. Search the media archive of WITNESS for hundreds of hours of original video from Latin America (e.g., interviews, testimonies, hearings, exhumations), many of them used in regional human rights proceedings. WITNESS is an independent organization that promotes the use of video to document human rights abuses. http://www.witness.org/option,com_mediaarchive/Itemid,212/.

Ghosts of Cité Soleil (2006). Powerful documentary about two brothers who use rap music to make sense of life in Haiti's most dangerous shantytown, showing UN peacekeepers. 85 minutes.

Useful Websites

Office of the United Nations High Commissioner for Human Rights (UN-HCHR). The ins and outs of the international human rights regime, including information relevant to Latin America. http://www.ohchr.org/english/.

Inter-American Commission of Human Rights. Official Website of the IACHR, a must-visit by anyone interested in human rights in the region. http://www.cidh.org.

Inter-American Court of Human Rights. Official Website of the region's human rights tribunal. http://www.corteidh.or.cr/index_ing.html.

Organization of American States. Official Website of the OAS, showing how human rights mechanisms fit into the region's leading intergovernmental organization. http://www.oas.org.

Inter-American Human Rights Database. Contains full text of IACHR documents since its inception, including case law, annual reports, and special reports. http://www.wcl.american.edu/humright/digest/#english.

Inter-American Commission of Women. Main policy forum in the region dedicated to advancing women's rights and gender equality; a specialized agency of the OAS. http://www.oas.org/cim/default.htm.

Inter-American Children's Institute. OAS body devoted to children's rights. http://www.iin.oea.org/default_ingles.htm.

Inter-American Indian Institute. Another specialized OAS body, focusing on indigenous affairs. http://www.indigenista.org/web/.

United Nations. General UN Website, with access to numerous programs and agencies whose work intersects with human rights. http://www.un.org.

Notes

[1] Interestingly, Asian-Pacific countries have not developed a formal regionwide human rights system. Some possible reasons include the enormous heterogeneity of the countries in that vast region and the preference for national systems of protection.

[2] Treaties "enter into force" when a prespecified number of states ratify—not just sign—them.

[3] Argentina, Bolivia, Colombia, Costa Rica, Chile, Ecuador, El Salvador, Guatemala, Haiti, Honduras, Nicaragua, Panama, Paraguay, Peru, Suriname, Uruguay, and Venezuela.

[4] The following states had signed bilateral immunity agreements with the United States in early 2007: Antigua and Barbuda, Belize, Bolivia (2003, but subsequently rescinded), Colombia, Dominica, Dominican Republic, Guyana, Honduras, and Panama, in addition to the non-state parties of El Salvador, Haiti, and Nicaragua. Resisting states in 2006 included Argentina, Barbados, Bolivia (after 2005) Brazil, Costa Rica, Ecuador, Mexico, Paraguay, Peru, Saint Lucia, St. Vincent & Grenadines, Trinidad and Tobago, Uruguay, and Venezuela.

[5] Tom J. Farer, "The Rise of the Inter-American Human Rights Regime: No Longer a Unicorn, Not Yet an Ox," *Human Rights Quarterly* 20, 4 (1998): 965–1035.

4

Transnational Networks

atin America has been almost revolutionized since the dark episodes of human rights abuse that characterized the Cold War. Despite the numerous and egregious violations that persist, it is difficult to exaggerate the changes that have occurred. Many countries have undergone transitions to democracy, and the overall level and intensity of abuses is incomparable with that of earlier decades.

Such changes would not have been possible without transnational advocacy networks (TANs). In contemporary politics, TANs are considered the key engines of human rights change. These networks include a broad range of actors: international and regional organizations like those discussed in the last chapter, international NGOs, local activists within repressive states, government agencies responsible for human rights in foreign policy, and people working anywhere on behalf of human rights campaigns—whether students, churchgoers, or even celebrities. Together, these actors mount transnational campaigns and, under the right circumstances, can elicit reforms.

Indeed, the human rights transformations that have swept the region cannot be understood simply as pressures from "above" or below." Top-down pressures from international organizations like the United Nations or from powerful governments like the United States have perhaps been necessary to raise the costs of repression for human rights violators. But without human rights allies within these countries, no amount of pressure from above would have caused such dramatic changes. Likewise, despite their valor and persistence, human rights activists—often operating during the height of repression—could not have emerged, often would not have survived, and could never have thrived without their foreign allies. It is a combination of multiple and reinforcing pressures, from a variety of actors, that has sparked human rights reforms across the region. And it is these alliances between state and non-state actors, across the global North and South, that help to explain remarkable human rights changes. Each actor brought something unique to the table; together they altered the human rights landscape. Where international actors lacked domestic allies, or vice versa, where domestic groups did not forge external ties, human rights abuses persisted defiantly.

After considering what TANS generally do, this chapter examines the specific role of non-state actors (both international NGOs and local activists) as well as foreign governments in applying human rights pressure. Regarding local activists in Latin America, we zero in on the unique contributions made by relatives of human rights victims and by religious groups, as well as prominent campaigns surrounding globalization. Despite numerous challenges, in a globalizing world of diffuse and loosely linked pressures, TANs may be the best hope for human rights change.

When Networks Apply Pressure

A TAN consists of any set of actors, traversing national borders, which is committed to a particular human rights campaign. Like any network, TANs are not regulated by a centralized coordinating authority; they are not hierarchical. Rather, they rely on dense interactions and information flows, loosely coordinating their campaigns. These actors form a complex web of linkages and interact—despite their differences—to promote human rights reforms in a particular context. For example, in recent years a transnational network has formed to counteract the disappearance of women in the Mexican border town of Juárez. Actors as varied as European and American student organizations, international NGOs like Amnesty International, members of the U.S. Congress, Mexican human rights organizations, world-renowned film directors, and celebrities like Jennifer Lopez work as part of a large informal transnational network. Connected across cyberspace, this network is dedicated to drawing attention to the disappearances in Juárez and eliciting reform.

Since transnational networks apply a broad and unique range of human rights pressures, it is particularly useful to think of TAN activities in terms of the multiple *audiences* they address and the *strategies* they employ. In terms of audiences, TANs target human rights perpetrators, powerful foreign governments, the world community, and even the victims of abuse. They also deploy a wide mix of strategies. When targeting perpetrators, they rely above all on the power of naming and shaming—exposing violations and invoking moral authority to embarrass a state into changing its behavior, or at the very least responding to accusations of abuse. Since TANs are not naïve about their capacity to elicit change, they can be quite skillful in lobbying powerful actors that may have more direct leverage, especially foreign governments. The hope is that governments will incorporate human rights concerns more fully into their foreign policies, applying material pressure like the threat of economic or military sanctions on human rights violators.

More broadly, TANs address the court of world opinion, knowing that the more people mobilize around an issue, the more likely intense human rights pressure will follow. In this regard, TANs tend to rely heavily on documentation, witness testimony, and vivid images of abuse. The assumption is that people are more likely to support a human rights cause once they are educated about what is happening, have heard victims speak for themselves, and are moved by powerful images of human suffering.

Within targeted countries, TANs tend to support human rights victims and organizations directly, offering them financial or legal assistance, training, and moral support. The goal is to lend them legitimacy, empowering them to continue functioning. These networks also cooperate with regional and international human rights mechanisms, submitting petitions on behalf of victims and presenting expert testimony. In practice, TANs rely on numerous mutually reinforcing strategies to achieve their goals.

As the concrete examples in this chapter illustrate, transnational networks often have unintended consequences, a phenomenon that has been described as a *boomerang effect*.[1] Here is the logic of the boomerang effect. Transnational networks often target countries that have both highly repressive regimes *and* strong human rights organizations. Human rights groups within such polities usually have no power over the government, since in many cases they are the direct victims of abuse. With their local avenues of influence blocked, these local groups will bypass the domestic sphere and forge alliances with international actors, feeding external groups with crucial information about the abuses taking place in their country. As a result of these transnational alliances, external groups are

UP CLOSE: MOTHERS ON THE FRONT LINES

On 30 April 1977, at the height of Argentina's dirty war, fourteen brave women began what would become one of the world's best-known local human rights organizations. All they had in common was that their children had disappeared. It was mostly a spontaneous gathering; the women had met at hospitals, morgues, and government offices where they went to demand information about their missing children. It was only a matter of time before they ended up at Plaza de Mayo, the central square in Buenos Aires where the presidential palace—the Pink House—is located. Between 1977 and 2006, they gathered every Thursday afternoon at the same place, donning white scarves on their heads; in total, they staged 1,500 demonstrations.

These white scarves, and the image of the mothers marching peacefully in the square, became emblazoned in the minds of observers around the world. Certainly, they were not alone in opposing the government's abuses, but they were unique as a human rights organization: they challenged the state overtly in a central public space, and they did so nonviolently and nonpolitically, as mothers. How could a government who so often invoked the traditional language of motherhood openly target a group that embodied its stated ideals? It did not. Instead, it chose to attack some of them clandestinely. Several of the organization's members, including three of its founders, were imprisoned or disappeared.

The influence of the Madres de Plaza de Mayo (Mothers of the Plaza de Mayo) took them to the capitals of Europe, the UN office in Geneva, and the steps of the U.S. Congress, where representatives of Las Madres forged transnational alliances that pressured Argentina's ruling junta. In the process, Las Madres garnered international awards; shared the stage with U2, which named a song after them; and inspired countless activists around the world. Argentine president Néstor Kirchner declared in 2003: "We are all Mothers of the Plaza de Mayo."

Source: President Kirschner's quote is from Regina M. Anavy, "Hope Ends 29-Year March of Mothers of the Plaza de Mayo," *San Francisco Chronicle*, 26 February 2006.

much more likely to pressure a government, bolstering and empowering local actors in the process. So, ironically, the same government that silenced or ignored local groups will become the object of even more intense international scrutiny and pressure. This is the boomerang effect: government violators may dismiss human rights pressure applied by local groups; but in a globalizing world, this strategy may backfire as international pressure returns manifold.

International NGOs

Of all the actors who apply human rights pressure, international NGOs may play the most unique role. Not technically beholden to governments, they can be credible brokers on behalf of human rights victims. In contrast, intergovernmental organizations like the United Nations are often limited by their perceived ties to states. International NGOs also rely more extensively on information and moral suasion (persuasion based on ethics); and in response to ongoing problems of funding, they turn to creative grassroots campaigns like letter writing to mobilize support. Local activists in repressive states may employ similar strategies, but they are ultimately constrained by the coercive environments in which they operate. In general, international human rights NGOs serve as bridges between local activists in repressive states and the world at large.

Since 1961, when Amnesty International was founded by a dedicated British lawyer, it has played an essential role in promoting human rights around the world. Its role in Latin America has been especially strong, leading transnational campaigns against virtually every repressive state in the region. During the Cold War, when some international NGOs clearly took sides, Amnesty was careful to apply human rights pressure against both left- and right-wing regimes and to denounce state and non-state actors committing abuses. This evenhanded activism won the organization the Nobel Peace Prize in 1977, further enhancing its global image and power. Amnesty has led fact-finding missions, issued reports (including its highly regarded annual reports), assisted human rights victims, and applied direct pressure on governments. While Amnesty is subject to criticism, it is difficult to understand human rights reforms across the region without taking into account this organization's powerful role.

Despite Amnesty's high profile and name recognition, other international human rights NGOs have also been very influential in the region.

For example, Human Rights Watch—the largest international human rights NGO headquartered in the United States—has published reports on various human rights topics in the Americas since the early 1980s, including prison conditions, women's rights, and the role of paramilitary groups. It has also been very active in providing legal assistance to human rights victims appearing before regional human rights bodies. Likewise, Human Rights First (originally called the Lawyers Committee for Human Rights) has relied mostly on legal strategies to promote change. In Latin America, they were the first group permitted to conduct a fact-finding mission to Chile under Pinochet in the 1970s. Well known for its neutrality, Human Rights First has been particularly active in working for the release of political prisoners.

Focusing exclusively on the region, the Washington Office on Latin America (WOLA) has played a historically significant role. Founded in the early 1970s by members of civil society groups and religious organizations, WOLA has worked to promote human rights, democracy, and socioeconomic justice in the region. Even a select list of its accomplishments spans numerous issues: WOLA sponsored the first U.S. delegations to monitor elections in the region, helped draft U.S. legislation critical for applying human rights pressure, criticized the U.S. anti-drug war and its implications for human rights, and made important inroads concerning femicide in Juárez and gang violence in Central America. Given its regional focus, WOLA has been especially well situated to shape U.S. human rights policy toward Latin America.

Other international NGOs work on particular human rights issues, such as the rule of law in Latin America. The highly regarded International Commission of Jurists, composed of dozens of renowned jurists from around the world and a legal staff stationed in Geneva, is one such organization. For decades, it has promoted the rule of law and the integrity of the judiciary in the region and beyond; founded in the early 1950s, it is one of the oldest international human rights NGOs in the world. Like other international NGOs, it has conducted fact-finding missions, issued reports, sponsored training courses, and applied direct pressure on governments. It has also tapped into its network of affiliated commissions, led in Latin America by the Andean Commission of Jurists (Comisión Andina de Juristas, CAJ). CAJ has been an influential and respected human rights organization within the Andean subregion. Along with the International Commission of Jurists, it focuses on developing international/regional human rights standards and promoting their subsequent implementation by states.

Other prominent international human rights NGOs promote human rights in the region for specific issues. These include major organizations working on humanitarian concerns (e.g., CARE), children's rights (e.g., Save the Children), health (e.g., Physicians for Human Rights), and torture victims (e.g., World Organization Against Torture). Still other international NGOs are actually coalitions of human rights organizations, such as the International Federation for Human Rights, which has been quite active in Latin America.

International human rights NGOs are of course imperfect, and they are most effective when they ally with other groups in civil society. Like all organizations, international NGOs face challenges, including adapting their mandates to changing circumstances, securing financial autonomy, and debating different strategies while avoiding unproductive infighting. Nor do the major international human rights NGOs operate in isolation; indeed, they work alongside hundreds of lesser-known organizations. Many of these civil society actors meet regularly at international conferences, where they develop crucial contacts and advance human rights campaigns. NGOs based in Latin America, moreover, hold frequent regional conferences, in addition to convening as a group before major global human rights conferences (including Vienna in 1993, Beijing in 1995, and Durban in 2001) to stake out regional platforms. These forums provide essential opportunities for networking among human rights activists, allowing them to mobilize broad support and pool scarce resources. International human rights NGOs are indeed most successful when they have activist allies, especially within abusive states.

Local Activists

Local human rights groups are on the front lines of everyday human rights struggles. Whether they consist of women's groups, indigenous advocates, relatives of human rights victims, legal aid agencies, religious or social justice organizations, or those fighting on behalf of lesbian, gay, bisexual, and transgender people, activists working for these organizations risk their lives to protect human rights. And those forced to leave their home countries due to a fear of persecution often continue to fight for human rights from abroad.

UP CLOSE: CHALLENGING SEXUAL-ORIENTATION DISCRIMINATION

Latin America is stereotypically known for its chauvinistic, *machista* culture, so it may come as no surprise that discrimination and violence on the basis of sexual orientation is rampant across the region. Lesbian, gay, bisexual, and transgender (LGBT) people regularly are murdered, imprisoned, tortured, raped, and otherwise harassed, while local laws and courts often reinforce discriminatory policies. The problem is so severe that hundreds of LGBT people every year seek asylum outside their home countries to escape brutality.

Despite these problems, the region's advocates—in conjunction with international advocacy groups—have made significant legal strides in challenging sexual-orientation discrimination. The success stories are impressive. Ecuador was the second country in the world to ban sexual-orientation discrimination. Federal laws in Venezuela, Uruguay, Mexico, and Peru grant equal protection to all peoples regardless of sexual orientation. City and state governments in Argentina, Bolivia, Brazil, and Mexico have responded to pressure from human rights advocates by prohibiting discrimination and, in some cases, even recognizing the rights of same-sex couples. All these developments would not have occurred absent an active and vibrant local LGBT human rights movement. Legal reforms, however, are only a first step toward respecting the rights of all people, irrespective of their sexual identities.

Source: "Latin America's Unheralded Global Human Rights Leadership," *Outspoken, International Gay and Lesbian Human Rights Commission Newsletter* (Winter/Spring 2007): 2–3.

Human rights defenders have in fact come to constitute one of the principal targets of human rights abuse in Latin America. While the situation is most dire in Colombia, thousands of the region's human rights workers in recent years have either been killed or live under death threats or continual harassment and intimidation. In Guatemala, for example, approximately 300 human rights activists are attacked every year.[2] Human rights lawyers have been shot dead in Mexico City; and the offices of human rights organizations throughout the region are regularly ransacked, and in some cases burned to the ground. Astonishingly, most governments fail to investigate attacks against human rights defenders adequately, and very few people are prosecuted for these crimes.

UP CLOSE: ACTIVISTS AT RISK

Human rights activists have always taken immense risks, including confronting abusive regimes during periods of extreme violence. Ironically, human rights defenders are now being increasingly targeted, despite rising democratization and the prominence of human rights discourse. In many parts of the world, including Latin America, it is quite dangerous to be a human rights activist today.

The situation has become so grave in Latin America that the Inter-American Commission on Human Rights released a special report in 2006 on the situation of human rights defenders. International organizations have issued special resolutions, large regional conferences have convened, and human rights organizations have created special programs to defend the defenders.

Not surprisingly, Colombia is one of the most dangerous countries for human rights workers, with dozens of activists killed or disappeared every year. And according to the international organization Human Rights First, "Women human rights defenders are routinely extra-judicially executed in Colombia," while their children and families are regularly threatened. In many instances, human rights defenders in Colombia are detained for no good reason and imprisoned indefinitely.

Activists also face very harsh conditions in Guatemala, where death threats and killing are common. In mid-2007, for example, a well-known forensic scientist and judge investigating past human rights abuses received death threats, triggering an international campaign. Guatemalan groups suggest that since 2000, death threats and disappearances against human rights defenders have quadrupled in number.

The patterns are similar across the region—whether the targets are Mexican activists asking too many questions about femicide, Venezuelan or Cuban protesters critical of the government, Honduran or Brazilian advocates working on behalf of vulnerable populations, or activists anywhere in the region promoting justice for past human rights crimes. In general, governments are failing to protect human rights defenders adequately or to investigate, let alone prosecute, these crimes. Despite the serious risks, Latin America's human rights activists continue bravely speaking truth to power.

Source: Human Rights First, "Human Rights Defenders in Latin America: Towards a Recognition of Their Importance," report to Inter-American Commission on Human Rights, 1 March 2007 (http://www.humanrightsfirst.info/pdf/07508-hrd-def-report-IACHR.pdf).

Despite these ongoing risks, the number of human rights organizations in the region has grown in recent decades (Figure 10). In 2007, the number of human rights organizations in most countries more than doubled what it had been in 1993. This growth in activism may seem surprising, since the overall level of human rights abuses declined significantly in many countries during the same period. Yet the rise in human rights advocacy may reflect a confluence of mutually reinforcing factors, which have emboldened human rights groups and enhanced their capacity to act: a region-wide wave of democratization, giving human rights groups greater opportunities to organize; global changes in technology, includ-

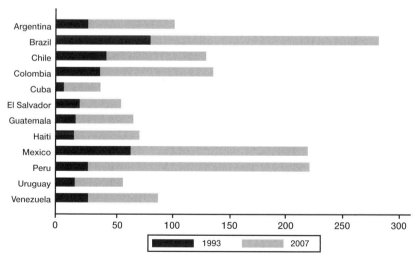

FIGURE 10. Number of human rights organizations in Latin America: trends in selected countries. Data from 2007 from Human Rights Organizations Database (Human Rights Internet, Canada); data from 1993 from Masterlist of Human Rights Organizations (Ottawa: Human Rights Internet, 1994).

ing access to the Internet, which have permitted the region's activists to forge more extensive transnational alliances; and the growing prominence of international human rights norms worldwide, which has legitimated the struggle of these groups and empowered them to mobilize. Ironically, while the conditions permitting human rights organizations to exist have improved dramatically, today's activists constitute one of the primary targets of abuse.

Relatives of the Detained-Disappeared

Human rights victims leave families behind. Perhaps not surprisingly, some of the strongest human rights organizations in the region consist of relatives of those clandestinely detained or disappeared. And with the practice of forced disappearances having originated in Latin America in the 1960s, it is only fitting that some of the world's strongest associations of "relatives of the disappeared" are in Latin America. These organizations have taken various forms, including groups of mothers, grandmothers, and relatives-at-large. Like the Madres de Plaza de Mayo (Figure 11), the Grandmothers (Abuelas de Plaza de Mayo) formed in the 1970s in Argentina; they relied on genetic science to identify their grandchildren who had been kidnapped during the dirty war. Broader organizations of

FIGURE 11. Madres de Plaza de Mayo stage a peaceful protest in Buenos Aires during the dictatorship. Daniel Garcia/AFP/Getty Images.

relatives also formed in over a dozen countries. It is not unusual for relatives to have spent twenty or thirty years searching for their loved ones, without proper investigations into their cases, bodies to bury, or answers to their most basic questions.

So many organizations of relatives formed that in 1981, groups in 14 countries joined forces and created the Latin American Federation of Associations for Relatives of the Detained-Disappeared (FEDEFAM). This federation, in turn, has played a crucial international role in bringing to light the problem of disappearances. As early as 1983, FEDEFAM presented a draft for an international treaty on disappearances. It took almost a decade for the international community to accept the idea, and in 1992 the United Nations approved the nonbinding Declaration for the Protection of All Persons from Enforced Disappearance. Only in 2006 did the General Assembly approve a binding international treaty on disappearance, which opened for signature in 2007; over one-fifth of the original signatories were Latin American countries. Without the efforts of local associations of relatives of the detained-disappeared in Latin America, similar groups in other parts of the world (for example, the Asian Federation against Involuntary Disappearances) might not have formed, and an important international human rights treaty might never have come to pass.

To this day, relatives of human rights victims continue to be targeted for stirring up the past. The sister of Velásquez Rodríguez, who was disappeared in Honduras and whose case made its way to the IACHR (Chapter 3), helped form the Committee of Relatives of the Detained-Disappeared in 1982. A few years later she had to leave Honduras after receiving multiple death threats for her attempts to pursue justice. Between 1998 and 2000, while Pinochet was being held in London, the Association of Relatives of the Detained-Disappeared in Chile received multiple death threats. The association of relatives in Colombia also has been subjected to repeated death threats and intimidation; in 2000, two of its members were disappeared.[3] Most recently, organizations of relatives of the young women disappeared in Ciudad Juárez, Mexico (such as Nuestras Hijas de Regreso a Casa, May Our Daughters Return Home) have had their offices broken into, and members have been physically intimidated.

Perhaps no one is better positioned to demand an end to human rights abuses than the relatives of those imprisoned and killed. Their grief propels them in the face of ongoing dangers, even as many of them become targets of abuse. These local activists have been driving forces across the region, exposing human rights violations and defiantly demanding change.

Religious Groups

People often assume that religious groups have an ethical obligation to denounce human rights violations. Indeed, in many cases, religious groups have been among the region's most courageous human rights defenders. At the same time, religious groups—like any group—can be quite diverse; and in practice the role of religious organizations vis-à-vis human rights violations has varied enormously. The reality is that some religious figures have been implicated in actual violations. And not all church officials in Latin America have challenged abusive national governments, let alone become stark defenders of human rights.

Many religious figures and associations are of course inspirational. The story of human rights change in Latin America cannot be told without mentioning groups like Chile's Vicaría de Solidaridad, El Salvador's Tutela Legal, Argentina's Servicio Paz y Justicia (SERPAJ, a Christian ecumenical group), and the international World Council of Churches. These organizations, among others, became widely known for their credible human rights reporting and their assistance to victims. Individually, people like newspaper editor Jacobo Timerman chronicled his captivity—in the classic human rights testimony *Prisoner Without a Name, Cell Without a Number*—including the abuses he suffered for being Jewish in Argentina. Popularized in film, San Salvador's Archbishop Oscar Romero being murdered at his pulpit in 1980 is an almost iconic image of a religious figure standing up to a repressive state. Even in countries where religious groups did not oppose the regime's human rights violations, individual members still risked their lives, sheltering political opponents and assisting relatives of victims. Hundreds of members of religious groups were killed in over a dozen of the region's countries for supporting human rights causes.

Within the higher echelons of the Catholic Church—historically, the most important religious actor in a region that is still home to the world's largest Catholic population—responses to human rights violations have also varied enormously. Chile and Argentina, despite being neighboring countries and in many ways similar, differed dramatically during the height of repression in the 1970s: the Catholic Church in Chile was an active force for human rights change (as it was in nearby Paraguay), while in Argentina the Church hierarchy was often silent, and under the worst

of circumstances, it was a collaborator with the regime. No better illus-
tration of this exists than the case of Christian von Wernich, a Catholic
priest and chaplain of the Buenos Aires police, who was put on trial in
2007 for kidnapping and torture (including the highly publicized case
of journalist Jacobo Timerman). In Brazil, the role of the Church shifted
over time, from tacit conspirator to a major advocate of reform. The reasons for these variations are certainly complex, reflecting the preferences
of individual religious leaders, the longstanding history of church-state
relations, and the political pressures that even members of the clergy face
when confronted with rights violations.

Globalization and Resistance

Local human rights activists have actively opposed state repression, just
as they have resisted violations of economic and social rights linked to
globalization. In doing so, local activists have joined strong transnational
solidarity networks, and they have relied extensively on modern tools like
the Internet. Globalization has indeed proved to be a double-edged sword
for human rights. On the one hand, it has given local actors the tools to
connect with sympathizers and allies in far-flung places. On the other
hand, critics assert that it has led to exploitation of the poor and erosion
of local cultures. Regardless of one's stance, human rights discourses and
struggles have inevitably been part of the globalization debate.

While globalization has arguably expanded opportunities for economic growth and facilitated the flow of information across borders,
its effects remain contested. Many local human rights activists in Latin
America emphasize the negative side of globalization, particularly its
harmful consequences for vulnerable groups like indigenous communities, unskilled laborers, poor women and children, and sex workers. The
rich are getting richer, critics argue, but Latin America is the region in
the world where the greatest gap exists between the rich and the poor.
And if globalization is so beneficial, why do over 20 percent of the region's populations continue to live off of less than $2 per day?[4] Ram-
pant corruption in business, local government, and law enforcement only
makes matters worse.

More specifically, antiglobalization activists in the region—like their
counterparts elsewhere—blame neoliberal capitalism, an economic ideology associated with low social expenditures, unfettered markets and free

trade, privatization, weak government intervention, and high consumer-ism. In the Latin American context, unsurprisingly, globalization is often viewed as a new form of imperialism and therefore a force to be resisted. As of 2006, when several of the region's governments shifted to the po-litical left, national leaders have joined the voice of those challenging globalization. They condemn Washington, D.C., international financial institutions like the IMF and the World Bank, and multinational corpo-rations. Defenders argue that the problems associated with globalization may have occurred anyway, and, at worst, they are short-term costs that must be endured for long-term progress. From a human rights perspective, however, basic rights (including the rights to food, housing, and health-care) cannot be suspended even temporarily—every person's right at any given moment is deemed just as valuable as the rights of later generations. The debate rages on.

Chiapas: Free Trade and Cyberprotest from the Mexican Jungle

One of the best-known cases where local activists have resisted globaliza-tion is Chiapas, Mexico (see Chapter 1). The uprising in Chiapas in 1994 was timed to coincide with the entry into force of the North American Free Trade Agreement (NAFTA). On the same day that NAFTA went into effect, January 1, 1994, the Zapatista Army of National Liberation (*Ejército Zapatista de Liberación Nacional,* EZLN) went public. The pro-test emanated from one of the poorest and remotest regions in Mexico, where the benefits of free trade and globalization seemed at best question-able to many of the area's indigenous Mayan inhabitants: for example, while the majority of Mexico's hydroelectric energy comes from Chiapas, many in the region ironically lack access to clean drinking water. Aided by the Internet and by their media-savvy leader (Subcomandante Marcos), the Zapatistas posted their materials on the Internet, and the group im-mediately forged strong alliances with sympathetic activists around the world.

The results of this transnational campaign are noteworthy. While the Mexican government engaged in low-intensity warfare with the Zapatistas and their purported supporters, the EZLN itself soon chose a nonviolent strategy. By 1996, they had signed an accord with the government; and in 2001 they marched peacefully into Mexico City, demanding that Vicente Fox's new government adhere to the agreement that would grant them some autonomy and control over resources. The Zapatistas have shown that they can adapt to changing circumstances; they now emphasize the relevance of their demands for all Mexicans and the importance of seeking social justice in the face of globalization. They have toured the country and hosted international meetings of indigenous groups. Remarkably, a group donning ski masks and red bandannas from remote southern Mexico negotiated with the national government, shaped political discourse, and became widely known abroad. To this day, the Zapatistas and their supporters continue to be targets of government abuse, but they also have worked with the government to implement antipoverty measures in the region.

FIGURE 12. Subcomandante Marcos, head of the Zapatistas, greets a crowd on a march from Chiapas to Mexico City in March 2001. Yoray Liberman/Getty Images.

The Chiapas case illustrates dramatically how human rights, globalization, and network activism intersect. Using modern technology, the Zapatistas reached out to a vast transnational audience, networking strategically to pressure the Mexican state. Human rights abuses in the form of physical coercion did take place, but the government also moved to address some economic and social issues and at least acknowledged the plight of indigenous people. Local groups called international attention to a range of human rights violations, protesting the costs of globalization for indigenous and poor people, and in some cases were responsible for improving people's daily lives.

The Amazon: Deforestation, Fair Trade, and Indigenous People

Globalization's effects often harm the natural environment, with important implications for human rights. Nowhere is this more acutely evident than in the Amazon, an area that includes the world's largest and most complex rainforest system. The arrival of multinational corporations to extract natural resources and exploit the land for commercial gain, as well as financing by international financial institutions like the World Bank, has led to environmental degradation and displaced indigenous people inhabiting the land. Activities like logging and mining, whether legal or illegal, have the dual effect of damaging the environment (e.g., through deforestation) and threatening indigenous people (e.g., by introducing diseases). In many cases throughout Latin America, violence has erupted and indigenous people—who constitute 10 percent of the region's population—have been killed simply because they were obstacles to commercial ventures. State agents have either participated directly in this repression or been silent bystanders.

Most surprising, however, have been the responses of indigenous people to human rights violations. While some groups have chosen to resist globalization, others have opted for a policy of participation. Like the Zapatistas, indigenous people throughout the Amazon—from Brazil to Peru and Bolivia—have staged ethnic rebellions and launched transnational campaigns protesting global market forces, including the construction of dams and the extraction of valuable minerals. Others have engaged global markets, incorporating ethnic goods and needs into capitalist schemes. For example, indigenous groups create local crafts, using the Internet and foreign partners to market their goods to a broad audience abroad. These businesses are typically treated as communal enterprises, where profits are shared equitably among the group's members. Similarly, local groups often participate in ecotourism, permitting foreigners to enter and experience their world. Of course, ethnic engagement in globalization does not come without risks; it is still possible that profits will not be evenly distributed, groups will be dislocated, and foreign partners will exploit fragile relationships.

This case also raises the question of how far responsibility for human rights conditions should extend in a globalizing world. For instance, is buying "fair-trade" products (i.e., those that have been certified to meet certain labor and ecological standards) from Ben and Jerry's or The Body Shop empowering local groups to become self-sufficient? Or are critics correct when they assert that buying local handicrafts made in the Amazon and taking exotic trips to rainforests are only hypocritical half measures that distract attention away from the inevitable collision course pitting globalization and indigenous peoples against one another? After all, despite growing recognition about the importance of indigenous rights and the right to a clean environment, these types of rights are among the most weakly institutionalized international human rights norms. A key challenge in coming decades, therefore, will be to integrate indigenous people into the global economy while protecting their rights.

Indigenous groups, typically viewed as powerless, have nonetheless managed in recent years to change political conditions, forming successful political parties in Bolivia, Colombia, Ecuador, Nicaragua, and Venezuela. They also have challenged powerful multinational actors and participated in market interactions to their advantage. Human rights improvements have not been uniform, but they show the power of local groups to claim rights even against historically dominant actors like states and markets.

UP CLOSE: INDIGENOUS PEOPLES
VERSUS MULTINATIONAL CORPORATIONS

Indigenous groups, remarkably, are resisting incursions by multinational corporations. In a typical scenario, a large oil, mining, or logging company comes into a country, with the support of both the government and powerful domestic business groups (and sometimes the World Bank). International law requires that local groups be consulted or participate in decisions that might harm them, following the principle of "free, prior, and informed consent." More often than not, however, the concerns of local indigenous groups are ignored. These groups then ally with international partners, together undertaking vigorous campaigns. Global Response, a U.S.-based NGO working at the intersection of the environment and human rights, is one of these international partners. It assists local indigenous groups in devising strategic campaigns, including letter-writing operations, often quite successfully.

Change has already come to Belize, for example. The country's government authorized a U.S. company to explore an area occupied by the Maya people, over the strong objection of indigenous groups. A transnational campaign ensued, in which NGOs pressured the government and assisted the Maya in preparing a legal case. In its decision, Belize's Supreme Court cited the 2007 UN Declaration on the Rights of Indigenous Peoples, noting the Maya collective ownership of the land based on their traditional use of it: they own it because they have occupied it historically. International activist Paula Palmer noted, "This ruling establishes a ground-breaking precedent in Belize and sends a signal of hope throughout the indigenous world."

Source: Paula Palmer, "Breathing Life into the Struggle: Victories for Indigenous Peoples and Transnational Allies," *PeaceWork* 381 (December 2007–January 2008).

Sweatshops: Multinationals, Labor Rights, and Violence Against Women

Maquiladoras are foreign-owned companies that operate in Latin America, especially in Mexican towns along the U.S. border. They are typically assembly plants, where a product is made from components that have been imported; the assembled good is then exported back to the original country. In the context of globalization, companies create *maquiladoras* because it saves them money. Assembling a product in the United States would require paying minimum wage and following labor regulations. In contrast, assembling a product across the border permits a multinational corporation to pay a fraction of what it would have to pay in the United States: if the minimum wage is $7.00 per hour in the United States, a multinational could get away with paying just over $5 per day in Mexico. Not surprisingly, these businesses are thriving in Mexico, where approximately 3,000 *maquiladoras* employ over one million workers whose earnings account for almost half of the country's imports.[5]

Cost-saving measures for multinationals translate into harsh conditions for those working in *maquiladora* factories. Resembling sweatshops, most employees are women, more desperate and willing to accept lower wages and perceived as easier to control by male supervisors. The working environment is often highly stressful and unhealthy, as workers can be exposed to toxic chemicals and dangerous conditions. It is not uncommon for *maquiladora* employees to work fourteen-hour days, or for company policies to target women specifically. For example, women are often given a pregnancy test before they are hired, forced to use birth control while employed, and fired if discovered to be pregnant. Intimidation, harassment, and violence also are commonplace.

Most disturbing, violence against *maquiladora* workers is linked to the rise of femicide throughout the region (Chapter 1). While gender violence and the targeted killing of women in the region does not happen only in the context of *maquiladoras*, many of the women who have been raped, tortured, and killed in Mexico's border towns and in Guatemala have been young and poor workers in foreign-owned factories. These women are especially vulnerable when it comes to criminal gangs, drug cartels, sex traffickers, and even serial killers, all of which are closely connected to growing violence against women in the region. In the aftermath of violence, moreover, local law enforcement officials usually do not investigate crimes adequately and the judicial system fails to punish perpetrators. The victims are perceived to be weak and insignificant, essentially invisible.

Local activists (including relatives of victims) have joined transnational networks to resist the wave of violence against women, especially in border towns like Ciudad Juárez and Chihuahua, where *maquiladoras* attract hundreds of vulnerable young women. Assisted by the prominent NGO Washington Office on Latin America, a delegation of Latin American women appeared before the IACHR in Washington, D.C.—on the eve of International Women's Day in 2006—to protest femicide in the region. U.S. congressional hearings have been held on the subject; and both the House and Senate passed concurrent resolutions in mid-2006 to express sympathy for the victims in Juárez and to offer increased U.S. assistance. More broadly, several celebrities, including Salma Hayek, Jennifer Lopez, and Jane Fonda, have called attention to the condition of women in Mexico's border towns. In other countries like Holland, citizens have urged transnational corporations to apply pressure and have appealed to the European Union. International organizations, such as the IACHR and the UN Special Rapporteur on Violence against Women, have visited the region to better understand femicide, as have international NGOs like Amnesty International. Transnational networks are quickly emerging to address the linkages between corporate responsibility, human rights, and violence against women south of the U.S. border.

Globalization, despite its advantages, creates demands and pressures that can produce new human rights violations. For example, something as seemingly innocuous as tourism, facilitated by cheaper air travel and greater accessibility to remote locations, has led in the Caribbean to increased demand for sex workers, itself associated with rising rights violations. Likewise, human traffickers have exploited Caribbean women's poverty to lure them abroad: almost 50,000 Dominican women have been trafficked into the global sex industry.[6] In a world where economic and human flows are intertwined, but not always well regulated by systems of governance, demands for cheap labor will often lead to violence—and resistance.

Top-Down Pressure: The United States and Beyond

If human rights pressure frequently rises from the bottom up, reflecting grassroots aspirations and mobilization, it also depends on top-down pressures from foreign governments. Foreign governments have an important role to play, given their vast resources and potential leverage over broader economic and military relations. The more dependent a state violator is on a foreign government, the greater the potential influence. Presumably, a Latin American government will care if human rights demands are made by the same French government that sells them weapons; by Spain, the former colonial power, now an EU member, which supports multinational firms in the region, tourism flows, and cultural exchanges; or by the United States, a neighboring global power that dominates the region's trade. Even if human rights pressure by these foreign governments and their allies is insufficient to assure substantial reform, it can be deeply consequential.

Complementing other human rights pressures, foreign governments have been influential in Latin America. In Europe, France, Spain, and other countries have long promoted human rights reform. Sweden, for example, has championed the protection of refugees, historically providing shelter to human rights victims in its embassies in the region or offering them exile in Sweden. The Netherlands has also been a consistently strong promoter of human rights in the region, especially in providing foreign assistance. Multilaterally, the European Union has applied a range of human rights pressures, from behind-the-scenes "quiet diplomacy" to public condemnations and punitive sanctions in more extreme situations. In the Americas, Canada has contributed to regional peace initiatives and facilitated human rights institution building. The United States has also pressured the region's countries since the 1970s to improve their human rights practices. While U.S. administrations have not applied these pressures consistently, thereby contributing to the region's violations, U.S. pressure has nevertheless had positive effects that should not be discounted.

Given the historical significance of the United States for Latin America, as well as its proximity to the region, it is useful to understand the origins of U.S. human rights policies. Beginning in the 1970s, the United States—like other Western countries—integrated human rights formally into its foreign policy. Human rights issues were gaining ground internationally, following the creation of Amnesty International and the drafting of major human rights treaties the previous decade. This was a period of rising social movements and of protests against state violence, racial and social inequality, and the war in Vietnam. The Cold War itself was entering a period when tensions were relaxed (known as détente). As human rights became the subject of both social protest and Cold War superpower discourse, human rights abuses in neighboring Latin America (especially Chile and Argentina) took on a sense of urgency. Partly in response, human rights concerns were formally incorporated into U.S. foreign policy.

Beginning with a set of hearings in 1973 before the House Subcommittee on International Organizations and Movements (known as the Fraser Subcommittee), human rights issues became institutionalized in the foreign policy apparatus of the United States. From then on, most foreign policy decisions would have to incorporate human rights criteria. Five developments were critical in this regard, three involving congressional actions and two focused on the executive branch. First, in 1974, the Jackson-Vanik Amendment was added to the Trade Act, threatening to restrict trade to countries that denied people the right to emigrate. (In practice, this applied mostly to Eastern Europe.) Second, the Harkin Amendment to the Foreign Assistance Act in 1975 made a country's economic aid contingent on its human rights performance, with crucial implications for Latin America. Third, Section 502B of the Foreign Assistance Act made a country's military aid dependent on its human rights practices. Fourth, a Bureau of Human Rights and Humanitarian Affairs was created in the State Department in 1976; under President Bill Clinton, the office was renamed the Bureau of Democracy, Human Rights, and Labor. Fifth, the State Department was charged with issuing annual reports on human rights conditions around the world, and a thick volume has been prepared every year since the late 1970s. Together, these steps have helped to assure that *institutional* incentives exist to apply human rights pressure, regardless of the administration in power. This explains why sometimes the United States applies contradictory pressure, with Congress or the State Department promoting human rights and other government officials turning a blind eye.

Why the United States or any government applies human rights pressure in some situations but not in others is a complex question. It depends partly on whether human rights constituencies have access to a government, allowing them to influence policy. In the case of democracies, the media can also play an essential role, bringing stories and images of abuse to people who can then pressure their elected officials. And just as ideology helps to explain why human rights abuses occur, ideology can also explain why states apply human rights pressure: anticommunism, for example, assured that the United States staunchly opposed leftist regimes in the 1980s in Central America, while antiterrorism today shapes U.S. human rights policy in Colombia. Ideologies also help to account for underlying problems that may not be readily apparent. For instance, U.S. human rights pressure against Haiti has been driven by concern over unwanted refugees spilling across U.S. borders. But this is only one source of U.S. policy. The question no one wants to ask is why these refugees are unwanted in the first place. Does race play a role? Would refugees from the Southern Cone, for instance, fare any better?

Since the 1970s, Latin America has been a litmus test for the effectiveness of U.S. human rights pressures. Recall that a wave of repression was spreading through the region precisely when human rights criteria were institutionalized in U.S. foreign policy. As Table 5 shows, the United States applied human rights sanctions to nine countries in the 1970s; all of these actions, with the exception of sanctions against Cuba, coincided with the formation of new human rights congressional mechanisms. Determining the success of these pressures, however, is not as straightforward as it may seem. One prominent human rights scholar has described the history of U.S. human rights pressures in Latin America as a story of "mixed signals," where the messages, signals, and cues sent to the region have more often than not been inconsistent and contradictory.[7] It is not surprising, then, that the effectiveness of these pressures continues to be debated. Some observers trace most human rights improvements to U.S. pressures, while others maintain that changes would have occurred even without these pressures. The real question, explored in the next chapter through case studies, is less polemical and more policy-relevant: when and how did human rights pressures matter.

Conclusion: The Politics of Networking

Transnational advocacy networks may promote principled change, including human rights reform, but they are still political actors. This means

**Table 5. Human Rights Sanctions by the United States:
Latin America in the Twentieth Century**

1960s–1970s	1980s	1990s
Cuba (1960–)	El Salvador (1987–88)	El Salvador (1990–94)
Chile (1975)	Nicaragua (1981–90)	Nicaragua (1992–95)
Uruguay (1976–81)	Haiti (1987–90)	Peru (1991–95)
Paraguay (1977–83)	Panama (1987–90)	Colombia (1991–95)
Argentina (1977–83)		Paraguay (1996)
Guatemala (1977–)		
El Salvador (1977–81)		
Brazil (1977–84)		
Bolivia (1979–82)		

Source: Institute for International Economics, "Chronological Summary of Economic Sanctions for Foreign Policy Goals, 1914–99," Institute for International Economics (Washington, D.C.: Institute for International Economics, 2006), http://www.iie.com/research/topics/sanctions/sanctions-timeline.htm.

that human rights campaigns in Latin America have targeted some issues and places more than others. For example, why have efforts on behalf of indigenous rights in the region been relatively weak? And why is there little activism regarding economic and social rights, including the right to health? When human rights networks do emerge, moreover, they remain hostage to the realities of power: they face funding shortages, political opposition, and unequal access to government decision making. Despite their strengths, the various actors comprising a network are always constrained by their political environments; they are never as autonomous as they may seem from afar. The most successful transnational human rights networks are precisely those that use politics to their advantage, mobilizing public opinion and transforming state interests.

As significant as transnational human rights networks are, therefore, it is important to think critically about when and why these networks emerge and which issues generate the most attention and are most likely to succeed. Existing research suggests that transnational groups are indeed more likely to mobilize around certain issues, especially those relating to bodily harm and vulnerable groups, for example, torture or child trafficking.[8] When the links between perpetrator and victim are more diffuse and complex, as they are with many economic and social rights—including rights to healthcare, housing, and education—transnational mobilization will be more difficult. Differences across human rights issues remind us to look for human rights problems that are *not* the focus of transnational campaigns. Paradoxically, how much attention an issue receives does not necessarily indicate its importance.

Even if the various parts of a transnational network work in unison, inequalities in power can still shape network dynamics. For example, powerful NGOs in the global North can be paternalistic, sometimes dictating the terms of interaction with local partners in Latin America. Governments that provide international NGOs with funding may also have expectations of these organizations, hoping in some cases that they will mimic their own foreign policies or at least not oppose them. Even the most powerful international human rights NGOs are constrained to some degree by their political environments and, ultimately, by state sovereignty. States still decide the basic rules that NGOs operating in their countries must follow. Likewise, no actor can enter a foreign country to conduct a fact-finding mission without the express permission of the government being investigated. Transnational flow may be greater than it has ever been historically, but state sovereignty does persist.

Unequal resources can be an additional source of strain in transnational relations. Accordingly, only some groups can afford to travel to conferences or to equip themselves with the latest technology. In general, for local NGOs to attract external support, they have to be relatively successful to begin with, potentially reinforcing existing power imbalances. They also have to be located, ironically, in particular kinds of states: coercive states that care about their international reputations and that have active civil societies. Human rights victims and NGOs that find themselves in less repressive climates, less globally interdependent economies, and weaker civil societies are not as likely to get connected to a transnational network. We may not be used to thinking about the conflicts that underlie transnational human rights networks, but they are quite real and should not be forgotten.

Observers are often dismissive of international human rights pressure. They point to the hypocrisy of powerful foreign governments, who themselves abuse human rights and then pressure developing countries. They question the political objectivity and effectiveness of international NGOs that rely on grassroots campaigns and strategies to counter egregious human rights violations far away. They can be skeptical of local human rights groups, questioning either their innocence (have they done something to deserve their plight?) or their power to resist abusive governments successfully. Taken in isolation, each actor that forms part of a transnational network is certainly limited in what it can do to change repressive human rights conditions.

The key is to view transnational human rights pressure as part of a complex network. Despite power imbalances and the individual weaknesses of actors, it is the linkages between the actors that are most significant. Debating which actor mattered most in eliciting human rights reforms in a particular country is pointless. Transnational human rights networks must be conceptualized as a multiplicity of complex pressures, pushing states to make concessions and alter their abusive practices. Within this scheme, local activists in repressive states—whether consisting of families of the disappeared, religious organizations, or activists combating entrenched discrimination or the inequalities of globalization—are nonetheless the crucial link. Local groups provide essential information about violations and unparalleled stories of abuse. Empowering them is crucial to the success of any human rights campaign. Armed with local allies, transnational human rights networks have mounted formidable assaults in Latin America, forcing state violators to respond and sometimes to change their behavior.

Questions and Debate

1. What exactly are transnational advocacy networks, and what makes them unique?
2. What specific role can international human rights NGOs play?
3. What do you find most interesting about local human rights activism in Latin America. Why?
4. Why do you think that transnational activism surrounding indigenous rights has been relatively weak?
5. Could multinational corporations be a positive force for human rights change? If not, why? If so, how so?
6. In your view, why does the United States (or any country) apply human rights pressure in some situations but not others?

References

Additional Reading

Rita Arditti, *Searching for Life: The Grandmothers of the Plaza de Mayo and the Disappeared Children of Argentina* (Berkeley: University of California

Press, 1999). The definitive account of Argentina's Grandmothers' organization, including extensive first-hand testimony.

Alison Brysk, *From Tribal Village to Global Village: Indian Rights and International Relations in Latin America* (Stanford, Calif.: Stanford University
Press, 2000). Unique look at indigenous movements in the region and
their influence on the world stage.

_____, ed., *Globalization and Human Rights* (Berkeley: University of Califor-
nia Press, 2002). Multifaceted examination of the relationship between
human rights and globalization, including Latin American cases.

Susan Eckstein and Timothy P. Wickham-Crowley, eds., *Struggles for Social
Rights in Latin America* (New York: Routledge, 2002). Leading text exploring a wide range of social struggles in the region.

Shareen Hertel, *Unexpected Power: Conflict and Change Among Transnational
Networks* (Ithaca, N.Y.: Cornell University Press, 2006). TANs for economic and social rights, in the context of globalization; including a Mexican case study.

Stephen Hopgood, *Keepers of the Flame: Understanding Amnesty International*
(Ithaca, N.Y.: Cornell University Press, 2006). Fascinating and critical
look at the leading international human rights NGO.

International Federation for Human Rights, *Mexico—The North American
Free Trade Agreement (NAFTA): Effects on Human Rights*, no. 448/2
(April 2006). Thorough report about the effects of NAFTA on labor
rights in Mexico.

Margaret Keck and Kathryn Sikkink, *Activists Beyond Borders: Advocacy
Networks in International Politics* (Ithaca, N.Y.: Cornell University Press,
1998). Award-winning text of transnational networks, including a chapter on human rights in Latin America.

Kerry Kennedy Cuomo and Eddia Adams, *Speak Truth to Power: Human
Rights Defenders Who Are Changing Our World* (New York: Crown,
2000). Journalistic stories of human rights defenders from around the
world.

Penny Lernoux, *Cry of the People: The Struggle for Human Rights in Latin
America—The Catholic Church in Conflict with U.S. Policy* (New York:
Penguin, 1982). Classic if partisan view of U.S. policy in the region, es-
pecially the role of progressive Catholics vis-à-vis human rights.

Rigoberta Menchu, *I, Rigoberta Menchu: An Indian Woman in Guatemala*
(London: Verso, 1987). Internationally acclaimed, though controversial,
oral testimony given by this Mayan woman who won the Nobel Peace
Prize in 1992.

Julie Mertus, *Bait and Switch: Human Rights and U.S. Foreign Policy* (New
York: Routledge, 2004). Fair but critical look at the role of human rights

in U.S. foreign policy; winner of the American Political Science Association 2004 Best Book Award in Human Rights.

María Elena Moyano, *The Autobiography of María Elena Moyano: The Life and Death of a Peruvian Activist*, ed. Diana Miloslavich Túpac (Gainesville: University Press of Florida, 2000). An unusual look at the life of a woman activist in Peru who was assassinated in the early 1990s.

Rosa Isolde Reuque Paillalef, *When a Flower Is Reborn: The Life and Times of a Mapuche Feminist* (Durham, N.C.: Duke University Press, 2002). Testimonial account of an indigenous activist woman in southern Chile.

John Ross, *Zapatistas! Making Another World Possible, Chronicles of Resistance 2000–2006* (New York: Nation, 2006). Overview of the Zapatistas' unique influence in recent years.

Kathryn Sikkink, *Mixed Signals: U.S. Human Rights Policy and Latin America* (Ithaca, N.Y.: Cornell University Press, 2004). The definitive read on U.S. human rights policy toward the region. Replaces the classic work by Lars Schoultz, *Human Rights and United States Policy Toward Latin America* (Princeton, N.J.: Princeton University Press, 1981).

Kati Suominen, *U.S. Human Rights Policy Toward Latin America*, Special Report 65 (Washington, D.C.: U.S. Institute of Peace, January 23, 2001). Concise and useful summary of U.S. human rights policy toward the region.

Winifred Tate, *Counting the Dead: The Culture and Politics of Human Rights Activism in Colombia* (Berkeley: University of California Press, 2007). A rich examination of human rights activism in a wartorn country, revealing competing perspectives.

Maria Teresa Tula, *Hear My Testimony: Maria Teresa Tula, Human Rights Activist of El Salvador* (Boston: South End Press, 1994). The story of one woman's transformation from a peasant to an international human rights activist.

Claude Welch, *NGOs and Human Rights: Promise and Performance* (Philadelphia: University of Pennsylvania Press, 2000). Overview of the work and effectiveness of human rights NGOs.

Filmography
Feature Films

Bordertown (2007) and *Virgin of Juarez* (2006). Two popular feature films on the femicide in Juárez. 112 and 90 minutes respectively.

The Violin (2005). The struggle between the Mexican government and indigenous people in Chiapas, featuring a family of traveling musicians who smuggle weapons to the rebels. 98 minutes.

The Burning Season (1994). Feature film based on the true story of a Brazilian rubber tapper who protests government violence and developers' plans to clear part of the rainforest. 123 minutes.

Romero (1989). Chronicle of the life, including political activism and assassination, of Archbishop Oscar Romero in El Salvador. 105 minutes.

La historia oficial (*The Official Story*) (1985). An Argentine woman's realization that her adopted daughter might have belonged to a *desaparecido*. 112 minutes.

The Eyes of the Birds (1982). Fictional film about a visit by an International Red Cross delegation to Libertad (Liberty) prison in Uruguay. 82 minutes.

Documentaries

Bajo Juárez: The City Devouring Its Daughters (2007), On *the Edge* (2006), *Señorita Extraviada* (*Missing Young Woman*) (2001). Three critically acclaimed films documenting the disappearance of women from Juárez, Mexico, including the role of the government and globalization. 96, 58, and 74 minutes respectively.

La dignidad de los nadies (*The Dignity of the Nobodies*) (2005). Women farmers, shantytown dwellers, and hospital workers discuss their struggle against globalization. 120 minutes.

La cueca sola (2003). Documentary tracing five Chilean women's struggles against Pinochet's dictatorship. 52 minutes.

25 Años, Madres de la Plaza de Mayo (2002) and *Las Madres de la Plaza de Mayo* (1985). Two documentaries that trace the history of this women's human rights organization in Argentina. 30 and 64 minutes respectively.

Life and Debt (2001). Social costs of globalization in Jamaica. 80 minutes.

Warrior of Light (2001). Inspiring story of a Brazilian woman activist working with street children. 94 minutes.

Botín de Guerra (*Spoils of War*) (2000). First-hand accounts by the Grandmothers of the Plaza de Mayo. 112 minutes.

Enemies of War (1999). The murders of six Jesuit priests in El Salvador, their housekeeper, and her daughter in 1989; the role of a U.S. congressional investigation. PBS special.

For These Eyes (1998). A woman's search for her missing granddaughter, whose parents were two Uruguayan activists disappeared during Argentina's dirty war. 52 minutes.

Useful Websites

Washington Office of Latin America. One of the most important organizations shaping U.S. human rights, democracy, and justice policies toward Latin America since the 1970s. http://www.wola.org.

Asociación Madres de Plaza de Mayo. Spanish-language Website of the original Las Madres group in Argentina. http://www.madres.org.

FEDEFAM. Small but very informative Website, detailing the efforts of relatives on behalf of disappearances. http://www.desaparecidos.org/fedefam/eng.html.

Bureau of Democracy, Human Rights, and Labor. U.S. government agency (part of the State Department), responsible for human rights in U.S. foreign policy. http://www.state.gov/g/drl/hr/.

Nuestras Hijas de Regreso a Casa (Our Daughters Return Home). The leading organization formed by relatives of young women killed in Ciudad Juárez, Mexico. http://nuestrashijasderegresoacasa.blogspot.com/.

Comisión Andina de Juristas. A leading regional human rights NGO in Latin America, focusing on the rule of law in the Andean region (Spanish site). http://www.cajpe.org.pe/.

Professionals for Human Rights (CEPRODH). Argentine center devoted to human rights defenders. http://www.ceprodh.org.ar.

Physicians for Human Rights. A major international human rights organization, mobilizing health professionals on behalf of human rights and promoting the right to health. http://www.physiciansforhumanrights.org/.

Notes

[1] Margaret Keck and Kathryn Sikkink, *Activists Beyond Borders: Advocacy Networks in International Politics* (Ithaca, N.Y.: Cornell University Press, 1998).

[2] Human Rights First, "President Bush Should Stand Up for Human Rights Defenders in Latin America," Press Release, 6 March 2007.

[3] Amnesty International, *Bulletin on Human Rights Defenders in Latin America and the Caribbean*, 15 March 2002.

[4] World Bank, *World Development Indicators 2007* (Washington, D.C.: World Bank, 2007)

[5] For an overview, see Edgar W. Butler, James B. Pick, and W. James Hettrick, "Maquiladoras," in *Mexico and Mexico City in the World Economy* (Boulder, Colo.: Westview Press, 2001).

[6] Pan American Health Organization, *Trafficking of Women and Children for Sexual Exploitation in the Americas* (Washington, D.C.: Pan American Health Organization, 11 May 2005).

[7] Kathryn Sikkink, *Mixed Signals: U.S. Human Rights Policy and Latin America* (Ithaca, N.Y.: Cornell University Press, 2004).

[8] See especially Keck and Sikkink, *Activists Beyond Borders.*

5

Human Rights Change

Across Latin America, endemic human rights abuses gave way to reform in the last two decades of the twentieth century. While violations continued to occur, human rights conditions also improved markedly by the new millennium. A thirty-year civil war ended in Guatemala and peace agreements were concluded in Central America. Further south, Uruguay went from having the highest per capita rate of political imprisonment anywhere in the world to one of the best human rights records in the developing world. In some cases, reforms have included truth commissions and human rights trials, discussed in the next chapter. Given the magnitude of these changes, the region is often held up as a model of how societies struggling with widespread killings and torture can undergo transformation.

Dramatic changes in human rights conditions can nonetheless be puzzling. It is unclear why state violators would initiate reform: transnational human rights pressures can be very intense, but they are rarely so burdensome as to make reform necessary. It is also perplexing why human rights practices, often applied for years, change when they do. Why does human rights pressure succeed when it does and to the extent that it does? And why do some human rights problems persist alongside reforms? As influential as transnational human rights networks can be, they cannot account entirely on their own for human rights change.

This chapter looks at case studies of human rights change across the region—from Latin America's Southern Cone to Central America, the Andean region, and the Caribbean. We examine the role of transnational human rights pressures as well as changes in the incentives that tempt states to violate human rights. First, however, we review the leading ways of thinking about human rights change: when and how do the human rights pressures discussed in the last chapter translate into concrete reforms? This chapter concludes by considering a spectrum of changes that can be attributed, at least in part, to transnational human rights pressure.

Models of Human Rights Change

Scholars have turned to two types of models to explain human rights improvements. One is a *static* model of change, emphasizing the conditions that must exist at any given moment for human rights to improve. This type of explanation often focuses on the importance of certain actors applying pressure (including foreign governments, international organizations, or human rights NGOs) or the significance of institutional preconditions like democracy.

While this model is appealing, static accounts can be problematic. Approaches that focus on the overriding importance of human rights pressure, for example, very often cannot explain why human rights changes occur when they do. After all, pressures are often applied for very long periods of time and reforms occur only sometimes. Furthermore, even when changes occur, sometimes the changes seem symbolic and even hypocritical; for instance, a government might reduce the number of disappearances but increase the level of torture, or abuses might fall in urban areas but rise in rural locations. In short, the effects of human rights pressure are far from uniform, so it is risky to assign such pressures overwhelming significance when trying to understand human rights change.

Likewise, approaches that focus mostly on institutional conditions can be problematic. For example, democracy is itself a complex phenomenon, difficult to explain and the product of an intricate mix of domestic and international conditions. Moreover, states often begin to improve human rights before they democratize; and even after a state embarks on democratization, human rights protections can be highly uneven. Human rights reforms cannot be understood, therefore, as simply a byproduct of democracy. Human rights conditions certainly may improve because states are subject to human rights pressure or they are undergoing democratization, but at best these are necessary—not sufficient—conditions.

Partly to address these gaps, some scholars have proposed a *dynamic* model to explain how human rights conditions transform over time. Foremost among these is the "spiral model." According to this model, human rights changes can be understood as passing through a series of phases. In the first phase, state repression is high, and local human rights groups begin mobilizing and forging transnational networks. In the second phase, repressive governments engage in a policy of denial, rejecting human rights pressures. By the third stage, they begin giving into human rights pressure by offering "tactical concessions"; their goal is to avoid damage to reputations or escape punishment. Some states will then move to internalize international human rights norms in the fourth phase, or change their domestic laws and institutions to accommodate human rights. Rule-consistent behavior, however, does not occur until the final phase, when norms and practices converge fully and state hypocrisy is a thing of the past. It is important to note that the spiral model is a model, so it deliberately simplifies a complex process. The assumption is that not every state will undergo every phase in precisely the same way, if at all; much will depend on the actual strength of human rights groups, the persistence of pressure, and the nature of the particular state in question.

The insights of dynamic and static models of human rights change can also be combined and amended. The spiral model usefully showcases how a state targeted for pressure will alter its practices over time, but it cannot entirely account for why states often respond in different ways to similar human rights pressures. A compelling model of human rights change must address both why reforms are appealing and why continued violations are no longer deemed appropriate. As discussed in Chapter 2, while human rights pressures can raise the costs of violating human rights, making it less appealing to do so, exclusionary ideologies and domestic instability often push states to violate human rights even in the face of countervailing pressures. Accordingly, if states initiate significant human rights reforms, it is only because they face pressures to do so *and* they no longer have an incentive to violate human rights. Very few governments, however, will reform their human rights practices during a period of domestic instability and turmoil, regardless of any pressure they face. Given these dynamics, it is important to combine insights from models of human rights change (discussed in this chapter) with an understanding of why states actually violate human rights (surveyed in Chapter 2).

UP CLOSE: MOBILIZING FOR DISABILITY RIGHTS

The rights of persons with disabilities, long overlooked, have at last received global attention. According to the United Nations, "Over 600 million people, or approximately 10 per cent of the world's population, have a disability of one form or another. While their living conditions vary, they are united in one common experience—being exposed to various forms of discrimination and social exclusion."

The landmark Convention on the Rights of Persons with Disabilities is the world's most recent human rights treaty, entering into force in mid-2008. Interestingly, about one-third of the countries that have ratified the convention are in Latin America. Only two countries in the Americas have not signed or ratified the convention to date (Venezuela and the United States), placing the region at the forefront of global support for the treaty.

Support for disability rights across the region is the direct result of transnational activism, as local groups have mobilized on behalf of the issue and partnered with global allies. In Nicaragua, for example, the Federation of Women with Different Capacities was created in 2002, consisting of 3,000 disabled women who lobby the government and promote social awareness. Fundación Solidez is a related Nicaraguan umbrella organization, supporting over a dozen disabled women's groups.

These local organizations are in turn allied with One World Action, an international NGO headquartered in London that has helped create a Regional Disability Rights Program in Central America. This transnational network strives to assure that disability rights are implemented locally, that governments are accountable for ongoing discrimination, and that the public is aware of the importance of disability rights. While implementation of these new internationally recognized rights is far from complete, the changes that have taken place in a relatively short amount of time are striking.

Sources: "Human Rights and Disability," Office of the UN High Commissioner for Human Rights (http://www.unhchr.ch/disability/index.htm); Nicaraguan case from One World Action (http://www.oneworldaction.org/our_partners/latin_america/nicaragua_partners.htm).

Cross-National Illustrations

Human rights pressure and its effects have varied throughout the region, but one common theme emerges: human rights pressures tend to have succeeded in countries where certain domestic conditions prevailed—local human rights groups were active, the government was internally divided, and armed violence was absent or minimal. When human rights pressures work, it is because they make it more costly for a government to continue violating human rights. They also make it clear that abuses are normatively unacceptable; such delegitimization is a basic step in moving toward reform.

The evidence shows that human rights effects can be subtle, as states respond in various ways to pressure human rights. In the short term, there can be changes in rhetoric, cosmetic improvements, or some decline in violations. Human rights pressures can also empower local groups and activists, and they can strengthen the position of regime soft-liners. In the long term, human rights pressure can be a catalyst for democratization. Regionally, moreover, countries in closest proximity to one another tend to mimic one another's behavior. Political scientists refer to this as *regional contagion*, when human rights violations or democratization seem to spread to neighboring countries. This might explain why, despite important differences in human rights pressures, countries in a subregion often show remarkably similar trends. The following subregional cases demonstrate some of these dynamics.[1]

The Southern Cone

Perhaps no two countries received more international human rights attention in the 1970s than Chile and Argentina. What is surprising about the military regimes in these countries is that they held out for relatively long despite the intensity of transnational pressure. Both faced an onslaught of pressure—from international NGOs, regional human rights institutions, international organizations like the United Nations and World Bank, transnational activist networks, as well as the United States and European governments. Locally, both countries enjoyed active human rights movements, including associations of relatives, women's groups, and legal organizations.

In both cases, pressure intensified under the Carter administration when it took office in 1977. Until then, many of the signals the military juntas had received from the highest echelons of the U.S. government had been highly contradictory: public condemnation of human rights violations alongside private encouragement to bring "terrorist subversives" under control as quickly as possible. Given these mixed signals, it is not surprising that human rights pressure initially seemed to produce nondramatic results.

Even as pressure intensified, however, the regimes responded with a mix of strategies. On the one hand, they denied violations and accused foreigners of interfering in their internal affairs. On the other hand, they simultaneously paid lip service to human rights and they made certain concessions, such as releasing prisoners (especially high-profile ones that had generated international attention), disbanding death squads, and permitting foreign human rights monitors into the country. Yet these were clearly concessions more than meaningful reforms.

In Chile, for example, the regime closed the intelligence service (Dirección de Inteligencia Nacional, DINA) that had overseen massive abuses, a welcome change; yet in its place it created the Centro Nacional de Información (CNI), which shared personnel and procedures with the former service—a makeover rather than a real transformation. Likewise, human rights monitors in Chile were escorted on carefully controlled visits, sometimes moving prisoners to other quarters or reconstructing parts of a prison. Among the most striking concessions was Pinochet's decision to issue a new constitution for Chile in 1980, one that included human rights safeguards.

The intensification of human rights pressures did lead to a decline in violations in both Chile and Argentina, although this decline was far from uniform. In both countries, the overall number of disappearances fell, while the level of torture either remained the same or increased over time. Differences also existed between urban and rural areas, with human rights violations improving in some locations but staying the same or even worsening in others. This variance suggests that the effectiveness of human rights pressures is never perfectly predictable. In the Southern Cone, human rights violations declined only when armed groups were no longer active, either because they had gone underground or been killed by the state. Yet absent transnational human rights pressures, the juntas in Santiago and Buenos Aires would have had little incentive to change their behavior at all.

More dramatic changes ensued with the advent of democratization in both countries, itself engendered by forceful human rights pressures. Despite years of authoritarian rule, the 1980s brought democracy to Argentina (1983) and Chile (1989). Argentina's transition occurred during an economic crisis and, more importantly, the military's crushing defeat in a short-lived war for the small Malvinas (Falkland) Islands against Britain. Given the military's weakness and the strength of the human rights movement, the regime collapsed, and civil society promoted democracy as a viable alternative. In December 1983, Raúl Alfonsín, running on a human rights platform, became Argentina's first post-dirty war president.

In contrast, Chile's transition occurred during a period of economic growth and intense transnational human rights pressures. A wave of local protests in Chile in 1983 and 1984 had been met by heavy repression. Unfortunately for the regime, this repression coincided with the Reagan administration's new policy of promoting human rights and democracy, which quickly led to a rise in transnational pressure against Chile's junta. A broad alliance of civil society groups joined forces in Chile; and in 1988 Pinochet stunned everyone by calling for a referendum that he expected to win. The gamble backfired, as 57 percent of Chileans voted to oust Pinochet. Pressured by different sectors, the Chilean general stepped down and democratization filled the void.

FIGURE 13. Young people in Chile celebrate Pinochet's defeat in 1988 plebiscite. Cindy Karp//Time Life Pictures/Getty Images.

The neighboring countries of Uruguay and Brazil offer interesting comparisons. Unlike their Chilean and Argentine neighbors, human rights groups in both countries were relatively weak. This reflected the particular paths followed by each country. The height of Brazil's repression had occurred in the 1960s, before a global explosion in transnational human rights pressures. By 1974, the Brazilian regime had initiated a political opening—*abertura*—which at least created the illusion of greater freedom. Brazil's vast geography and federal system of governance (like Mexico) also meant that local groups faced more hurdles in forging national alliances, at the same time that local state agents were more autonomous from the central government and free to violate human rights. The relatively weaker role played by human rights pressure in Brazil's transition to democracy has translated, in turn, into an ongoing climate of violations and impunity.

In the case of Uruguay, the military regime ruled in such a totalitarian manner that local human rights activists were not free to organize until the eve of democratization—recall that Uruguay had the highest per capita rate of political imprisonment in the world. Despite the existence of international human rights pressure against Uruguay, a weaker human rights movement meant a weaker transnational network. This did not stop Uruguay, or Brazil, from democratizing in the 1980s. But weaker transnational networks did have implications for the pursuit of post-authoritarian human rights justice, as democratic governments moved to forget the past (see Chapter 5).

UP CLOSE: PROTEST THROUGH ART

Resistance to human rights abuses often takes the form of art—poetry, music, tapestry weaving, dancing, photography, or theater. Art has intersected with human rights violations throughout Latin America in numerous ways. Dictatorships often targeted artists, detaining or disappearing them, while artistic work inspired people even at the height of repression. Among the most famous cases of a targeted artist is Victor Jara, the popular folk singer in Chile, who was tortured and killed in the days following the 1973 coup. Witnesses say he sang his protest songs until the end, and the stadium where he was detained now carries his name. Pablo Neruda's poems, which had earned him the Nobel Prize for Literature in 1971, were burned by the Chilean dictatorship but still move generations today.

Others have used art courageously to protest rights violations. From the Bolivian highlands to Brazil's *favelas* to the Salvadoran jungle, artists have composed and performed music criticizing human rights abuses, often inspired by indigenous traditions. In Chile, women whose partners had disappeared sewed colorful tapestries by hand chronicling their loss and hope for the future. These *arpilleras* were taken around the world and became powerful symbols of human rights resistance. And in El Salvador, an armed group of folk musicians known as Torogoces ("songbirds") accompanied leftist insurgents on their missions and mobilized people with their songs on a clandestine radio station. More recently, one of Mexico's biggest rock bands (Jaguares) teamed up with Amnesty International to release a Spanish version of John Lennon's "Gimme Some Truth" and held benefit concerts to draw attention to the killings in Ciudad Juárez. On the streets of Colombia, young people use hip hop as social resistance, while other hip-hop artists are fighting human trafficking in Brazil through their art. Likewise, street theater across the region regularly commemorates poignant scenes of abuse.

Music has also inspired foreign artists, who in turn have spread awareness of rights violations in the region. Sting's "They Dance Alone" was motivated by a scene he witnessed: women dancing the *cueca* (Chile's national dance) alone, while carrying photos of their disappeared partners. Chile's National Stadium, where hundreds of people were held immediately following the 1973 coup, has become a site for commemorating human rights: a high-profile Amnesty International Concert was held there in 1989; and in early 2005 Chilean president-elect Bachelet presented U2 with a human rights award in the stadium. If blaring music was used to cover the terrorizing screams of people being tortured at detention centers, music and art have also been used as weapons of hope and resistance.

Central America

Unlike the Southern Cone, human rights violations in Central America peaked mostly in the 1980s. Given how dependent Central American countries historically have been on the United States, the role of the Reagan administration during this period needs to be taken into account. Indeed, the Reagan administration's human rights policy went through two important phases. The first phase was dominated by the Kirkpatrick Doctrine, named after Jeanne Kirkpatrick, the first female U.S. ambassador to the United Nations. The Kirkpatrick Doctrine maintained that right-wing authoritarian regimes (as opposed to Soviet bloc totalitarian regimes) should be tolerated if not supported by the United States: in the context of the Cold War, authoritarian regimes were deemed an effective balance against leftist counterinsurgents. The second phase occurred in the mid-1980s, when U.S. foreign policy shifted toward promoting democracy abroad, especially in Latin America. Both the Kirkpatrick Doctrine and democracy promotion were strategies for countering Soviet influence in the context of the Cold War.

Central America was a crucial arena during the Cold War of the 1980s, shaping U.S. human rights policy towards the region. The intensity with which the United States applied human rights pressures against a country basically depended on the Cold War camp to which the country belonged. *Nicaragua*, where leftist Sandinistas took power in 1979, loomed as the largest threat for the United States. Sanctions lasted until 1990, when the Sandinistas were narrowly ousted from power in a free election and Violeta Chamorro became the region's first female president. In contrast, El Salvador, Honduras, and Guatemala were treated as buffer states that could block the spread of communism; this served to limit the effectiveness of human rights pressures against these countries.

Contradictions in U.S. policy were significant. U.S. diplomats and the military would often send one set of messages, while Congress would send another. For example, while Congress imposed human rights sanctions against Guatemala and El Salvador, the Reagan administration and U.S. military aided and abetted these same Central American states.

El Salvador, Nicaragua's northwestern neighbor, embroiled in civil war, was considered particularly vulnerable. The United States supported the repressive government, arming the military and actively reinforcing counterinsurgency attacks against leftist rebels (especially the Farabundo Martí National Liberation Front; FMLN). Peace came to El Salvador partly through UN involvement, beginning in 1991 with the arrival of the UN Observer Mission in El Salvador (ONUSAL). A peace accord was signed in 1992, and the UN remained in the country for a few years, overseeing the transition, demilitarizing parties, and playing a direct role in many aspects of governance.

Although *Honduras* did not suffer the bloodshed of its neighbors, the United States considered it on the front lines of the battle to save the Americas from communism. The United States thus used the country as a staging ground to attack Nicaragua. Some of the *contras*, the anti-Sandinista groups supported by the United States, were armed and trained in Honduras before being sent across the border to wage war in Nicaragua. Despite the egregiousness of some of the human rights violations the country endured, the scale of abuse in Honduras was relatively low. The country was not on the world's radar compared to its neighbors, and so it escaped much transnational pressure until the 2009 coup.

In contrast, *Guatemala*'s genocidal violations led to its international isolation, while the United States privately supported the government. The Reagan administration gave its Guatemalan allies a green light, arming and assisting them. These contradictory pressures explain why Guatemala's repression peaked in 1982 (Chapter 1), at precisely the same time that U.S. military and economic aid was relatively low. Given these inconsistent pressures and the ongoing conflict, Guatemala's turn to democracy did not occur until a 1996 peace agreement—two years after a UN peacekeeping force had arrived and the United Nations had helped broker a peace deal to end the decades-old civil war.

A key figure in changing Guatemala's human rights landscape was Rigoberta Menchú, an indigenous woman who suffered at the hands of the regime. Menchú's internationally popular book—*I, Rigoberta Menchú*—in the early 1980s catapulted her onto the world stage. Despite controversies surrounding the veracity of all of her claims, she won the Nobel Peace Prize in 1992. Having lost some of her closest relatives to the genocide, Menchú became a symbol of the indigenous peasants repressed at the hands of a vicious state. For many she came to embody the face of human rights in Central America.

The Central American cases illustrate a different set of dynamics from the Southern Cone. First, with many Central American countries experiencing civil wars, U.S. involvement consisted of more direct (if still covert) military action. U.S. government actions, moreover, sometimes clashed with congressionally imposed human rights sanctions, sending contradictory messages to the region's regimes. The extreme case is Panama, which the United States invaded in 1989 to depose General Manuel Noriega, a former U.S. ally. The invasion was justified on the grounds that Noriega was a corrupt leader, involved in drug trafficking and human rights violations. The U.S. action was nonetheless internationally controversial, criticized for imposing regime change forcibly.

Second, while human rights groups certainly existed in these countries, they had a more difficult time mobilizing and forging transnational alliances under conditions of war; the relative weakness of human rights groups was further compounded by the poverty and illiteracy that characterized these countries. Finally, the United Nations, building on a peace process initiated by the region's leaders in the 1980s, played a crucial role in securing peace and democracy. In general, these cases suggest that under conditions of civil war and high U.S. involvement, international organizations may play a relatively stronger role than transnational networks in improving human rights.

UP CLOSE: NEW INTERFACE—TECHNOLOGY AND HUMAN RIGHTS

Just as human rights abuses rely on technologies of terror—from firearms to electroshock weapons—activists have used technology to their advantage. It began with fax machines, which bombarded government offices with letters demanding the release of a political prisoner or an improvement in human rights conditions. Since the post-1990 Internet age, human rights activists have used online resources to broadcast their messages to a global audience, enroll in distance-learning courses, and draw on otherwise inaccessible data and documents. These developments were only the beginning of the technology revolution for human rights.

*   *   *

The use of *digital technology* by human rights activists today is expanding rapidly. Text-messaging has become an especially popular way of mobilizing human rights pressure quickly, while online video blogs and camera cell-phones can record and disseminate images of violence to an unimaginably broad audience. Geospatial technologies like GPS employ satellites to pinpoint the location of human rights violations; they have been used to map internal displacements and environmental damage in the Andes. Local groups and their transnational allies, in turn, can incorporate this evidence into legal proceedings against abusive powers.

*   *   *

NGOs are also employing *open source software* (free and accessible software) to collect and protect human rights information. Activists in both Colombia and Guatemala, for example, have used such software to store sensitive human rights data. With NGOs in these countries compiling evidence of past violations that can be used in legal cases, activists' computers are increasingly being stolen to remove confidential information. Using special open source software allows NGOs to encrypt their data so that in the event of a theft or break-in, only they can retrieve their material off a secure server.

Likewise, new software is being used to input and analyze large volumes of human rights data statistically, an invaluable tool for truth commissions and local NGOs. In Peru, technologically sophisticated information management systems assisted that country's truth commission by creating a massive database of past violations. The result was a much more reliable estimate of the number of abuses, one much higher than initially thought. Similarly innovative work is being done in Colombia to document as accurately as possible the number of people killed and disappeared in that country's armed conflict.

This technology is also being used to document ongoing abuses. In the Mexican border town of Reynosa, for instance, the Center for the Promotion of Human Rights and Frontier Studies (CEFPRODAC) uses human rights software to monitor child trafficking and abuses against migrants. By digitizing human rights violations data, the Center can cross-reference and retrieve information quickly, in some cases helping locate missing persons.

*   *   *

More traditional forms of technology, including *video*, are having equally dramatic effects on human right work. Across Latin America, people are being armed with video cameras to record existing abuses. Witness, a New York-based organization, has been at the forefront of these efforts, empowering local people to produce human rights videos that it then distributes. For instance, in Paraguay, Witness participated in preparing a documentary on mental disability rights, until then a largely invisible issue. Zeroing in graphically on the plight of two brothers in a psychiatric hospital, the film showed the extreme and inhumane, prisonlike conditions in which almost 500 patients were kept. The video was presented to the Inter-American Commission on Human Rights and to high-level government officials, leading eventually to improved hospital conditions and region-wide attention to mental disability rights. And in Mexico, Carlos Pérez Rojas—winner of a prestigious Reebok Human Rights Award for young activists— works with the Chiapas Media Project so that indigenous people like himself can document mistreatment. Film has always been a powerful medium, but now it is also a tool of rights empowerment.

*   *   *

Technology is a double-edged sword, though it has produced dramatic changes for human rights. Text-messaging is helping to mobilize human rights pressure, even if it is also used regularly to send death threats to human rights activists. As advocates push the boundaries of new technology, adapting them to the needs of human rights, some governments will certainly attempt to control access to and use of these technologies. Restrictions aside, technology will continue to change how human rights struggles are waged. So far, the results in Latin America have been impressive: new technologies expose local human rights concerns globally; help to disseminate and protect sensitive information; and in some cases improve human rights conditions.

Sources: Material on open source software from Benetech Website (http://www.benetech.org); on video technology, see Witness Website (http://www.witness.org); for the Chiapas Media Project, see http://www.chiapasmediaproject.org.

The Andean Region

Despite recent progress elsewhere, Andean countries remain in turmoil, home to some of the region's worst human rights violations. While there is no shortage of rights defenders, the violence has reached such proportions in a country like Colombia that it is difficult for social groups to mobilize effectively. Human rights conditions in this subregion cannot be separated from the war on drugs, the role played by large indigenous and rural populations, conflicts over natural resources, and more recently the turn toward leftist politics. For the United States, it appears that the Cold War conflict of the 1980s in Central America has now shifted to the Andes.

Colombia, one of the largest countries in Latin America, is a humanitarian disaster. It has more internally displaced people than any other country in the world, other than Sudan.[2] Fighting rages between the armed forces, paramilitary groups supported by the government, leftist armed guerrilla groups like FARC (Revolutionary Armed Forces of Colombia), and gangs sponsored by drug cartels. The FARC is triply reviled as a communist-inspired group, participant in the drug trade, and designated terrorist organization.

Colombia also constitutes the heart of the U.S. war on drugs (Plan Colombia), so that the United States aggressively assists the government in eradicating the drug trade and looks the other way when it comes to human rights abuses. Particularly controversial was the failure of the Clinton and Bush administrations to comply with the Leahy Provision, a law sponsored by Senator Patrick Leahy of Vermont and passed in 1997 that forbids the United States from offering military assistance to foreign armed forces that violate human rights. In the name of the drug war, U.S. governments have used a series of loopholes to circumvent having to comply fully with the law in Colombia. In short, the enormity of the drug war has undermined human rights in Colombia and made peace elusive for this conflict-torn country.

The 2005 election of Evo Morales, an indigenous (Aymara) leader, as *Bolivia*'s president was partly a reaction to past human rights abuses and a drug eradication campaign. While Bolivia had been a major producer of coca, used in cocaine, the heavy-handed (foreign-sponsored) use of fumigation and repression had succeeded in reducing the country's contributions to the global drug trade. The human toll was nonetheless heavy in a country that has Latin America's highest income inequality (see Appendix 3, Table 1). Like similar programs in Colombia, fumigation of coca fields has had enormous rights implications, displacing poor people from their homes, creating health and environmental hazards, and destroying the economic livelihood of innocent people with no other source of income. In many cases, moreover, the state has resorted to violence against indigenous peasants to assure the eradication of coca.

President Evo Morales has attracted worldwide attention because of his uniqueness: he is indigenous, a leader among coca growers, and a socialist opposed to U.S. policies and global markets. Morales ran on a

FIGURE 14. Aymara peasants in Bolivia demand "de-neoliberalization" of hydrocarbon resources and justice for past genocide. Aizar Raldes/AFP/Getty Images.

platform of protecting indigenous rights, opposing fumigation programs, and supporting the legal growing of coca. Despite winning a majority of the vote, his opponents still openly challenge—in sporadic clashes and protests—his right to extend too many privileges to the country's indigenous population (the largest of Latin America, at over 50 percent), his hostility to the United States and market forces, and his intent to place control over natural resources like hydrocarbons (used for petroleum) in state hands.

The Bolivian case suggests the challenges that governments face when they try to remedy past human rights abuses too quickly, especially in a political context where powerful elites stand much to lose. Leaders like Morales need to walk a fine line between changing human rights conditions and assuring a climate of political stability. Absent such stability, even the most well-intentioned of regimes may find themselves resorting to abuse.

No country better dramatizes Latin America's political "left turn" in the new millennium than *Venezuela*. Hugo Chávez has been the country's democratically elected socialist president since 1999, opposing both the United States and globalization. Despite making strides to improve economic and social rights for the country's poor, Chávez has come under fire in recent years for limiting freedom of expression (including closing media outlets) and curbing the judiciary's independence. The country also remains a dangerous place for human rights defenders, prisoners, or those at the mercy of police forces. The United States has been highly critical of Venezuela's political stance, especially given this oil-rich country's shared border with Colombia. Just as Bolivia's recent experience cautions against pursuing too many human rights changes too quickly, Venezuela under Chávez suggests that human rights policies must be balanced: economic and social rights cannot be pursued at the cost of civil and political rights.

Why have transnational human rights networks not been able to exert more positive influence in the Andean region? The overriding importance of anti-drug efforts by the region's governments in alliance with the United States, as well as the ongoing presence of armed guerrilla groups, has dwarfed the role of human rights activists—local and foreign. For instance, although the OAS has had a mission in Colombia since 2004, funded partly by European governments, it has not been able to make significant headway. The human rights changes that have occurred, involving indigenous rights and economic-social rights, have been more the result of partisan politics than transnational forces, and it remains to be seen whether they can survive ongoing clashes with the United States and global market pressures. For Colombia, still mired in a bloody and long-standing conflict, human rights change will be contingent on a dramatic shift in U.S. drug policy and eventual peace between the warring parties.

The Caribbean

Two of Latin America's most notorious human rights violators are found in the Caribbean: Cuba and Haiti. Each of these countries exemplifies a particular set of dynamics. Cuba illustrates state resistance to human rights pressure; the case also shatters conventional assumptions about the type and extent of rights violations that plague the island state. Haiti shows the limits of using force to impose democracy and human rights. Both reveal the significance of poverty in impeding human rights progress. Given their proximity to the U.S. mainland, the cases also raise crucial issues about the role of immigration in shaping human rights policies.

It may seem puzzling that *Cuba* has been subject to sanctions by the United States for so long—since 1960—yet it continues to resist human rights pressure. Contrary to popular views, Cuba's human rights practices have varied enormously over time.[3] The highest level of violations occurred between 1959, immediately after Fidel Castro launched the Cuban Revolution, and 1970. Even then, the dominant form of abuse in Cuba consisted of political imprisonment. Killings and torture have been used, but they have not been systematically deployed by the government as a preferred form of social control. The period after 1970 saw the use of other strategies by the regime, namely a reliance on mass migrations to remove opponents. It was not until after the collapse of the Soviet Union, when economic crisis set in, that Cuba resumed more forcefully the use of repression to quiet dissidents.

Since the early 1990s, moreover, the regime has permitted the formation of human rights organizations, which have more than tripled. This has been partly the result of pressures from European countries attempting to cultivate ties with Castro's political opponents. At the same time, freedom of movement and association have been curtailed, limiting the capacity of these groups to mobilize effectively, and the regime continues to hold prisoners of conscience. While some economic and social rights (for instance, the right to education and healthcare) are protected to relatively high degrees, many people see the poverty that consumes the country as the negation of any commitment to economic and social rights.

In response to ongoing abuses, a group of women—relatives of political dissidents rounded up and arrested in 2003—created the Ladies in White group (Damas de Blanco). Emulating Las Madres of Argentina, on Sundays the women wear all white and march peacefully though Havana's streets. In 2005, the European Parliament awarded the group the Sakharov Prize for Freedom of Thought.

These developments notwithstanding, at the core of any human rights debate about Cuba is the question of sanctions. Have the sanctions worked, and should they be continued? If they do not work, why do U.S. administrations—Democrats and Republicans alike—persist in applying them, especially when so much of the world (including Canada and European countries) opposes them? The U.S. position on the sanctions is closely shaped by the Cuban-American lobby in Florida and other states, which represent a large voting bloc. Experts note, however, that changing demographics due largely to immigration by other Hispanic groups may dilute the power of this lobby over time, allowing a U.S. administration to join the groundswell of support for lifting the sanctions. While President Barack Obama's administration eased some travel and trade restrictions in 2009, the broader embargo remains in place.

In the meantime, sanctions against Cuba do not seem to have improved human rights conditions. The government has violated human rights despite the sanctions, mostly in response to rising social demands associated with periods of economic decline. Some contend that U.S. sanctions arguably have exacerbated the human rights situation by keeping the majority of Cubans in poverty. It is interesting to note in this regard how the Cuban case differs markedly from U.S. policy to China, where engagement (not sanctions) has been the preferred choice.

While the United States has attempted to isolate Cuba through sanctions, it has intervened forcibly in *Haiti* to protect human rights. Despite forceful intervention, however, Haiti remains mired in extreme poverty, violence, and corruption. Just as the history of Haiti between 1957 and 1986 was dominated by the repressive rule of François Duvalier and then Jean-Claude Duvalier, the post-Duvalier period introduced new upheavals.

The trouble began in 1991, when a military coup replaced Jean-Bertrand Aristide as president and a flood of refugees attempting to flee to the United States were turned back. Aristide, a Roman Catholic priest, had been elected a year earlier in UN-supervised elections; as he was the first democratically elected president in Haitian history, much was at stake. The United Nations responded to the 1991 coup by imposing sanctions and established a joint mission with the OAS two years later. With no change on the horizon, the United States intervened with force, briefly occupying the island in 1994 and reinstating Aristide (who ruled until 1996).

In an interesting twist of events in 2001, Aristide won a controversial election, facing numerous opponents who charged him with corruption and his own brand of repression. Aristide ruled again with a heavy hand, encouraging the use of extralegal vigilante justice to deal with crime and human rights violations. February 2004 was a decisive date. In what is often considered a U.S.-inspired coup (supported by France and Canada), Aristide left the country for Africa, and American marines (along with Chilean and Canadian allies) briefly occupied the country. Widespread violence erupted between members of Aristide's leftist party and their opponents, the former being brutally targeted and attacked. A UN peacekeeping force has been in Haiti since 2004 to establish stability, but it too has come under criticism for committing human rights abuses.

The Haitian case reminds us of the limits and dangers of relying on foreign intervention to secure human rights and the importance of a strong rule-of-law system. Despite the violence, human rights groups in Haiti have grown impressively since the early 1990s, quadrupling in number. It is difficult to gauge whether the use of force by the United States and others has made matters better or worse than they otherwise would be. It is also unclear whether the United States would have intervened in the absence of the refugee issue, or whether France would have supported Aristide's ouster if it did not have a colonial legacy in Haiti.

The motives of powerful states aside, can a small, poor country with the highest illiteracy rate in Latin America escape corruption and violence? Is development, including education, at the core of human rights progress? Would the international community have been better off helping Haiti to develop equitably and democratize state institutions like the police and judiciary? International actors linked human rights to democracy in Haiti, but they made a few fatal errors: they defined democracy mostly in electoral terms; they assumed that rights abuses could be reduced by a single person or political party and supported one side at the expense of the other; and they relied too heavily on a military solution to a conflict with more complex politico-economic-social roots.

From the perspective of international politics, small Caribbean states appear to epitomize weakness and dependency vis-à-vis the hegemonic United States. U.S. interests have combined with poverty and the absence of democracy—at the root of many human rights violations—to isolate Cuba and occupy Haiti. Yet the rise of local human rights groups challenges the view that small states are entirely helpless and human rights change is impossible.

In more democratic but still dependent corners of the Caribbean, social forces have had notable success in opposing U.S. power and rights violations. Vieques, a tiny island that is part of Puerto Rico, was used after World War II as a place for the U.S. navy to conduct munitions testing, including of bombs and missiles. Much of the island's population was displaced after 1940 so that the U.S. base in Vieques could be created. Weapons testing then placed the island's residents in harm's way, both in the immediate sense of being wounded or killed and by way of longer term environmental hazards.

Beginning in 1999, after a resident was killed by a stray bomb, a transnational network of protest rose against the U.S. presence in Vieques. Four years later, the U.S. Navy withdrew from the island as a direct result of transnational pressure. Even if the legacy of historical inequali-

FIGURE 15. Puerto Rican demonstrators block entrance to U.S. naval base in Vieques in early 2003. Humberto Trias/Getty Images.

ties resulting from earlier forced displacement went unaddressed, the U.S. withdrawal was significant. Despite the fact that military withdrawal occurred in a democratic context—Puerto Rico is technically part of the United States—Vieques still illustrates how seemingly weak actors can forge transnational alliances and change the practices of powerful actors.

Conclusion: A Spectrum of Influence

Transnational human rights networks have varied a great deal in terms of their success, both cross-nationally and over time. Across the region, widely divergent human rights changes are evident. The highest concentration of success occurred in the Southern Cone, where human rights pressures led to democratization; but even here, countries differed substantially from one another, depending on the strength of local activists and the incentives that tempted governments to violate human rights.

Changes over time are perhaps illustrated best by the case of Mexico, where 300 students were massacred in a public square days before the 1968 Summer Olympics in Mexico City (Chapter 1). Despite the magnitude of the abuse, weak internationalization of human rights norms led to little pressure. In contrast, the Mexican government's repression of the

Chiapas uprising twenty-six years later elicited an unprecedented wave of global support.

In other parts of the region, transnational pressure often seems constrained by overwhelming U.S. interests, warlike conditions, and massive poverty. Still, despite the vast scale of violence once evident in Central America, UN assistance and regional diplomacy led to negotiated peace agreements. The Caribbean countries of Cuba and Haiti seem relative failures on the human rights front, as does violence-driven Colombia, yet even in these cases there has been an impressive growth in human rights groups. Furthermore, the type of abuse at stake may be significant in explaining transnational influence: state repression may be more easily targeted than more systemic and socially engrained patterns of discrimination against groups like women, indigenous people, and homosexuals, or the somewhat diffuse effects of globalization on economic and social rights.

A close look at human rights changes also reveals that the influence of transnational networks is complex. On the one hand, it would be wrong to assume that human rights have improved based on single indicators, such as a decline in one type of violation, government ratification of a human rights treaty, or willingness to invite foreign monitors or change domestic laws. It is crucial that we look for counterevidence of ongoing abuse. On the other hand, any improvement can be significant. One political prisoner freed is one life improved. Even symbolic gestures can have disproportionate effects over time, as activists push a government to build on its previous commitments. In this way, in the to-and-fro of small hypocritical gestures and activist demands, more consequential human rights changes can occur.

If the story of human rights violence is one of terror, the story of human rights reform inspires hope. Transnational networks can exert both symbolic power (through testimonials, documentation, and shaming) and material power (through sanctions and condemnation by powerful actors). Their influence is nonetheless constrained by powerful structures: violence, poverty, dependency. It would therefore be naïve to expect the mere application of human rights pressures, however intense, to lead to dramatic improvements—just as it would be cynical to dismiss small gestures on the part of violators, since even these can improve individual conditions and set in motion unintended processes of change.

To borrow Margaret Mead's memorable quote, "A small group of thoughtful, committed citizens can change the world. Indeed, it is the only thing that ever has." At the end of the day, this is the force that lies behind human rights change: ordinary people's empathy for the way that other human beings are treated, their willingness to mobilize for the rights of others. The process of human rights reform is both political and visionary.

Questions and Debate

1. Is the human rights rhetoric of governments significant? Even when it is hypocritical?
2. Should the United States lift sanctions against Cuba? Would doing so improve human rights conditions?
3. Do human rights improvements occur along a continuum, or in fits and starts? Discuss.
4. What is the relationship between human rights protection and democracy? Does one cause the other?
5. Is it only a matter of time until human rights conditions improve in places like Colombia and Haiti? Why?
6. Why would countries in a region (or subregion) mimic one another's human rights practices?

References

Additional Reading

Susan Burgerman, *Moral Victories: How Activists Provoke Multilateral Action* (Ithaca, N.Y.: Cornell University Press, 2001). Analysis of human rights change, especially in the Central American context.

Sonia Cardenas, *Conflict and Compliance: State Responses to Human Rights Pressure* (Philadelphia: University of Pennsylvania Press, 2007). Overview of why states respond to human rights pressure; includes extensive case studies of Argentina and Chile.

Ann Marie Clark, *Diplomacy of Conscience: Amnesty International and Changing Human Rights Norms* (Princeton, N.J.: Princeton University Press, 2001). Study of how the most prominent international human rights NGO has shaped global norms, focusing on physical integrity rights and drawing extensively on Latin American examples.

Mayra Gómez, *Human Rights in Cuba, El Salvador, and Nicaragua: A Sociological Perspective on Human Rights Abuse* (New York: Routledge, 2003). A look at human rights changes over time in three understudied cases.

Frances Hagopian and Scott P. Mainwaring, eds., *The Third Wave of Democratization in Latin America: Advances and Setbacks* (Cambridge: Cambridge University Press, 2005). The authoritative volume on the progress and challenges facing countries in the region that have democratized since 1978.

Thomas Risse, Stephen C. Ropp, and Kathryn Sikkink, eds., *The Power of Human Rights: International Norms and Domestic Change* (Cambridge: Cambridge University Press, 1999). Influential book explaining human rights change, including a comparative case study of Chile and Guatemala

Kenneth Roth, "Human Rights in the Haitian Transition to Democracy," in *Human Rights in Political Transitions: Gettysburg to Bosnia*, ed. Carla Hesse and Robert Post (London: Zone Books, 1999). Critical look at international human rights policies in Haiti, written by the head of Human Rights Watch.

Christopher Welna and Gustavo Gallon, eds., *Peace, Democracy, and Human Rights in Colombia* (Notre Dame, Ind.: University of Notre Dame Press, 2007). Probes the connections between conflict, democracy, and human rights as they have played out in Colombia.

Filmography

The City of Photographers (2006). A group of photojournalists who captured life in Chile under Pinochet's regime; art as social resistance. 80 minutes.

Favela Rising (2005). Account of how a Brazilian man rose from the slums of Rio to lead a nonviolent cultural/musical movement. 78 minutes.

Resistencia: Hip Hop in Colombia (2003). Rare look at hip hop as social resistance in wartorn Colombia. 53 minutes.

The Agronomist (2002). Story of a Haitian national hero, journalist, and freedom fighter. 90 minutes.

A Force More Powerful: Chile—Defeat of a Dictator (2000). Examines the forces that led to Pinochet's removal from office. 34 minutes.

Prohibido (1997). Interviews with artists, theater directors, and journalists showing Argentina's dirty war from the perspective of the arts. 105 minutes.

Threads of Hope (1996) and *Scraps of Life* (1992). Stories of Chilean women sewing *arpilleras*, mosaic quilts made with scraps of fabric and depicting scenes of political violence. 51 and 28 minutes respectively.

Dance of Hope (1989). Documents the challenges faced by relatives of the disappeared; includes footage of international rock concerts held in solidarity. 75 minutes.

Chile: Hasta Cuando? (*Chile: Until When?*) (1986). Clandestine record of human rights abuses committed by the Pinochet regime in the mid-1980s, on the eve of democratization. 57 minutes.

Useful Websites

Human Rights Watch. In its annual report, Human Rights Watch documents the role of leading international actors vis-à-vis countries in the region and elsewhere. http://www.hrw.org.

Institute for Justice and Democracy in Haiti. Haitian organization producing groundbreaking reports of human rights in that country; key site for those interested in Haiti. http://www.ijdh.org.

Human Rights in Latin America, U.S. Central Intelligence Agency. Searchable database of documents relating to human rights changes; dating mostly between 1964 and 1995 and focusing largely on El Salvador and Guatemala. http://www.foia.cia.gov/human_rights.asp.

Chiapas Media Project. Award-winning organization that equips indigenous communities in Mexico with video and computing equipment to document their own conditions. http://www.chiapasmediaproject.org.

Benetech. Leading organization committed to using technology on behalf of human rights, including throughout Latin America. http://www.benetech.org/human_rights/.

Notes

[1] For discussions of Mexico, see the sections on Chiapas and *maquiladoras* in Chapters 2 and 5.

[2] United Nations High Commissioner for Refugees, *The State of the World's Refugees 2006: Human Displacement in the New Millennium* (Oxford: Oxford University Press, 2006).

[3] This section draws partly on Mayra Gómez, "Patterns of Human Rights Violations in Cuba," in *Human Rights in Cuba, El Salvador, and Nicaragua: A Sociological Perspective on Human Rights Abuse* (New York: Routledge, 2003).

PART III

Securing Justice

6

Accountability Versus Impunity

Societies undergoing democratization and post-conflict reconstruction must confront past human rights abuses sooner or later. Who was responsible for violations under the old regime, and who should be held accountable now? Should truth be pursued at all costs, even if it threatens a new and perhaps fragile stability? Can violators be punished without sacrificing democracy? Can human rights and democracy thrive in the absence of national reconciliation? In the aftermath of a long period of egregious violations, it is tempting to assume that human rights issues are a thing of the past. But victims and their relatives are unlikely to let go of the past. They will demand answers, bodies to bury, and some semblance of justice—fragmentary measures to bring them closure.

While Latin America is not entirely unique in this regard, the region has played a pathbreaking role. It is, along with Africa, the region of the world with the highest concentration of truth commissions. It is also the region where the most human rights trials have occurred. European attempts to prosecute Chile's Pinochet shone a spotlight on the possibilities and challenges of prosecuting dictators. Likewise, as detailed below, the region's proximity to the United States has meant that an increasing number of Latin Americans have been prosecuted in U.S. courts for their past human rights crimes. The pivotal experience gained by forensic scientists in investigations into past abuse in Latin America has been exported around the world. Yet despite these gains, impunity remains the Achilles' heel of human rights reform throughout Latin America.[1] Politics explains why accountability has proved so elusive.

Democratic Transitions and the Quest for Justice

For a country undergoing a profound transformation—moving from a past of systematic human rights abuses to a democratic future where rights are protected—the pursuit of justice can appear daunting. Members of the old regime and their supporters have had the tables turned; they must now coexist with the new regime and its prodemocracy forces. In many cases, former torturers and abusive policemen continue to live alongside their victims, crossing each other on the street and seeing one another at movie theaters. In the higher echelons, abusive officers may still be in the government or military or pursuing lucrative careers in the private sector, while repressive leaders continue to live comfortable and undisturbed lives in their villas and clubs. One victim described the urge to seek revenge in unsurprising terms: "The ones who took them and killed them are right there, on active duty. They are still mocking us. When I see them a change comes over me. Just looking at them makes you sin, because so many things come to your mind."[2] As long as no one confronts the past openly, old wounds are likely to fester and threaten democratic consolidation.

The question is how to address past human rights abuses. Justice is subjective, after all, and it can take various forms. The narrowest conception equates justice with legal punishment. According to this definition, human rights justice occurs only when violators are tried in courts and sentenced for their crimes. A broader view of human rights justice focuses on the *process* that a society goes through to confront and address past abuse. From this perspective, truth itself can be a form of justice. Another approach is to seek revenge on violators, resulting in the kind of vigilante justice that gripped the streets of Port-au-Prince and other Haitian cities. The problem is that precisely because there are different avenues to justice, people will disagree over which course to take. The pursuit of justice is therefore likely to be contentious, even among human rights supporters.

In practice, the policy options for countries undergoing democratic transitions typically have focused on truth commissions and human rights trials. Human rights trials, as will be discussed in subsequent sections, can be held either in the country where the abuses were committed or in a foreign country. Regardless of the path chosen, the pursuit of justice requires exhaustive investigations to compile concrete facts about the past, recreate chains of command, and establish clear evidence for accusations. Different options are not necessarily mutually exclusive—a country can have both a truth commission and human rights trials—but there are always trade-offs associated with a particular choice, as this chapter reveals.

While Latin American countries have taken different trajectories on the road to establishing human rights accountability, they all have struggled with the challenges of impunity. The various options chosen throughout the region have tended to reflect the relative strength of the military versus the dynamism of the human rights movement in a given country. Where militaries have remained powerful under democracy but the human rights movement has been relatively weak, human rights accountability has also been rather weak (e.g., Brazil). The strongest cases of accountability are found in countries with a weak military and strong human rights movement (e.g., Argentina). Where both militaries and human rights groups have been strong, however, a more complicated path has been chosen (e.g., Chile).[3] In all cases, human rights accountability has depended on a clear democratic transition; absent this (e.g., Mexico), governments have resisted the systematic pursuit of human rights justice.

The Role of Truth Commissions

A dozen countries in Latin America have created truth commissions to expose human rights violations. Truth commissions, temporary institutions created to pursue justice retroactively, are far from simple or noncontentious creations. They can have numerous purposes, and they require extensive resources and political commitment. In general, the region's truth commissions have tended to fulfill—to varying degrees—two primary functions: documentation and reparations. Truth commissions vary further in terms of their mandates, independence, and resources.

In addition to the truth commissions on Table 6, some countries have created special, more limited commissions of inquiry to investigate a particular episode of abuse; in others, "unofficial" truth commissions by non-state actors have arisen. For example, Brazil's Archdiocese of São Paulo published a widely circulated report in 1985, titled *Brasil: Nunca Mais*. The Brazilian government itself created a special commission in 1995 to accept petitions for compensation from families of those killed or disappeared since the 1960s; a 500-page report, *The Right to Memory and Truth*, was issued in 2007.[4] And whereas Uruguay technically had a truth commission, its report was considered so inadequate that an NGO stepped in to document past abuses.

The mandate of a truth commission can be relatively broad or narrow, depending on the range of abuses covered. In this regard, a truth commission's name can reveal a great deal about it (see Table 6). Many commissions in the region chose to focus narrowly on cases of disappearance, as is most evident in Argentina's case, while disregarding abuses like torture. Interestingly, only two commissions incorporated the notion of "reconciliation," borrowed from the South African context, into their own bodies: Chile and Peru. Guatemala's commission uniquely emphasized "historical clarification," provocatively alluding to a rewriting of history, while Uruguay's drew attention to the pursuit of peace. Even if many commissions have been unable to fulfill their stated purposes, a truth commission's mandate still highlights each country's preferred approach to retroactive justice.

Table 6. Truth Commissions in Latin America

Country	Year created	Details
Bolivia	1982	National Commission of Inquiry into Disappearances (8 members) Report released: None Documented 155 cases of disappearance, 1967–82
Argentina	1983	National Commission on the Disappeared (16 members Report released: 1984 Documented 9,000 disappearances, 1976–83
Chile	1990	National Commission for Truth and Reconciliation (8 members) Report released: 1991 Documented abuses, 1973–90
El Salvador	1992	Commission on the Truth for El Salvador (3 members, UN-mandated) Report released: 1993 Documented abuses, 1980–92
Honduras	n/a	Prepared by National Commissioner for the Protection of Human Rights Report released: 1993 Documented over 180 disappearances, 1979–90
Guatemala	1994	Commission for Historical Clarification (3 members, UN-mandated) Report released: 1999 (3,500-page, 9-volume report) Documented abuses, 1962–96

Country	Year created	Details
Haiti	1994	National Truth and Justice Commission (7 members) Report released: 1996 Documented abuses, 1991–94
Ecuador	1996	Truth and Justice Commission (7 members) Disbanded soon after creation
	2007	Truth Commission (4 members) Report released: Ongoing Investigation into over 300 cases of disappearance, torture, and political killings
Paraguay	2003	Truth and Justice Commission (9 members) Report released: 2008 Documenting hundreds of disappearance, 1954–2003
Peru	2000	Truth and Reconciliation Commission (12 members) Report released: 2003 Documented over 69,000 deaths and disappearances, 1980–2000
Uruguay	2000	National Peace Commission (6 members) Report released: 2002 Documented disappearances, 1973–85
Panama	2001	Truth Commission (7 members) Report released: 2001 Documented abuses, 1968–89

Regardless of their purposes, truth commissions have been granted differing levels of independence and resources, which in turn has affected their overall impact. On the weak side of the spectrum, the Bolivian commission, despite being the first created in the region in 1982, was disbanded prematurely and never issued a final report. Its limited independence was apparent from the outset, with the commission being placed under the direction of the Defense Ministry—itself implicated in past violations. Likewise, Ecuador's first commission was dismantled shortly after being created for lack of political support; over a decade later, another commission was created, showing how persistent societies can be in pursuing retroactive justice. On the other side of the spectrum, Argentina's commission has perhaps been the region's highest profile institution, having more members than any other. Guatemala's internationally supported commission has also been among the most extensive and prominent in the world, with 100 to 200 staffers and more than a dozen field offices in the country. Peru's more recent commission reached an all-time high in staff, numbering at one time about 500. The independence and resources of a truth commission reflect, above all, the extent to which members of the former regime retain power and continue to enjoy societal support.

Documenting the Truth

Truth commissions are perhaps best known for documenting past human rights abuses, in the process exposing an overlooked, distorted, or otherwise silenced truth. Documentation itself is a complex task, involving a great deal of coordination and resources. The emphasis is on collecting detailed evidence of abuses, including testimony from witnesses (17,000 statements, in the case of Peru's commission); physical evidence, including evidence from decomposed bodies; and paper trails revealing responsibility in a complex chain of command. The effort can require years of work on the part of NGOs, relatives of victims, police officers, teams of lawyers, and forensic scientists. It can require traveling to remote parts of a country to interview hundreds of people, or holding hearings at which people—victims, bystanders, and perpetrators—recollect past horrors.

FIGURE 16. Bodies of nine students and one professor killed in La Cantuta, Peru, in 1992 (see Chapter 4) are exhumed from a common grave in 2007, following an order from the Inter-American Court of Human Rights. Eitan Abramovich/AFP/Getty Images.

A common challenge truth commissions face is how much truth to reveal. For example, should hearings be open to the public or held behind closed doors? Most commissions in the region have held private hearings; but if public hearings are chosen, should they be televised as they were in Peru? Additionally, should truth commissions name names—that is, reveal the identity of perpetrators, as they did in El Salvador and Honduras? And if names remain sealed to avoid retribution against violators, what steps should be taken to assure that the names are not leaked, as they were in Argentina and Chile? The consensus is that revealing the truth about human rights abuses must be done in a way that honors victims without further polarizing society.

In the end, the final product usually takes the form of a report. While a report may sound relatively innocuous compared to the scope of human rights atrocities, it can serve valuable functions. Reports can be extensive, detailed, and widely disseminated. One of the most best-known truth commission reports in the world, Argentina's *Nunca Más* (*Never Again*), documented approximately 9,000 cases of disappearance; an abridged version quickly became a national best-seller. Guatemala's report, *Memory of Silence*, was over 3,500 pages and spanned nine volumes. It named more than 40,000 people who had been killed or disappeared, accusing the state and its armed forces of having committed genocide against the indigenous Mayan population.

Truth commission reports can serve multiple ends. They often provide appendixes with a substantial amount of data that shows how abuses changed over time or how they were distributed across the country. Any student researching human rights conditions in a country that has had a truth commission should consult the commission's report, an indispensable tool for understanding human rights violence. Beyond providing valuable data, truth commission reports can be cathartic for a society coming out of a period of intense repression: they help to restore justice by acknowledging victims, revealing the scope of past abuse, and accusing state and non-state actors of violence.

UP CLOSE: FORENSIC SCIENCE UNCOVERS THE TRUTH

Forensic anthropologists—who study human remains to identify victims and their form of death—have joined the effort to establish the truth about past human rights violations. The use of forensic science to promote human rights justice was first used most extensively in Latin America. Under the leadership of world-renowned North

American forensic scientist Clyde Snow, the Argentine Forensic Anthropology Team (Equipo Argentino de Antropología Forense) was created in 1986. This was the first forensic team in the world to identify the remains of human rights victims. Their work relied on close collaboration with human rights groups, such as the Mothers and Grandmothers of the Plaza de Mayo. Using DNA testing, the goal was to establish genetically the identity of the victim, often found in an unmarked, mass grave—whether to bring relief to grieving relatives, establish the truth for the truth's sake, or challenge the legal impunity of perpetrators.

The Argentine Team model, supported by international human rights organizations and scientific associations, soon began proliferating around the region and world. Within Latin America, forensic scientists have played an especially important role in Guatemala, Peru, and Chile. Outside the region, the Argentine Team has trained similar teams in dozens of countries recovering from past abuses, in places as far-flung as Bosnia, East Timor, and South Africa.

Source: Argentine Forensic Anthropology Team Website (http://www. eaaf.org/).

Compensating Victims

Another valuable, if downplayed, function of truth commissions is to recommend reparations and compensation for victims and their families. Though the terms "reparation" and "compensation" are often used interchangeably, their difference is subtle but not insignificant. Reparations seek to make amends for a wrong, a token gesture acknowledging past pain and suffering. The purpose of compensation is to reimburse someone for losses incurred, such as loss in income.

The amount of reparations and compensations allocated tends to follow specific formulas. For example, recommendations by Argentina's commission led to a reparation scheme wherein relatives of a disappeared person could receive a lump sum of $220,000, the equivalent of 100 months of salary for the highest-paid civil servant. In other countries like Chile, relatives of those killed receive a monthly lifetime pension, as well as health and educational benefits; additionally, tens of thousands of civil servants who had been dismissed from their jobs for political reasons were eligible for compensation.

The notion of "paying" victims or their relatives for past human rights abuses tends to elicit strong reactions. Some observers (especially those viewing the situation from afar) consider it tasteless to attach a monetary price tag to indescribable suffering and abuse; monetary compensation cannot be commensurate to a victim's pain. Others worry that reparations for past abuses may hurt unstable economies or divert resources from present-day poverty. A more pragmatic view, in contrast, emphasizes the responsibility of the government to give something to the victim or his or her relatives and to compensate for the concrete if intangible losses suffered as a result of abuse, including losses from a victim's income or the lost opportunity to pursue an education. They note that the amounts in question are relatively small for government coffers, while the payoffs for political—and therefore economic—stability are much larger. Virtually no one, however, would claim that reparations or compensations are sufficient to make amends for human rights violations.

Reparations and compensation should certainly be viewed cautiously when governments use them to bypass more painful human rights prosecutions, substituting a monetary solution for fuller justice. Guatemala's government initiated a reparations program in response to the truth commission report, approving over $2.5 million to compensate families of victims. Yet, to this day, the government has not delivered on its promise to pay reparations.

One exception was the case of Myrna Mack, a Guatemalan anthropologist educated in England. In 1990, while she was researching indigenous populations in Guatemala City, state agents murdered her, stabbing her more than twenty times. Despite the high-profile nature of the case, the government conceded responsibility, apologized, and awarded Mack's family $800,000 in compensation only after the case went to the Inter-American Court for Human Rights in 2003. Guatemala's Supreme Court also convicted a high-ranking member of the military for Mack's killing in 2004. (He escaped and went into hiding before serving his sentence.)

Other governments have used compensations to stave off further prosecutions. The Brazilian government in the 1990s refused to investigate past crimes or prosecute human rights violators. Instead, it responded to human rights pressure by compensating survivors and their relatives. In other cases, including Chile, the fact that compensation has not been extended to all victims (for example, victims of torture who were not killed) has led skeptics to be wary of government motives in issuing compensation.

The key question is whether countries undergoing transitional justice would be better off without monetary compensations or a truth commission. Human rights organizations, on balance, tend to support the idea that governments should pay reparations. Even when governments are pressured to take such steps, official recognition of past abuse contributes to a stronger climate of accountability and justice. For example, as a result of pressure from both the Inter-American Court of Human Rights and the Inter-American Commission on Human Rights in 2003, Honduras's president issued his country's first official apology for past human rights violations and initiated a program to compensate dozens of claimants.[5] Documentation and reparations, the main outputs of truth commissions, may seem sorely incomplete steps, but the alternatives—official silence and forgetting—may not be feasible as long as enough people remember the past and continue to demand justice.

UP CLOSE: REMEMBERING VICTIMS IN PUBLIC MEMORIALS

"Striking in its simplicity, the memorial employs few basic materials—glass, rock, concrete, and light—in a natural forest setting close to the water. A white bridge juts out over a pool of exposed jagged rocks. Two large glass panels flank the sides of the bridge. The names of the 176 disappeared and detained citizens are etched in the glass" (Description of the Memorial of Disappeared and Detained Citizens in Montevideo, Uruguay, the first in the region dedicated solely to the disappeared).

*   *   *

Truth commissions often propose ways in which the past might be memorialized for future generations. Typical recommendations call for statues and monuments to be erected, museums and parks to be built, public spaces to be labeled as sites of former abuse, and national days of remembrance to be marked permanently. In practice, nongovernmental groups and civil society have been the driving forces behind the region's human rights memorials.

Villa Grimaldi in Chile, a former villa in the outskirts of Santiago that was frequented by artists and intellectuals in the nineteenth century and used as a notorious detention center under Pinochet, is one of the most widely known and powerful memorial sites in Latin America. While the military razed most of the complex in the final days of Pinochet's rule, it has been converted to a Park for Peace under democracy.

Very little has been reconstructed. Instead, there are discreet plaques on the ground that mark the location of cells. A tree from the past where a soldier was once hanged for sympathizing with prisoners, and a rose garden where female detainees were raped, still stand. Eerily, the original swimming pool, used by officers—and on weekends by their children, whose laughter and squeals could be heard by detainees nearby—also remains. A fountain marks the spot where prisoners were beaten, just as a wall lists the names of hundreds killed at the camp and plaques commemorate women victims. A tower where prisoners were tortured is one of the only things that has been reconstructed. The symbolism of Villa Grimaldi cannot be overstated, as former prisoners visit alongside foreign dignitaries, while outside its gates relatives of the disappeared have continued demanding accountability.

Even the seemingly innocuous step of creating a memorial can be contentious, as societies debate the most appropriate ways in which past human rights atrocities should be remembered. Where should memorials be erected? On the site of former places of abuse? In more neutral spaces? Is it acceptable to place them near military facilities? More generally, how can a memorial capture the horror of the past while remaining relevant to future generations? These dilemmas were compounded in the case of Guatemala, where Western notions of memorializing clashed with indigenous traditions: rather than memorials emphasizing national reconciliation, indigenous groups demanded—but have not gotten—reconstruction of the traditional shrines that were destroyed by the army during the country's thirty-six-year civil war.

*   *   *

"The military dictatorship's principal camp for torturing and killing has been converted into a symbol of state repression and violence. It is a place of horror and memory. It is a place from which we can help tell the story of a generation eliminated by the dictatorship. . . . Finding the tools to tell that story to new generations is the Gordian knot before us" (Marcelo Brodsky, on how to memorialize Argentina's most notorious detention camp, the Navy Mechanics School).

Sources: Molly Dondero,"The Power of Design, Memory, and Civic Participation in the Southern Cone," *Latin Americanist* (University of Florida Center for Latin American Studies) 37, 2 (Fall/Winter 2006): 4; Marcelo Brodsky, ed., *Memoria en construcción: el debate sobre la ESMA* (Buenos Aires: La Marca, 2005), 44 (author's translation).

Human Rights Trials

For some members of society, the "restorative justice" of truth commissions is insufficient: without perpetrators being held accountable for their crimes, there can be no justice. Despite the enormous documentation and truth telling of Guatemala's commission, for example, many Guatemalans were left wanting more. "As the conclusions (of the CEH's report) were read at a solemn ceremony at the National Theatre, rights workers, relatives of victims and others among the 2,000 people broke into standing ovations, sobs, shouts and chants of 'Justice! Justice!'"[6] They wanted human rights violators to be punished for their past crimes.

The cry for "retributive justice"—or punishment—has been so strong throughout the region that in every country in which a truth commission has been formed, human rights trials have also been held. In fact, the majority of domestic human rights trials in the world have taken place in Latin America, followed in far second by Eastern Europe.[7] Part of this may be explained by the fact that Central and South American countries have civil law systems (as opposed to the common law systems that predominate in the Caribbean). Civil law systems, influenced by continental Europe, permit victims and third parties like human rights groups to file *criminal* complaints with courts; in contrast, Anglo-American common law systems only permit public prosecutors to file criminal complaints. While human rights trials have been common throughout the region, some countries—Argentina, Chile, Guatemala, Honduras, Panama, Paraguay, and Peru—have made more use of them. Recent data further indicates that human rights trials tend to occur, on average, about ten years after a democratic transition has been initiated.

UP CLOSE: 80 MILLION PAGES OF PAPER TRAIL—
THE GUATEMALAN POLICE FILES

An explosion at a munitions dump in the outskirts of Guatemala City in mid-2005 led to an unexpected discovery. It all started when local residents contacted the Human Rights Ombudsman office, requesting that area buildings be searched for further explosives. When Ombudsman representatives entered an abandoned building, owned by the National Civil Police, they were shocked by what they found. The rat-infested dark, dank rooms in the building contained the archives of the former National Police. A closer look at the documents revealed astounding evidence of abuse: written orders, interrogation notes, and photos of corpses. Investigators even uncovered documents coded with numbers that stood for specific orders, such as "kill" or "disappear."

Rebuilding the archive is an arduous process, under the direction of the Ombudsman office that made the initial discovery. First, the documents need to be preserved. Many Guatemalans who lost relatives to state-sponsored violence are now working on-site, hopeful that their endeavor will lead to greater truth and justice. Special software is being used to input much of the data, with several European governments having donated funds to facilitate the project. While the process is years from completion, some of the material is already being used in human rights investigations. According to the Human Rights Data Analysis Group, "The Guatemalan National Police Archive is the largest single cache of documents that has been made available to human rights investigators in history."

Source: Human Rights Data Analysis Group (http://www.hrdag.org/about/guatemala-police_arch_project.shtml).

Argentina Paves the Way

Just as Argentina's truth commission was path-breaking, the South American country has played a unique role in prosecuting human rights violators, revealing both the possibilities and challenges of securing justice. In conjunction with the truth commission, Argentina's new democratic government in the mid-1980s pursued several human rights trials. Remarkably, when compared to other countries, Argentina charged nine of the highest ranking members of the dirty-war junta with human rights violations.

In a widely publicized set of trials beginning in 1985, high-ranking officers were sentenced to life imprisonment—including General Jorge Videla, head of the ruling junta. (Note that life imprisonment is the highest acceptable punishment in international human rights law.) Immediately after the prosecutions, however, the government came under political fire for opening a Pandora's box: Where would the government stop in prosecuting violators? Would the legal system be overwhelmed? And would further prosecutions polarize society and undermine democratic stability?

Caving in to the pressure, Argentina clamped down on accountability. Congress passed two controversial laws in 1986 and 1987 respectively: the Final Stop Law (Ley de Punto Final) and the Due Obedience Law (Ley de Obediencia Debida). The Final Stop Law put an end to any further prosecutions involving human rights crimes during the dirty war; the Due Obedience Law made it impossible for lower-level members of the military to be prosecuted for human rights crimes on the basis that they were "following orders." And in 1990, in an unexpected move, President Menem pardoned General Videla and other members of the dirty-war ruling junta. The door appeared to be effectively shut on further prosecutions.

Demands for human rights accountability, however, can be surprisingly resilient. In 2005, Argentina's Supreme Court declared the Final Stop and Due Obedience Laws unconstitutional, claiming that amnesty laws were inapplicable to crimes against humanity. In a landmark case in 2006, a former Buenos Aires police officer was found guilty of genocide, but not before one witness was disappeared and judges were threatened. Likewise, in 2007 a federal court in Argentina overturned Menem's pardons, reopening human rights trials. While these advances are welcome, they remain of limited impact. The more than 250 officers awaiting trial in Argentina constitute a fairly small percentage of perpetrators; the legal system, moreover, is proving overwhelmingly slow and cumbersome. Still, Argentina remains a leader in transitional justice. In addition to prosecuting human rights crimes domestically, the country serves as a forum for judging human rights violations committed elsewhere in the region, passing trendsetting legislation to support universal jurisdiction (the right to prosecute human rights violations committed anywhere) and upholding international law.

The Pinochet Case: New Legal Frontiers

General Pinochet's arrest in London in fall 1998 set in motion a wave of unanticipated hope around the world. For the first time, a former head of state was subject to prosecution for human rights crimes committed while in office. This is a remarkable development, since traditionally heads of state have been immune from prosecution—state sovereignty has always trumped human rights accountability. All of this appeared to change with Pinochet's arrest in a London hospital room late one October night in 1998.

Extradition to Spain?

An interesting twist on Pinochet's London arrest is that it originated in Spain. Indeed, Spain's request to try Pinochet may seem strange at first glance: why would Spain have jurisdiction over Pinochet? Moreover, why should the United Kingdom extradite a Chilean leader temporarily on its territory to another country? The rationale was simple but revolutionary. According to the concept of *universal jurisdiction* in international law, anyone can be held accountable in any country for human rights crimes committed anywhere. Thus, the Spanish government requested that the Chilean general be extradited to Spain for having tortured Spanish citizens.

The 500-day detention of Pinochet in London proved to be a roller-coaster ride. After an international arrest warrant was issued, British officials took the unexpected step of detaining the Chilean general. A British lower court, charged with deciding whether Pinochet could be extradited, first concurred with Pinochet's defense that he had immunity as a former head of state. The higher House of Lords, however, reversed the decision on appeal, noting that crimes against humanity (including torture) were international crimes subject to universal jurisdiction.

Another twist occurred when a judge in the case was found to have a connection to Amnesty International, and therefore a purported conflict of interest. The case was reheard; in the end, the House of Lords found that Pinochet could be extradited for cases of torture, but only for crimes committed after December 1988—long after the worst abuses had taken place.[8]

Unfortunately, governments and not courts often have the last word in extradition. Although British courts had considered the question of whether the UK had jurisdiction to extradite Pinochet, extradition itself was the government's decision. These divisions were apparent once Pinochet petitioned that he was ill and mentally unsound to stand trial. British Home Secretary Jack Straw, though an active opponent of Pinochet's regime in the 1970s, chose to disregard the House of Lord's decision. Political calculations carried the day; and on 3 March 2000, the British government allowed Pinochet to return to Chile.

The Pinochet case could not have gotten as far as it did, however, without the zeal and determination of teams of lawyers, judges, and NGOs, as well as victims and their relatives. The lawyer who filed the first case against Pinochet (Joan Garcés) was a Spanish-born twenty-year-old adviser to socialist President Salvador Allende when the 1973 coup broke out in Chile; he managed to flee the burning presidential palace in Santiago and escape to his native Spain. Two decades later he began working assiduously to prosecute Pinochet. Another key figure was Judge Baltasar Garzón in Spain, a maverick Spanish judge who has made a career of pursuing high-profile controversial cases.

Equally important was the role played by human rights organizations and Latin American exile groups in Europe. For example, Amnesty International in London, which had been tracking Pinochet's visits to Britain for years, was first to notify Spanish lawyers that Pinochet was in London for surgery. Once the case went to court, groups like Amnesty International and Human Rights Watch offered invaluable legal assistance. The contacts, publicity, and information that exile groups in Spain generated also played a crucial role in early litigation. These groups facilitated information flow from Latin America, which proved essential for documenting evidence of past abuse. Exile groups also mobilized public support by disseminating stories in the media and protesting publicly, including holding daily vigils outside Pinochet's London hospital.

The case went further than any previous attempts to prosecute a former head of state in a domestic court for human rights crimes committed elsewhere. In this regard, the Pinochet case set an essential precedent. Even if Pinochet's return to Chile was not the preferred outcome of activist and exile groups, the case made history.

Back to Chile

A maelstrom of controversy was set off with Pinochet's return to Chile. By the time he landed on the tarmac in Santiago, more than 60 complaints had been lodged against him in Chile. This did not stop hundreds of supporters from greeting him or prevent confrontations between Pinochet supporters and opponents.

Judge Juan Guzmán, the leading judge in Chile prosecuting Pinochet,

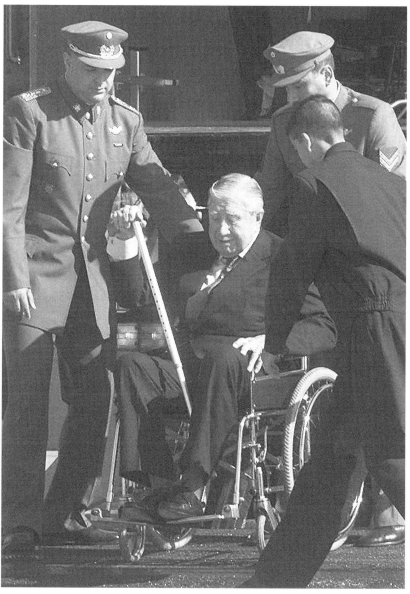

FIGURE 17. Augusto Pinochet arrives in Santiago in March 2000, after being under house arrest in England. Cris Bouroncle/AFP/Getty Images.

had his work cut out for him. The major challenge he faced was how to bypass a 1978 amnesty law, which Pinochet had saavily put in place so that no one in the regime could be held accountable for human rights crimes committed after the 1973 coup. Judge Guzmán nonetheless found a loophole: he portrayed disappearances in which bodies had not been recovered as ongoing crimes subject to prosecution.

Not helping matters was a policy that Chile's president after Pinochet (Patricio Aylwin) had issued on the heels of the truth commission report. The policy stated that human rights crimes committed during the amnesty period could be investigated but not prosecuted. The idea behind the policy—which came to be known as the Aylwin Doctrine—was to provide relatives of the disappeared access to the truth, helping them to determine the fate of their loved ones in exchange for not pursuing punishment. Given the government's desire to secure investor confidence, admitting past abuses promised to achieve two simultaneous goals: appeasing human rights demands while avoiding punishment of the armed forces. Partial accountability would be the price of regime stability.

A dramatic turn occurred in 2004, when Santiago's Court of Appeals issued the first sentence for forced disappearances, a crime until then protected by the amnesty law. In its judgment, reminiscent of the Spanish court's own nonrecognition of Chilean amnesty laws, the Court drew heavily on international law. It cited the Inter-American Convention on Forced Disappearances, which was signed by Chile; the *Barrios Altos* case of the Inter-American Court of Human Rights, which found that forced disappearances constitute crimes against humanity not subject to national amnesties (Chapter 3); and Pinochet's 1980 constitution, which ironically granted human rights treaties constitutional status. This judgment would not have been possible without a series of reforms that began in 1998 and expanded the size of the Supreme Court while implementing a mandatory retirement age for justices. Consequently, a generational shift in about half of the justices moved the court to a post-Pinochet era, where rule of law outweighed political allegiances and human rights accountability was at least possible.

Between the time of his return to Chile and his death in 2006, Pinochet was periodically placed under house arrest. He was released every time either due to ailing health or by posting bail. Chilean courts also went back and forth, stripping him of his immunity for certain crimes, then declaring him unfit to stand trial, then reversing back to place him under house arrest. His last indictment in 2006 was for torture and killings committed in Villa Grimaldi, Chile's most notorious detention center. Beginning in 2004, moreover, Pinochet faced charges of massive tax fraud and embezzlement, leading some to believe that he was more likely to be prosecuted for these crimes than for human rights abuses.

In the end, Pinochet would not face sentencing for any crimes. He died on 10 December 2006, ironically International Human Rights Day. (In a similar twist, General Stroessner of Paraguay died in mid-2006 on the opening day of Paraguay's Museum of Memory, built on the site of a former detention center.) Protestors took to the streets, and Chilean society—still polarized about Pinochet's legacy—was at least no longer silent about past abuses and the possibility of human rights accountability.

Within Chile, the Pinochet case broke societal silence about past violations and legitimized the notion of human rights prosecutions. Only two months after Pinochet's return to Chile, about 100 cases were filed against him. By 2003, more than 200 people were in prison or had been indicted for human rights crimes. In 2006, when Pinochet died, he faced hundreds of charges against him. On balance, the Pinochet case had far-reaching effects in Chile, especially by empowering the human rights movement. As a Chilean sociologist and rights advocate put it, "We finally felt free to discuss and say things that were considered taboo even after years of civilian rule."[9]

More broadly, the Pinochet case left a profound mark on transnational justice. His arrest in London turned on its head centuries of conventional wisdom. State security was no longer a legally valid rationale for violating basic human rights. The case in Europe also pressured the Chilean government to pursue human rights accountability more wholeheartedly than it otherwise would have. Within Chile, the Pinochet case empowered human rights victims and groups, and it demonstrated the possibilities of prosecuting powerful violators.

Pinochet was not extradited to Spain or ever sentenced in Chile, but it would be misguided to assume that the case waged against him had no repercussions. It challenged impunity for human rights crimes, both by lifting a wall of silence in society and showing the possibilities of legal prosecution. If there is any poetic justice in Pinochet having died on International Human Rights Day, it is this: Pinochet may not have been punished for his crimes, but the atrocities he committed turned him into a global symbol of a dictator on trial: even national leaders can be pursued for crimes against humanity.

Table 7. Brief Chronology of the Pinochet Affair

1978	Amnesty issued for human rights crimes committed since 1973
1988	Pinochet loses national plebiscite; declares himself head of armed forces and senator-for-life
1990	Pinochet steps down from office
1998	Arrest in London
2000	Return to Chile; Chilean court strips Pinochet's immunity as senator; Pinochet placed under house arrest in Chile for first time
2002	Chilean court rules Pinochet medically unfit to stand trial; Pinochet resigns as senator
2004	Chilean court reverses decision, finding Pinochet fit to stand trial (based on foreign television interview by Pinochet); multiple indictments follow
2006	Final indictment and house arrest for human rights crimes committed in Villa Grimaldi; Pinochet dies of a heart attack 10 December (International Human Rights Day)

Moving the Battle into U.S. and European Courtrooms

The Pinochet case is part of a global trend toward transnational justice, or an increasing reliance on legal processes in countries outside of the territory where a crime is committed. The basis for these cases is found in U.S. and European national laws, which increasingly acknowledge international human rights norms, as well as in broader recognition of the relevance of universal jurisdiction. Given its proximity to Latin America, the United States has seen in the last two decades an increasing number of human rights cases involving the region's citizens. Likewise, following the Pinochet case, European countries have increasingly decided to prosecute human rights cases originating in other countries.

In the United States, domestic laws have been used in recent decades to try people for human rights crimes committed elsewhere. Two laws in particular have been influential. First, the Alien Tort Claims Act, which has been on the books since the eighteenth century, allows foreign nationals (aliens) to bring claims before U.S. courts for violations of international law. In recent years, it has been used for human rights cases and in lawsuits against multinational corporations accused of violating human rights. Second, the 1991 Torture Victim Protection Act requires the United States to "extradite or prosecute" torturers, even if they are foreign.

The first case in which the United States applied domestic laws to try someone for a human rights crime involved Latin America. In the now famous *Filártiga v. Peña-Irala* case (1980, U.S. federal court), the Filártiga family from Paraguay confronted the alleged killer of their teenage son. Peña-Irala, a Paraguayan police inspector at the time of the killing, had purportedly overseen the torture of their son, leading to the young boy's death. As is common in these cases, the Filártiga family caught wind of the fact that Peña-Irala had illegally overstayed his visa in the United States, and they contacted U.S. immigration services. Peña-Irala was arrested and eventually charged with wrongful death by torture. The court found Peña-Irala guilty of torture, a clear violation of international human rights law. Referring to the Alien Tort Claims Act to justify its jurisdiction, the Court awarded over $10 million in damages to the Filártiga family.

While human rights cases from around the world have been tried in the United States, cases focusing on Latin America have constituted the largest percentage. In another important case, a federal jury in Miami awarded $4 million in damages to the family of Winston Cabello, a twenty-eight-year-old who had been killed by a former member of the Chilean military and secret police (Armando Fernández Larios).[10] Fernández Larios had retired in the United States as part of a plea bargain, having exchanged information about Chile's role in two 1976 assassinations committed in Washington, D.C. The case's importance, however, stems from the fact that it is the first time a U.S. *jury* charged someone with crimes against humanity. The Alien Tort Claims Act and the Torture Victims Protection Act were both used to prosecute Fernández Larios, who otherwise would have been protected by Chile's amnesty law.

The United States becomes a viable legal option when relatives of victims hit roadblocks in Latin America. Take the example of Velásquez Rodríguez (Chapter 3). In 2002, his sister and son filed a civil lawsuit in the United States against Lt. Col. Juan Evangelista López Grijalba, who had headed Honduras's military intelligence agency. While no one had been prosecuted in Honduras for the disappearance of Velásquez Rodríguez, the evidence clearly pointed to López Grijalba's role and responsibility. A federal court in Miami concurred and found him guilty in March 2006, ordering him to pay $11 million in damages to the family.

Following the Pinochet case, European countries have also become quite active in prosecuting human rights cases, especially Latin American ones, even if these cases do not always result in arrests or convictions. Countries like Belgium, France, Switzerland, Sweden, Germany, and Italy all brought charges against Pinochet and other Latin American violators. Italy, for example, issued almost 150 arrest warrants in 2007 for former military and police officers throughout South America apparently involved with Operation Condor (Chapter 2). And in 2005, Spain convicted Adolfo Scilingo, a member of Argentina's military, for having drugged and thrown people from helicopters during the dirty war; he was sentenced to more than 1,000 years in prison (though he will serve only thirty). Numerous similar cases are pending throughout Europe.

A related post-Pinochet trend is that countries no longer want to be seen as harboring human rights violators. Thus, Mexico became the first country to extradite a non-national to a country (Spain) for crimes committed in a third country (Argentina). Unlike past efforts, which had focused only on cases involving European victims, the Pinochet case revealed the fuller possibilities associated with universal jurisdiction—anyone could be prosecuted anywhere for committing grave human rights abuses.

Interestingly, most foreign human rights trials in the world today deal with Latin American cases. Argentina, for example, accounts for one quarter of all foreign human rights cases in the world. And since 2004, when Argentina's amnesty laws were found to be unconstitutional, Argentina has also been the country in Latin America that has been most active in trying human rights crimes committed elsewhere in the region. Indeed, twelve percent of all foreign human rights trials occur in Latin American states.[11] This suggests that, despite the widespread problem of impunity, human rights accountability is at least on the region's political agenda.

Political Trade-Offs: Order Versus Justice

At the heart of most debates over transitional justice is a trade-off: What are the costs of pursuing justice, and should justice be pursued at all costs? What if the cost of pursuing justice is instability, which could undermine democratic rule and potentially lead to longer term human rights violations? These dilemmas help to explain why human rights accountability is so often imperfect and impunity persists.

Post-conflict societies face a number of options in pursuing human rights accountability. The political trade-offs associated with transitional justice are evident, for example, when designing truth commissions. Choices have to be made about whether to hold public versus private hearings, to identify perpetrators, or to compensate victims. Latin America's experiences with truth commissions reveal the complex alternatives underlying truth telling. In some cases, societies with very weak legal systems have opted instead for personal retribution, represented most vividly by vigilante justice in Haiti.

Human rights trials also present societies with a range of options, including whether to hold trials nationally or abroad. Recent evidence suggests that foreign human rights trials—whether in the United States, Europe, or other Latin American countries—are more prevalent when domestic legal avenues are foreclosed. By emphasizing the importance of universal jurisdiction, foreign trials can have an unintended consequence: revealing the egregiousness of human rights violations, they give primacy to international norms. Human rights trials in national courts may in turn have certain advantages over international mechanisms like the International Criminal Court. Rather than being top-down approaches, domestic trials tend to emphasize victims, potentially contributing more fully to national reconciliation.

The region has also played a significant role globally vis-à-vis human rights trials. The Pinochet case, despite its ultimate limitations, set an invaluable precedent. At a minimum, it put dictators on guard, who must now curtail their travel itineraries. Note the dramatic example of Alberto Fujimori, Peru's former head of state, who was placed under house arrest in Chile while traveling there in 2005 and was extradited to Peru for human rights crimes—the first leader to be extradited by a national court to his country of origin. In 2009, he was convicted by a domestic court in Peru for human rights crimes and sentenced to more than twenty-five years in prison, becoming the first democratically elected leader in Latin America to be found guilty of crimes against humanity by his home country. In 2006, Juan María Bordaberry, the head of Uruguay's dirty war regime in the 1970s also was arrested for human rights crimes. In Central America, Guatemala's notorious Efraín Ríos Montt (1982–83) has an international arrest warrant for human rights crimes, issued by Spain; while he moves freely within Guatemala, he must be cautious about his travels abroad. Like Pinochet, General Alfredo Stroessner, who ruled Paraguay for thirty-five years (1954–89), died in 2006 having escaped punishment; but he had to live in exile in Brazil or face arrest at home.

Among the Pinochet case's other effects, it has challenged the role of national amnesties, so crucial in perpetuating impunity throughout the region. After the Inter-American Court of Human Rights ruled in 2001 that national amnesties were illegal in the case of disappearances, creative lawyers have taken advantage of loopholes in amnesty laws (such as the exclusion of minors in Chile or civil servants in Uruguay) to pursue justice on behalf of specific categories of victims.

Given limited resources and the costliness of human rights trials, the question of who should be prosecuted continues to plague human rights defenders. Should human rights trials focus mainly on the rank-and-file, as they have in Guatemala, or should they target the top of the command chain, as they did in Argentina and Chile? Also, how far into the past should prosecutions reach? Is there a point when the political costs of a trial exceed the benefits of justice? Though a Mexican federal judge declared in 2007 that the Tlatelolco massacre of 1968 was a crime of genocide, prosecutions have not proceeded due to the difficulty of retrieving evidence from so long ago. The costs of a human rights trial are indeed logistical as much as political. As full-blown legal proceedings, these trials have a high legal threshold to meet. They must trace responsibility for human rights violations meticulously, providing concrete evidence and crafting an airtight legal argument, regardless of the alleged perpetrator's notoriety.

Latin America has been at the forefront of human rights accountability *and* impunity in the world. The proliferation of truth commissions and human rights trials across the region reflects what some scholars have called a "justice cascade."[12] Despite this activism on behalf of transitional justice, and evidence that transitional processes are not necessarily destabilizing, the net effects of truth commissions and trials are still difficult to pinpoint.

One disagreement is over whether human rights trials can deter future violations. Will national leaders think twice before violating human rights, aware that they might face prosecution or at least public humiliation? Chapter 2 indirectly challenges this deterrence argument by suggesting that human rights violations cannot be reduced to individual calculations. Some people maintain that truth commissions and trials can at best have a catalytic effect, opening the door to incremental improvements. By this logic, impunity persists because—depending on the nature of a political transition and the conditions under which the former regime left office—those implicated in past abuses retain positions of power under democracy. Lifting the cloud of impunity therefore depends on securing a sound democratic transition and redefining the interests of the state's security apparatus. This can only occur incrementally.

The choice between accountability and impunity is in practice a false one. The most that many transitional societies can hope to do is to balance competing demands imperfectly, weighing the value of justice against the risk of instability. The varied experience of Latin America and other regions with truth commissions and human rights trials confirms this pattern. In South Africa, those who stepped forward and told the truth were given amnesty: punishment was forgone for the sake of national reconciliation. Societies grappling with how to restore justice after a period of horrific violations will reach different conclusions, painfully aware that their future may depend on their handling of the past.

Questions and Debate

1. Is truth without punishment ever sufficient for establishing human rights accountability?
2. Do truth commission reports matter? How so?
3. Does compensating human rights victims do more harm than good? Why?
4. Do human rights trials deter future violations? Why?
5. Is the Pinochet case, on balance, cause for hope or disappointment?
6. Should human rights violators be tried in their home countries or abroad?
7. Why has the "justice cascade" been so prevalent in Latin America compared to other regions of the world?
8. How, if at all, can human rights impunity be overcome?

References

Additional Reading

Alexandra Barahona de Brito, Carmen González Enríquez, and Paloma Aguilar, eds., *The Politics of Memory: Transitional Justice in Democratizing Societies* (Oxford: Oxford University Press, 2001). Broad overview of transitional justice, with chapters devoted to the Southern Cone and Central America.

Roger Burbach, *The Pinochet Affair: State Terrorism and Global Justice* (London: Zed Books, 2004). Extremely concise account of Pinochet's rule in Chile and attempts to prosecute the former Chilean dictator.

Priscilla Hayner, *Unspeakable Truths: Facing the Challenges of Truth Commissions* (New York: Routledge, 2002). The definitive text on truth commissions, surveying the global landscape.

Jon Elster, *Closing the Books: Transitional Justice in Historical Perspective* (Cambridge: Cambridge University Press, 2004). A sophisticated, historical overview of transitional justice around the world, including Latin America.

Christopher Joyce and Eric Stover, *Witnesses from the Grave: The Stories Bones Tell* (Boston: Little Brown, 1991). Dated but fascinating look at the work of Clyde Snow, leading forensic anthropologist, in Latin America and elsewhere.

Carlos A. Parodi, "State Apologies Under U.S. Hegemony," in *The Age of Apology: Facing up to the Past*, ed. Mark Gibney, Rhoda E. Howard-Hassmann, Jean-Marc Coicaud, and Niklaus Steiner (Philadelphia: University of Pennsylvania Press, 2007). An overview of how truth commissions in Latin America have accepted state responsibility for past abuses.

Teresa Godwin Phelps, *Shattered Voices: Language, Violence, and the Work of Truth Commissions* (Philadelphia: University of Pennsylvania Press, 2006). Innovative study of the importance of language in post-conflict societies struggling to balance truth, justice, and revenge.

Naomi Roht-Arriaza, *The Pinochet Effect: Transnational Justice in the Age of Human Rights* (Philadelphia: University of Pennsylvania Press, 2005). Detailed examination of the Pinochet case and its implications for transnational justice.

Kathryn Sikkink and Carrie Booth Walling, "The Impact of Human Rights Trials in Latin America," *Journal of Peace Research* 44, 4 (2007): 427–45. Excellent overview of the influence of human rights trials in the region.

Lawrence Weschler, *A Miracle, a Universe: Settling Accounts with Torturers* (New York: Pantheon, 1990). Eyewitness accounts of how citizens in Brazil and Uruguay dealt with their former torturers.

Richard Alan White, *Breaking Silence: The Case That Changed the Face of Human Rights* (Washington, D.C.: Georgetown University Press, 2004). Fast-paced account of the *Filártiga-Peña-Irala* case.

Filmography

A Promise to the Dead (2007). Follows human rights activist Ariel Dorfman's return to Chile while Pinochet is dying. 92 minutes.

Killer's Paradise (2006). Portrays the brutal killings of women in Guatemala and ongoing problems of impunity, as the government fails to seek justice. 59 minutes.

Justice (2004). Behind-the-scenes look inside a Brazilian criminal court, magnifying broader social inequalities. 102 minutes.

Justice and the Generals (2002). Two Salvadoran generals face trial in U.S. civil courts for human rights abuses; PBS documentary. 86 minutes.

The Pinochet Case (2001). Investigation into Pinochet's crimes against humanity. 109 minutes.

Caravan of Death (2000). Interviews with Judge Juan Guzmán, and retracing the "caravan of death's" route in 1974. 45 minutes.

Fernando Is Back (1998). The work of Chile's Forensic Identification Unit. 31 minutes.

Patio 29: Historias de silencio (*Stories of Silence*) (1998). Chilean victims buried in unmarked graves are exhumed. 84 minutes.

Chile, Obstinate Memory (1997). Portrays both survivors of Pinochet's regime and a new generation of Chileans who do not recall life under Pinochet, addressing the themes of memory and forgetting. 58 minutes.

Death and the Maiden (1994). Feature film about a woman who encounters the man who tortured her in a Latin American prison years earlier. 103 minutes.

Denial (1993). Uncovering the truth about the El Mozote massacre in El Salvador, despite government denials of responsibility and knowledge. 57 minutes.

One Man's War (1993). Feature film depicting the story of Dr. Joel Filártiga seeking justice for his son's assassination. 91 minutes.

Useful Websites

Truth Commissions Digital Collection. Sponsored by the U.S. Institute for Peace, the site includes links to truth commission reports in Latin America and elsewhere. http://www.usip.org/library/truth.html.

International Center for Transitional Justice. A wealth of information about transitional justice and human rights accountability. http://www.ictj.org.

Trial Watch. In-depth information about human rights trials around the world, including the Pinochet case. http://www.trial-ch.org.

Memoria y justicia (Memory and Justice). Website dedicated to human rights trials against Pinochet in Chile. http://www.memoriayjusticia.cl/index.html.

Pinochet Case Timeline. Detailed timeline of the Pinochet case, 1996–2006, by Amnesty International. http://news.amnesty.org/pages/Pinochet_timeline.

Asociación de Ex-Detenidos-Desaparecidos (Association of Ex-Detainees). First-hand testimonies by survivors of detention and disappearance in

Argentina, including information about perpetrators (Spanish). http://www.exdesaparecidos.org.ar

Notes

[1] Impunity refers to a political situation where human rights violators go unpunished; immunity occurs when specific individuals are legally exempt from prosecution.

[2] *Report of the Chilean National Commission on Truth and Reconciliation*, 2 vols. (Notre Dame, Ind.: University of Notre Dame Press, 1993), Part III, Chapter 4.

[3] A similar point is made in Alexandra Barahona de Brito, "Truth, Justice, Memory, and Democratization in the Southern Cone," in *The Politics of Memory: Transitional Justice in Democratizing Societies*, ed. Alexandra Barahona de Brito, Carmen González Enríquez, and Paloma Aguilar (Oxford: Oxford University Press, 2001).

[4] Archdiocese of São Paulo, *Brasil: Nunca Mais* (1985); *A Shocking Report on the Pervasive Use of Torture by Brazilian Military Governments, 1964–1979*, trans. Jaime Wright (Austin: University of Texas Press, 1998); Human Rights Secretary of Brazil, *Direito á Memória e á Verdade* (*The Right to Memory and Truth*), August 2007.

[5] "Country Report—Honduras," in Freedom House, *Countries at the Crossroads 2007* (New York: Freedom House, 2007), http://www.freedomhouse.org.

[6] Mireya Navarro, "Guatemalan Army Waged 'Genocide,' New Report Finds," *New York Times*, 26 February 1999, A1.

[7] This section draws on Kathryn Sikkink and Carrie Booth Walling, "The Impact of Human Rights Trials in Latin America," *Journal of Peace Research* 44, 4 (July 2007): 427–45.

[8] This was the date Britain ratified the Convention against Torture. According to the "double criminality rule" in international law, people can be extradited only for actions that are crimes in both the requesting state and the state where the criminal is located.

[9] Roger Burbach, *The Pinochet Affair: State Terrorism and Global Justice* (London: Zed Books, 2004), 124.

[10] For thorough coverage of this case, see Center for Justice and Accountability, http://www.cja.org/cases/cabello.shtml.

[11] Kathryn Sikkink and Carrie Booth Walling, "Errors About Trials: The Political Reality of the Justice Cascade and Its Impact," paper presented at annual meeting of the American Political Science Association, Washington, D.C., 31 August–3 September 2005.

[12] See Ellen Lutz and Kathryn Sikkink, "The Justice Cascade: The Evolution and Impact of Foreign Human Rights Trials in Latin America," *Chicago Journal of International Law* 2, 1 (2001): 1–33.

7

Never Again?

George Santayana, the philosopher and writer, famously remarked at the turn of the twentieth century that "Those who cannot remember the past are condemned to repeat it." If Santanaya was right, confronting past human rights atrocities is not simply a matter of justice. It may be part of preventing future abuses. Latin Americans realized this in the 1980s and 1990s when they echoed the words proclaimed decades earlier, after the horrors of the Holocaust were exposed: *Nunca Más, Never Again*. Noble intentions aside, it remains unclear just how much the region has overcome the human rights legacies of the past.

The last few decades in the region and elsewhere suggest that, despite notable attempts to establish human rights accountability, history has repeated itself in important ways. Disturbing similarities with the not-so-distant past persist. Despite the region's democratization, power imbalances still perpetuate the idea that human rights can be suspended in the name of national security or that certain groups are not as fully human as others. With rising global attention to human rights, some Latin American leaders—like many of their counterparts elsewhere—seem to have learned that mass-scale detention, disappearance, and killing of domestic political opponents is unacceptable, or at least too risky on the world stage. This sometimes requires limiting targets to already vulnerable groups, cloaking excuses more than ever in legal guise, and hiding the traces of abuse as much as possible. Societies still struggling with issues of impunity and ongoing abuses remind us that "never again" remains a partially unfulfilled hope.

Yet despite the challenges, human rights progress in the region has been nothing short of remarkable. Both the number and scope of human rights violations have declined considerably in recent decades and many countries show evidence of democratic consolidation. The region has played a leadership role in international human rights forums, while human rights discourse is familiar jargon in most countries. Though progress remains incremental and punctuated by setbacks, human rights reforms are amply evident throughout Latin America. The trick is to see how human rights conditions have improved without being blinded to real and enduring violations.

Institutional Reforms

Human rights conditions have improved dramatically in Latin America, undergoing a profound transformation from past decades. Violations are generally much more infrequent and the number of victims is far lower in most countries. Human rights standards, moreover, are now part of national constitutions and legislation, and regulatory bodies exist to oversee human rights compliance, even as the region's actors promote human rights education. Reforms extend to the judiciary and to security forces like the police, which often receive human rights training. Elections also tend to be fairly free, resulting in candidates that would have been unthinkable a few decades ago, including women, indigenous activists, and populist leaders; military coups are all but anomalous. Some candidates have won office partly due to their human rights platforms. Human rights organizations operate openly; and people from a broad spectrum of society, including peasants living in remote areas, have heard or embraced the language of rights. Certain practices for which the region was so widely known in the past, including disappearances and torture centers, are now largely taboo. Many of these changes can be traced to democratization and its emphasis on creating rights-protective institutions.

The creation of human rights ombudsman offices (*defensores del pueblo*)—otherwise known as "national human rights institutions"—is one noteworthy example of institutional progress. The regional diffusion of these state agencies follows a global trend, as these institutions have proliferated largely in the context of democratization. After Guatemala created the region's first national human rights institution in 1985, virtually every country followed suit. Chile, Brazil, and Uruguay are exceptions, but even they have taken steps to do so. These institutions tend to investigate accusations of abuse or maladministration by public authorities. They can also typically accept human rights complaints from the public, issue recommendations, and promote human rights education. Technically independent from the government, their role is to implement international human rights norms domestically, mediating between the state and society. While these institutions are not always as independent as they could be and do not always enjoy sufficient resources to fulfill their mandates, they are increasingly playing a valuable role.

Reforming specific state institutions, including the judiciary and police, has also been essential for human rights reform. Recognizing this, international actors (including foreign governments and the United Nations) have assisted Latin American countries, with both financial and technical assistance. The results have been mixed. Judicial reform, for example, has been most extensive in Chile. While some may attribute this to Chile's historically strong commitment to the rule of law, political leadership has also played a pivotal role, providing resources for institutional change and promoting progressive reforms. The case of Venezuela in turn reveals how, despite an outpouring of resources, judicial reform is unlikely in the absence of political commitment. And a country like Peru further shows the importance of reforming local, not just national, judiciaries. In many cases, judicial reform must move beyond the ad hoc commitment of individual judges to more enduring forms of institutionalization.[1] Setbacks aside, such reform is an integral aspect of human rights protection. An independent judiciary that earns the public's confidence can be crucial for human rights accountability.

Police reform, also intertwined closely with human rights protection, has followed a similar trajectory. Important steps have been taken to retrain law enforcement agencies that were previously taught to repress and punish political opponents. This has included equipping police forces with new skills that emphasize the investigatory aspects of their work. Yet despite unprecedented attention to reform, police violence remains high in Brazil, El Salvador, Mexico, Guatemala, Haiti, and Jamaica. High levels of crime—including trafficking in drugs, people, and arms—lead private business owners and others to call for a tough approach to crime (*mano dura*). Many politicians respond by approving or at least ignoring police violence and militarization, especially against marginalized groups. Poor or indigenous peoples provide convenient scapegoats for politicians and police forces eager to meet public demands for crime control. The region, of course, is not unique in this regard. Reform of state institutions is a basic challenge confronting post-conflict, democratizing societies around the world.

UP CLOSE: BRAZIL'S POLICE FORCE—ABUSE OR REFORM?

Brazil's police forces illustrate vividly both the capacity for corruption and the potential for reform. As the country has democratized, police forces have been called to protect public—not national—security. High levels of violence and crime, however, have made this transition especially challenging. While police reform is a priority, and even international actors are supporting Brazilian authorities in these efforts, progress remains far too limited.

Crime serves as a powerful rationale for police corruption and violence, which most often targets marginalized groups in the country's urban and poor centers. On the one hand, violent criminal gangs carry out kidnappings and attack police officers, often in revenge killings, leading to a spiral of conflict. On the other hand, police respond with extrajudicial executions and torture, while death squads (sometimes apparently linked to the police) murder indiscriminately. In total, about 50,000 people are murdered in Brazil every year. And in Rio de Janeiro alone, police are believed to have killed over 1,200 people in 2007 with impunity.

If Brazil's police are known worldwide for their abusive practices, this also exemplifies the challenges associated with reform. Thousands of police officers have participated in training courses, learning about human rights as well as training in crime-scene and investigatory procedures. International actors, from New Scotland Yard to the International Committee of the Red Cross, have assisted and helped train Brazil's police forces. Reform has also involved creating special oversight agencies and review boards. While these have been generally positive developments, the pressures of responding to violent crime with draconian measures seem overwhelming. The difficulties are magnified by a federal system (consisting of a federal police system alongside civil and military police forces at the local level), which makes cohesive reform more cumbersome.

Police reforms are essential for democratizing countries like Brazil. More substantial change, however, will require comprehensive reforms of domestic institutions, including the judiciary and even the private business sector. Without broader systemic change, it will be very difficult for political leaders and police forces to break out of the cycle of combating crime by sacrificing human rights.

Source: "Brazil," *Amnesty International Report 2008: State of the World's Human Rights* (New York: Amnesty International, 2007).

Human rights education offers a related and basic strategy for promoting long-term reform. It consists of incorporating human rights into school curricula, training government workers and others about human rights standards, and disseminating information about human rights norms through public and media campaigns. The goal is to socialize people into accepting human rights norms, replacing exclusionary ideologies with human rights ideas. While human rights education is not a panacea or a simple solution that can be applied on its own to yield dramatic results, it may be vital for combating discrimination and abuse. Not surprisingly, national governments and regional actors, assisted by international partners, have promoted human rights education throughout the region.

Despite significant advances in the region's democratic institutions, crafting regimes that are more fully rights-protective requires the political will to reform state institutions more effectively. Elections are insufficient on their own. Without a stable rule-of-law system, including an independent judiciary, a climate of impunity is likely to persist. Similarly, institutions like the police need to desist from responding to violence with violence. The challenges associated with democratic and human rights reform signal the importance of comprehensive policies: reforming state institutions requires addressing the systemic sources of social violence and corruption that are deeply implicated in a country's political economy. Put differently, political leaders need to confront the complex origins of domestic instability. Only then will the region's democracies be more equitable and sustainable. Democracy has brought enormous progress, but from a human rights perspective, the persistent exclusion and abuse of marginalized groups is unacceptable. While dramatic changes have occurred, too much remains the same.

Cold War Redux

September 11 doubly affected many Latin Americans, who long had associated the date with the first 9/11: the date of Chile's military coup in 1973. As Ariel Dorfman, Chile's renowned writer and human rights activist, put it: "my first September 11th had been in 1973, when terror was also inflicted on the innocent, when death also rained down from the sky, sending me into exile, making me into the man I have now become."[2] While the two events are very different—committed by state versus non-state agents of terror—they both led to periods where national security goals were used to justify the suspension of human rights. The human rights violations that ensued were of course also radically different: military regimes targeted large segments of the national population during the Cold War; post-2001, the region's democratic states focused on pursuing potential terrorists.

Even if the end of the Cold War is considered a watershed event in international politics that led to the proliferation of human rights norms worldwide, the period since the 1990s has seen particularly cruel human rights violations in Latin America. These have often taken vicious forms and targeted indigenous people, women, human rights defenders, and other marginalized groups. Today's human rights violations may not be as visible or widespread, but they are fundamentally similar to the atrocities of the Cold War, revealing persistent sources of abuse.

Perhaps the principal legacy of the Cold War on human rights is that it provided an ideological rationale for terrorizing people. Polarization into two competing global blocs served as a simplifying device for determining who was labeled an enemy of the state. The Cold War struggle was considered so fundamental—the view was that national survival itself was at stake—that virtually any means were deemed acceptable to fend off a perceived threat. This set the stage for committing widespread human rights violations throughout Latin America.

As the Cold War ended, new enemies replaced communism. In Latin America, the Cold War was first substituted by the *anti-drug war*. Whereas the drug trade had been flourishing for some time, it was not until the 1990s that efforts to counter it became much more systematic. No longer distracted by the fight against communism, the United States spearheaded counterdrug programs in the region. While the drug war targets several countries—Bolivia, Brazil, Colombia, Ecuador, Panama,

Peru, and Venezuela—the major producers in the region are Colombia, Peru, and Bolivia, and the bulk of counternarcotic activity remains heavily concentrated in Colombia.

Both Democratic and Republican administrations in the United States have had complicated records vis-à-vis the region's drug trade. In 1987, the Reagan administration was implicated in the Iran-Contra scandal, where the illegal drug trade was used to fund the anticommunist contras fighting in Nicaragua. The Clinton administration then initiated Plan Colombia in the late 1990s, with immediate consequences for human rights. Plan Colombia was a comprehensive project to counter the drug trade in Latin America, much of which would find its way to U.S. communities. The Plan involved military assistance, including a U.S. on-the-ground presence, and perhaps most controversially, aerial fumigation—the use of pesticides to wipe out coca production.

The problem is that pesticides can be hazardous, and they often fall outside their target zone. They also eliminate basic crops, including the coca leaf, which peasants (often indigenous) rely on for their livelihood. In some cases, this has led to refugee flows and displacement of already vulnerable populations. To be fair, the United States has provided countries with funds to grow alternative crops and support democratic institutions. It has also participated in discussions among the region's militaries regarding the role of human rights. On balance, however, anti-drug efforts have undermined human rights.

In addition to economic, social, and cultural rights, the drug war has led to other human rights abuses, as the region's militaries use violence liberally to achieve their anti-drug mission. This has led some observers to criticize close U.S. collaboration with security forces, especially Colombia's (the country with the most graduates from the School of the Americas implicated in human rights abuses), in the war on drugs. Likewise, anti-drug efforts have exacerbated existing political conflicts, feeding into a cycle of ever escalating violence. For example, in Colombia the FARC—affiliated with the Communist Party during the Cold War—has been involved since the 1980s in the drug trade and labeled a terrorist group internationally. The military, in turn, has responded to the FARC with a heavy hand, bypassing legal avenues and often opting for outright repression.

Post-9/11, the drug war in Latin America has been expanded and, interestingly, linked to the "war on terror." Drugs, suspected of financing terror, have been redefined as a key weapon of "narcoterrorists." The United States, at the helm of the global "war on terror," now focuses the majority of its efforts in the region on an Andean Counterdrug Initiative. More recently, the Merida Initiative (also known as Plan Mexico) provides a large volume of assistance to Mexico (a potential transit point for terrorists into the United States) for fighting drug trafficking and crime. The plan has been criticized for bolstering the military, which is known for a rising number of human rights abuses, and for paying inadequate attention to reform of the Mexican state. Drug traffickers and suspected terrorists may seem more sensible targets than Cold War ideological opponents. Critics nonetheless assert that the drug war—and more recently the war on terror—has led to disproportionate human rights abuses, serving as a new post-Cold War rationale for suspending basic human rights.

FIGURE 18. In an annual Silence March in mid-2007, Uruguayans—who now live in one of the most rights-protective regimes in Latin America—commemorate victims of the former military dictatorship, vowing "never again" to state terrorism. Pablo Porciuncula/AFP/Getty Images.

The Impact of the Global "War on Terror"

Following the 9/11 attacks, the United States intensified its attention to the issue of terrorism in Latin America and increased antiterrorism assistance to the region.[3] While most Americans may not think of the region as being on the front line of terrorism, the area has not escaped antiterror-ism efforts. Antiterrorism assistance takes the form of training and equip-ment, focusing on areas like airport security, anti-kidnapping programs, bomb detection, and counterterrorist financing. For example, in 2002 Congress approved more than $17 million to train members of the re-gion's militaries in antiterrorism. The program has now trained thousands of Latin Americans. Since antiterrorism assistance is funded through the Defense (rather than State) Department, it is not subject to the human rights checks of regular foreign assistance.

Attention today has focused on narcoterrorism in Colombia, leftist insurgents in Peru, and an apparent hub of funding for extremist Islamist groups in the borders between Argentina, Brazil, and Paraguay. While Cuba is the only country in the region listed by the United States as a sponsor of terrorism, Venezuela was put on a list of countries in 2006 that do not cooperate on the antiterrorism front, leading some defense equip-ment sales and services to be cancelled. In 2002, the United States moved beyond counternarcotics assistance to Colombia to include counterterror-ism assistance. As House Resolution 338 (12 June 2006) notes, the United States "recognizes the potential threat that sympathizers and financiers of Islamist terrorist organizations that operate in the Western Hemisphere pose to the United States, our allies, and interests."

Overall, however, governments in the region have cooperated on the antiterrorism front. Following the 9/11 attacks on the Untied States, countries in the region invoked the 1947 Rio Treaty (also known as the Inter-American Treaty of Reciprocal Assistance), which requires parties to the treaty to defend one another in case of an attack. In 2002, an Inter-American Convention on Terrorism passed, under the auspices of the OAS. It was the first international treaty after 9/11 to combat terrorism.

UP CLOSE: PUBLIC OPINION IN LATIN AMERICA AFTER 9/11

Latin American elites, along with their counterparts elsewhere in the world, were polled in December 2001 to see how the world had changed after 9/11. Those polled represented a cross-section of the most influential people in a country, not limited to political leaders. The results suggest that Latin Americans have been much harder hit by the "war on terror" than the conventional wisdom in the United States holds.

When asked whether personal freedoms and privacy in their countries had been hurt after 9/11, the majority of Latin Americas interviewed thought that it had (54 percent for personal freedoms and 59 percent for privacy). In terms of personal freedoms, the only regions where more people perceived a decline in conditions were Western Europe and the Middle East. Regarding privacy, only Western Europe scored lower.

When asked whether war was worth the risk of destabilizing Muslim states, fewer people in Latin America than anywhere else in the world (46 percent) thought that war was worth the risk.

Public opinion leaders were also asked whether Latin Americans had a favorable view of the United States. While most (63 percent) held a favorable view, the region scored second lowest after the Middle East.

Regarding whether the United States was "doing the right thing" in the war on terror, fewer than half of Latin Americans thought it was. Again, Latin America scored second lowest (46 percent) following the Middle East (41 percent)—compared to Asia (63 percent), Eastern Europe (64 percent), and Western Europe (90 percent).

Source: Pew Research Center for the People & the Press, "America Admired, Yet Its New Vulnerability Seen as a Good Thing," 19 December 2001 (http://people-press.org/report/145/).

Regional Ramifications

The U.S.-led global "war on terror" has had several concrete ramifications for human rights in Latin America. First, as discussed above, the focus on terrorism now shapes longstanding efforts to combat the drug trade. Second, the controversial detention of suspected terrorists in Guantánamo, Cuba, along with the Military Commissions Act of 2006 which legitimized these detentions, elicited a particularly strong reaction across Latin America.

Third, antiterrorism has gone hand in hand with rising militarization. With U.S. support, militaries in the region have increasingly engaged in standard policing functions, including combating gang violence and controlling crowds during protests; militaries have even moved to protect oil-rich areas like Chiapas. Support for militarization was reflected, for example, in the resumption of U.S. military aid to Guatemala in 2005 (suspended in 1990), a decision widely opposed by human rights groups who warned that the Guatemalan military still had to undertake long-promised reforms. More recently, U.S. military aid to the region has almost equalled economic aid (Figure 19). And the largest recipient of U.S. military aid outside the Middle East is still Colombia.

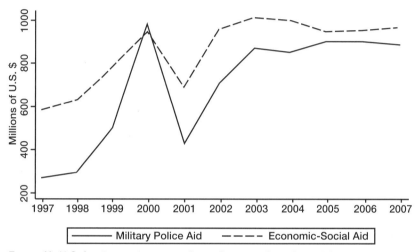

FIGURE 19. U.S. foreign assistance to Latin America. Data from Adam Isacson, Joy Olson, and Lisa Haugaard, *Below the Radar: U.S. Military Programs with Latin America, 1997–2007* (Washington, D.C.: Center for International Policy, Latin American Working Group Education Fund, and Washington Office on Latin America, 2007), 27.

Fourth, foreign economic relations have become closely linked to anti-terrorism measures. For example, free trade has been conceptualized as an integral aspect of national security. This means that any cooperation that states have extended in the war on terror has translated into preferential trade, just as the lack of cooperation has led to reprisals. Despite efforts like the Leahy Law to link military assistance and human rights (Chapter 4), military aid destined for combating terrorism in the region has rarely been linked in practice to human rights conditions.

Fifth, governments in the region, including those in Peru and Colombia, have passed antiterrorism legislation in direct response to the global war on terror. This type of legislation, not unique to the region, has defined national security and terrorist threats broadly, leaving the door open for human rights violations. In the process, opponents of antiterrorism legislation, human rights defenders, and other political critics have been targeted by states anxious to demonstrate their antiterrorism credentials.

A Shifting Political Landscape

If the global war on terror is one theme that has characterized the region in the twenty-first century, a dramatic shift to the political left and a general rise in populism are other crucial trends. These developments are far more important for human rights and social justice concerns than they may appear. They reveal people's discontent with basic living conditions, including endemic poverty, corruption, and rising militarization. If the composition of governments matters for understanding human rights (including their ideological orientation or electoral base of support), then recent political shifts in Latin America may be consequential.

While some dispute the extent and significance of the shifting political landscape in Latin America, the region clearly has undergone notable changes. The election of presidents with socialist credentials, for example, marks a particular electoral turn, especially in South America—Argentina, Bolivia, Brazil, Chile, Ecuador, Guyana, Peru, Uruguay, and Venezuela. Add to this the near-electoral win of a leftist president in Mexico in 2006, the Castro family's continued rule in Cuba, and even Paraguay joining the leftward trend in the 2008 elections. It is indeed the first time that so many presidents from the political left hold power across the region.

In a related vein, the new millennium has seen the rise of governments in the region who emphasize economic and social rights. This new line of leaders has often rejected the "Washington Consensus," dominant in international economic relations since the 1980s. The consensus refers to the set of market-driven, free-trade policies that international financial institutions and the United States tend to promote. Critics assert that these policies have hurt the poor disproportionately even if in some areas they have spurred national economic growth.

The populist theme has also featured prominently in these developments. As people have tired of decades of elite rule, especially in countries where social inequalities are particularly dramatic, national leaders have adopted the discourse of revolution and radical transformation. Latin American politics in the new millennium have emphasized a break from the past, from "business as usual" to an era of reform. To this end, many of the leaders—including in the heavily indigenous Andean countries of

Bolivia and Ecuador—can be characterized as populist, committed to responding to the popular will. Skeptics express concern that, despite the loftiness of some of their goals, populist leaders could undermine democratic stability. Historically, after all, populism has often led to a high concentration of power in the hands of the executive to the detriment of legislative and judicial authority.

Similar dynamics are apparent in foreign policy, especially in relations with the United States. The new brand of national leaders has often been highly critical of the United States, including its global war on terror. U.S. involvement in the region, from counternarcotics programs to economic trade, has been labeled imperialism-in-disguise. Additionally, active opposition by the United States to leaders in Venezuela and Haiti has spurred accusations that the United States has undermined democracy by attempting to orchestrate coups in these countries. Leaders have varied in the extent to which they have been willing to criticize the hegemonic power to the north, but the general tone of criticism cannot be denied.

These trends were first evident with the election of Hugo Chávez in Venezuela in 1999, and most recently with populist politics in the Andes. Chávez came into office calling for widespread social reforms and regional integration, but he has been criticized for concentrating too much power in his own hands and failing to control widespread corruption. Chávez's ties to Castro's Cuba, his country's oil richness, and his critique of U.S. policies have also made him a controversial figure in some circles, leading the Bush administration to label him a threat to regional security. If Chávez's election marked the beginning of a leftward turn in the region, the 2006 elections of Evo Morales in Bolivia and Rafael Correa in Ecuador sealed the influence of populism. Both have been vocal opponents of U.S. policies, including anti-coca programs like the fumigation campaigns. Morales, himself indigenous and a former *cocalero* (coca grower), has shattered expectations about Latin American leaders.

Other leaders have been somewhat more pragmatic. For example, former union leader Luiz Inácio "Lula" Da Silva, who took over Brazil's presidency in 2003, has been critical of free-trade policies but has worked not to alienate the United States. Domestically, he has undertaken a widespread campaign to combat poverty and inequality. Michele Bachelet, Chile's first woman president, has followed a similar track since 2006. Bachelet is a particularly interesting national leader, having replaced Ricardo Lagos—

Chile's first socialist president since Allende's death in 1973. A socialist, surgeon, and self-declared agnostic, Bachelet has broken deeply engrained gender barriers to head the heavily Catholic country. A torture survivor from the 1970s, she was also imprisoned and tortured with her mother in Villa Grimaldi, Chile's principal detention camp (Chapter 6). Her election raises fascinating questions about the potential human rights implications of a new generation of leaders who were direct victims of state violence.

Until recently, the United States responded to these trends with concern and in some cases alarm, interpreting them through the prism of national security. U.S. officials often indicated that a conspiracy existed between Cuba and Chávez's Venezuela to remake Latin America in their image. According to this perspective, electoral changes in the region were framed as national security threats. U.S. resistance to these trends, in a region that before 9/11 was slated to be a priority for the Bush administration but was subsequently neglected, did not win many friends. This was evident when President Bush met widespread opposition on a week-long trip to the region in spring 2007. Obama's election two years later augured a new era for the hemisphere, promising at least to engage leftist regimes in dialogue.

More neutral observers note that, while unbridled populism can be dangerous and undermine democracy, leftist victories may actually indicate democracy's strength in the region. Just as political parties in established democracies wax and wane in influence, Latin America's trend may be temporary and largely insignificant. Leftist governments in the region will emphasize new issues, while facing their own challenges and committing their own mistakes. Others warn that it is counterproductive to treat electoral-political trends as security issues. Inequality and social injustice—basic violations of economic and social rights—reflect people's concerns about their humane treatment and should be viewed as nonpartisan items on any political agenda.

UP CLOSE: TRAIL-BLAZING PRESIDENTS SPEAK OUT

Excerpts from President Michele Bachelet's Inaugural Address from the Balcony of La Moneda Palace, Santiago, Chile, 11 March 2006:

"Aside from the technological revolution unfolding before our eyes, I think that there is another revolution afoot in the way we relate to each other, the way we interact within our communities, and our manner of combating individualism, indifference and hopelessness.

"The past is what it is: the past. We will never forget it.

"I personify a whole history, which had dark and bitter moments, but I knew how to recover.

"The world is watching us. The world is closely observing what is happening in this small country in the south of the world that was able to restore freedom and rights—with effort and pain, yes—but it built a solid democracy. It brought about reconciliation and it is progressing."

*   *   *

Excerpts from President Evo Morales's Inaugural Address at the Congress in La Paz, Bolivia, 22 January 2006:

"The 500 years of Indian resistance have not been in vain. From 500 years of resistance we pass to another 500 years in power.

"We have been condemned, humiliated . . . and never recognised as human beings.

"We are here and we say that we have achieved power to end the injustice, the inequality and oppression that we have lived under."

Sources: English text of Bachelet's address is available from the Archive of Women's Political Communication, Iowa State University (http://www.womenspeecharchive.org/). For Morales's address, see "Morales Inaugural Speech: Excerpts," BBC News (http://news.bbc.co.uk/2/hi/americas/4638030.stm).

Pockets of Resistance

Despite a drastic reduction in state repression, a rise in democratization, and calls for economic and social reform, the future of human rights in the region remains uncertain. Pockets of resistance continue to challenge the cry of Latin Americans throughout the continent for basic decency and humane treatment. This cry is expressed through popular protest, social demands for change, immigration flows, activism and art, voting, violence, and personal anguish. Contemporary human rights abuses, in turn, reflect deeply embedded structural inequalities that are difficult to reverse.

Three elements, in particular, constrain the possibilities for more drastic change: poverty and inequality (which produce domestic instability), a climate of impunity (associated with weak democratic institutions, including the rule of law), and entrenched ideas about national security (or exclusionary ideologies). As Figure 8 suggests, these are the sources of human rights abuse. Powerful international actors will shape human rights outcomes to the extent that they influence these fundamental tensions. While much has changed—far fewer armed groups and wars exist, most regimes are democratizing, and anticommunism remains largely in the past—there are ongoing reasons why human rights violations continue.

Poverty and inequality are root causes of human abuse. When the gap between the haves and have-nots is particularly wide, so that basic human needs go unmet, social demands can turn violent, and social conflict is much more likely to erupt; those in power are also more inclined to resort to force to retain their privileged status. If violence erupts, decision-making elites will likely turn to repression as their preferred mode of social control. These dynamics help to explain shockingly high levels of human rights abuse in the 1970s, primarily taking the form of civil and political rights violations.

As democratic transitions helped societies institutionalize ways of solving conflict nonviolently, the region's more recent history has been one where ongoing violations of economic and social rights have led to popular discontent, both with the failure of traditional politicians to deliver on their promises and the perceived inequities perpetuated by neoliberal policies promoted by powerful foreign actors. Discontent in recent years has manifested itself in essential political shifts, whose long-term effects on human rights still are unclear. New leftist and populist leaders may aspire to improve economic and social conditions, but their legacy will depend largely on how well they are able to ameliorate conditions in their countries without sacrificing democratic institutions or civil and political rights.

While democracies clearly are associated with greater levels of human rights protection, they remain complex institutional phenomena: if a key piece of the democratic puzzle is missing (e.g., rule of law), the overall outcome will not live up to its potential. Latin America's democracies have proved relatively resilient and capable of weathering change, but the problems of impunity and lack of accountability remain deeply problematic.

Impunity underlies the widespread corruption that characterizes the region—from fraud and embezzlement by state and non-state elites to the police abuse feeding femicide and human trafficking across the region to the targeting of human rights defenders and members of the media who dare to expose injustices that otherwise would go unpunished. The sources of impunity are no doubt complex, yet at a minimum they reflect weaknesses in the rule of law. Democracies that score high in electoral terms can still be illiberal if basic abuses are left unpunished. The recent history of Latin America supports this contention.

Militaries may no longer have an iron grip on the region as they did in the past, but they still exert pronounced influence. In the context of the war on terror, moreover, their impact has only risen. As militaries have turned increasingly to domestic security issues, many critics worry that the armed forces are overstepping their appropriate institutional roles in democratic regimes. Broader militarization has also meant that police and other security forces resort to violence freely rather than work through legal channels.

The strength of militaries is in turn closely tied to prevailing *conceptions of national security*, which define when and how military responses are appropriate in domestic politics. An ever-expanding definition of national security, sparked largely by the global war on terror, broadened states' perceptions of what constitutes a threat to their security. Reminding one of the Cold War, today's national security enemies can include drug traffickers, political opponents, human rights activists, and vulnerable indigenous populations. Any political challenge to the state is potentially a justification to suspend legally protected rights. From afar, the victims and methods may not shock us as much as do tales of mass-scale genocide and disappearances. Up close, the pain and suffering of countless human beings who are beaten or killed, displaced from their homes, threatened on a daily basis, allowed to go hungry, or otherwise marginalized and discriminated against is a different story.

In practice, poverty, impunity, and militarization are closely intertwined. Former Brazilian president Fernando Henrique Cardoso declared to the French National Assembly in October 2001: "Fight vigorously against terror but also against the underlying causes of terror: hunger, ignorance, inequality and distorted perceptions of other cultures."[4] Almost eight years later, at the 2009 Summit of the Americas, regional progress on the human rights front had arguably stalled. According to Amnesty International, "The governments of the Americas have failed to recognize that human rights must be placed at the centre of efforts to confront the many fundamental challenges facing the region, including poverty, the global economic crisis, public security, climate change and energy security."[5] The 2009 coup in Honduras did not bode well. Human rights protections across Latin America hang on the ability of national leaders, at long last, to devise comprehensive policies—to find a balance between national security and personal integrity, between civil and political rights on the one hand and economic and social rights on the other.

Progress and Challenge

The history of human rights in Latin America is one of alternating terror and hope. This is a political reality. Depictions of human rights events in the region as characterized entirely by either terror or hope are overly simplistic and ultimately wrong. Horrific abuses have occurred in the region in the not-so-distant past, just as the continent has been a model of human rights activism and progress. It is crucial that societies commit to the idea that they will not return to the horrors of the past—*nunca más*—while remaining vigilant to a disturbing possibility: no society, under the right circumstances, is immune from widespread human rights violations.

Human rights atrocities rarely happen overnight. They occur in small steps, usually criticized by a brave few whose voices go unheeded. The tell-tale warning signs are social discontent (evident in armed conflict, widespread protests, or gaping inequalities), unresponsive governments (whether because they are nondemocratic, legally weak, or otherwise unaccountable in a system of impunity and corruption), and institutionalized ideas that legitimate abuse under certain conditions (from national security doctrines to ideas discriminating against groups on the basis of social markers, including race, religion, ethnicity, gender, and sexual orientation). After the fact, understanding past violations is essential, both for promoting reconciliation and justice and for assuring that historical memory protects future generations from similar atrocities.

The human rights changes that have swept across the region are nonetheless cause for hope. Regional mechanisms are among the strongest in the world. Domestically, groups targeted for repression have championed the cause of human rights in the face of overwhelming duress—from torture survivors to grieving relatives to marginalized groups. Canadian journalist Naomi Klein referred to this tension between terror and hope when she described the rising power of indigenous movements in Latin America: "Their power comes not from terror but from a new terror-resistant strain of hope, one so sturdy it can take root in the midst of Colombia's seemingly hopeless civil war. And if it can grow there, it can take root anywhere."[6]

Latin America's human rights trajectory is rich and complex. It serves as a mirror to the political factors underlying human rights abuse, reform, and the quest for justice everywhere. The twin themes of terror and hope expose the worst and the best that the region—and humanity—has to offer. When the basic treatment of people is at stake, political struggles are inevitable and change is at least possible.

Questions and Debate

1. How does the war on drugs undermine human rights? Do critics exaggerate its negative consequences?
2. Are recent counterterrorism efforts in the region comparable to human rights abuses during the Cold War? Why?
3. Can states abide by the rule of law when responding to "national security" threats? Should they?
4. Why do Latin American elites react so negatively to the U.S.-led war on terror, compared to their counterparts around the world?
5. Will the populist-leftist trend in Latin American politics improve human rights conditions? Why has Central America been largely excluded from this trend?
6. Does contemplating the future of human rights in Latin America make one more hopeful or more concerned? Please refer to specific countries and issues while considering sources of abuse.

References

Additional Reading

John Bailey and Lucia Dammert, eds., *Public Security and Police Reform in the Americas* (Pittsburgh: University of Pittsburgh Press, 2005). Useful overview of police reform efforts across the region.

Herbert Braun, *Our Guerrillas, Our Sidewalks: A Journey into the Violence of Colombia* (Lanham, Md.: Rowman and Littlefield, 2003). Chronicle of a kidnapping, as a window into the complexities of Colombia.

Daniel Brinks, *The Judicial Response to Police Killings in Latin America: Inequality and the Rule of Law* (Cambridge: Cambridge University Press, 2007). Novel examination of the connections between the judiciary and police, focusing on Argentina, Brazil, and Uruguay.

Steven Dudley, *Walking Ghosts: Murder and Guerrilla Politics in Colombia* (New York: Routledge, 2006). Detailed and intriguing account of the violence in Colombia.

Martha Knisely Huggins, Mike Haritos-Fatouros, and Philip G. Zimbardo, *Violence Workers: Police Torturers and Murderers Reconstruct Brazilian Atrocities* (Berkeley: University of California Press, 2002). Unique look at the perspective of Brazilian police forces committing human rights violations.

Juan A. Mendez and Javier Mariezcurrena, "Human Rights in Latin America and the Caribbean: A Regional Perspective," November 1999 (Notre Dame, Ind.: Center for Civil and Human Rights, 2000). A very useful discussion of democratic human rights reforms in the region, as well as ongoing social exclusion, pre-2000.

Lars Schoultz, *National Security and United States Policy Toward Latin America* (Princeton, N.J.: Princeton University Press, 2007). First-rate overview of U.S. policy toward the region, focusing specifically on national security issues.

Mitchell A. Seligson, "The Rise of Populism and the Left in Latin America," *Journal of Democracy* 18, 3 (July 2007): 81–95. Excellent survey of two key trends in the region.

Timothy P. Wickham-Crowley and Susan Eva Eckstein, eds., *What Justice? Whose Justice? Fighting for Fairness in Latin America* (Berkeley: University of California Press, 2003). Collection of case studies examining how social justice in the region is faring under democracy.

Deborah J. Yashar, *Contesting Citizenship in Latin America: The Rise of Indigenous Movements and the Postliberal Challenge* (Cambridge: Cambridge University Press, 2005). Sophisticated study of growing indigenous influence in the region.

Filmography

Elite Squad (2007). Award-winning film about a special-operations police force combating crime and abusing rights in a Brazilian *favela*. 115 minutes.

The Road to Guantánamo (2006). Part documentary, part drama, this film focuses on three British Muslims held in Guantánamo Bay. 95 minutes.

Behave (2006). A sharp look at Brazil's juvenile courts and detention centers. 80 minutes.

Cocalero (2006). Award-winning documentary tracing the trajectory of Evo Morales from coca farmer to president of Bolivia. 94 minutes.

Land of the Blind (2006). Feature film depicting ideas about terrorism, revolution, and political memory as played out repeatedly throughout history. 101 minutes.

State of Fear: The Truth About Terrorism (2005). Based on Peru's Truth Commission, this film uses the country's experiences with the Shining Path to tell a cautionary tale about the ongoing global war on terror. 94 minutes.

Switch Off (*Apaga y Vámonos*) (2005). Story of the foremost hydroelectric company in Latin America, revealing government complicity in environmental degradation and human rights violations in Chile; shows the government failing to protect indigenous rights and using antiterrorism legislation to arrest protestors. 87 minutes.

The Fourth World War (2004). Drawing on images and voices from around the world, including Mexico and Argentina, the film documents issues that unify people despite the global "war on terror." 60 minutes.

Useful Websites

Latin American Public Opinion Project (LAPOP). A variety of public opinion polls conducted throughout the region. http://sitemason.vanderbilt.edu/lapop.

Ombudsnet. Part of the Inter-American Institute of Human Rights, a site focusing on ombudsman offices in Latin America and the Caribbean. http://www.iidh.ed.cr/Comunidades/Ombudsnet/english/.

U.S. Defense and Security Assistance to Latin America. Most comprehensive database of U.S. military assistance to the region. http://www.ciponline.org/facts/.

Congressional Research Service Reports. Search "Latin America" to access hundreds of reports on the region, many dealing with terrorism and U.S. foreign relations. http://digital.library.unt.edu/govdocs/crs/searchform.tkl.

CELS (Legal and Social Studies Center). One of Latin America's leading human rights centers, focusing on Argentina; includes Spanish-language blog on state terrorism. http://www.cels.org.ar.

Notes

[1] Peter DeShazo and Juan Enrique Vargas, *Judicial Reform in Latin America: An Assessment*, Policy Papers on the Americas 17, Study 2 (Washington, D.C.: Center for Strategic and International Studies, September 2006).

[2] *A Promise to the Dead* (2007), film by Peter Raymont.

[3] This section draws on Mark P. Sullivan, *Latin America: Terrorism Issues*, CRS Report for Congress (Washington, D.C.: Congressional Research Service, 22 January 2007).

[4] Carlos Fuentes, "You Scare Us: Bush Is Giving Latin America the Willies," *Los Angeles Times*, 26 September 2004.

[5] Amnesty International, "Fifth Summit of the Americas: Human Rights Left Behind," Public Statement, 21 April 2009.

[6] Referring to an indigenous community in Cauca, southwestern Colombia. Naomi Klein, "The Threat of Hope in Latin America," *The Nation* (4 November 2005).

Appendix 1.
American Convention on Human Rights
(Pact of San José, Costa Rica)

Preamble

The American states signatory to the present Convention,

Reaffirming their intention to consolidate in this hemisphere, within the framework of democratic institutions, a system of personal liberty and social justice based on respect for the essential rights of man;

Recognizing that the essential rights of man are not derived from one's being a national of a certain state, but are based upon attributes of the human personality, and that they therefore justify international protection in the form of a convention reinforcing or complementing the protection provided by the domestic law of the American states;

Considering that these principles have been set forth in the Charter of the Organization of American States, in the American Declaration of the Rights and Duties of Man, and in the Universal Declaration of Human Rights, and that they have been reaffirmed and refined in other international instruments, worldwide as well as regional in scope;

Reiterating that, in accordance with the Universal Declaration of Human Rights, the ideal of free men enjoying freedom from fear and want can be achieved only if conditions are created whereby everyone may enjoy his economic, social, and cultural rights, as well as his civil and political rights; and

Considering that the Third Special Inter-American Conference (Buenos Aires, 1967) approved the incorporation into the Charter of the Organization itself of broader standards with respect to economic, social, and educational rights and resolved that an inter-American convention on human rights should determine the structure, competence, and procedure of the organs responsible for these matters,

Have agreed upon the following:

PART I—STATE OBLIGATIONS AND RIGHTS PROTECTED

CHAPTER I—GENERAL OBLIGATIONS

Article 1. Obligation to Respect Rights

1. The States Parties to this Convention undertake to respect the rights and freedoms recognized herein and to ensure to all persons subject to their jurisdiction the free and full exercise of those rights and freedoms, without any discrimination for reasons of race, color, sex, language, religion, political or other opinion, national or social origin, economic status, birth, or any other social condition.

2. For the purposes of this Convention, "person" means every human being.

Article 2. Domestic Legal Effects

Where the exercise of any of the rights or freedoms referred to in Article 1 is not already ensured by legislative or other provisions, the States Parties undertake to adopt, in accordance with their constitutional processes and the provisions of this Convention, such legislative or other measures as may be necessary to give effect to those rights or freedoms.

CHAPTER II—CIVIL AND POLITICAL RIGHTS

Article 3. Right to Juridical Personality

Every person has the right to recognition as a person before the law.

Article 4. Right to Life

1. Every person has the right to have his life respected. This right shall be protected by law and, in general, from the moment of conception. No one shall be arbitrarily deprived of his life.

2. In countries that have not abolished the death penalty, it may be imposed only for the most serious crimes and pursuant to a final judgment rendered by a competent court and in accordance with a law establishing such punishment, enacted prior to the commission of the crime. The ap-

plication of such punishment shall not be extended to crimes to which it does not presently apply.

3. The death penalty shall not be reestablished in states that have abolished it.

4. In no case shall capital punishment be inflicted for political offenses or related common crimes.

5. Capital punishment shall not be imposed upon persons who, at the time the crime was committed, were under 18 years of age or over 70 years of age; nor shall it be applied to pregnant women.

6. Every person condemned to death shall have the right to apply for amnesty, pardon, or commutation of sentence, which may be granted in all cases. Capital punishment shall not be imposed while such a petition is pending decision by the competent authority.

Article 5. Right to Humane Treatment

1. Every person has the right to have his physical, mental, and moral integrity respected.

2. No one shall be subjected to torture or to cruel, inhuman, or degrading punishment or treatment. All persons deprived of their liberty shall be treated with respect for the inherent dignity of the human person.

3. Punishment shall not be extended to any person other than the criminal.

4. Accused persons shall, save in exceptional circumstances, be segregated from convicted persons, and shall be subject to separate treatment appropriate to their status as unconvicted persons.

5. Minors while subject to criminal proceedings shall be separated from adults and brought before specialized tribunals, as speedily as possible, so that they may be treated in accordance with their status as minors.

6. Punishments consisting of deprivation of liberty shall have as an essential aim the reform and social readaptation of the prisoners.

Article 6. Freedom from Slavery

1. No one shall be subject to slavery or to involuntary servitude, which are prohibited in all their forms, as are the slave trade and traffic in women.

2. No one shall be required to perform forced or compulsory labor. This provision shall not be interpreted to mean that, in those countries in which the penalty established for certain crimes is deprivation of liberty at

forced labor, the carrying out of such a sentence imposed by a competent court is prohibited. Forced labor shall not adversely affect the dignity or the physical or intellectual capacity of the prisoner.

3. For the purposes of this article, the following do not constitute forced or compulsory labor:

a. work or service normally required of a person imprisoned in execution of a sentence or formal decision passed by the competent judicial authority. Such work or service shall be carried out under the supervision and control of public authorities, and any persons performing such work or service shall not be placed at the disposal of any private party, company, or juridical person;

b. military service and, in countries in which conscientious objectors are recognized, national service that the law may provide for in lieu of military service;

c. service exacted in time of danger or calamity that threatens the existence or the well-being of the community; or

d. work or service that forms part of normal civic obligations.

Article 7. Right to Personal Liberty

1. Every person has the right to personal liberty and security.

2. No one shall be deprived of his physical liberty except for the reasons and under the conditions established beforehand by the constitution of the State Party concerned or by a law established pursuant thereto.

3. No one shall be subject to arbitrary arrest or imprisonment.

4. Anyone who is detained shall be informed of the reasons for his detention and shall be promptly notified of the charge or charges against him.

5. Any person detained shall be brought promptly before a judge or other officer authorized by law to exercise judicial power and shall be entitled to trial within a reasonable time or to be released without prejudice to the continuation of the proceedings. His release may be subject to guarantees to assure his appearance for trial.

6. Anyone who is deprived of his liberty shall be entitled to recourse to a competent court, in order that the court may decide without delay on the lawfulness of his arrest or detention and order his release if the arrest or detention is unlawful. In States Parties whose laws provide that anyone who believes himself to be threatened with deprivation of his liberty is entitled to recourse to a competent court in order that it may decide on the

lawfulness of such threat, this remedy may not be restricted or abolished. The interested party or another person in his behalf is entitled to seek these remedies.

7. No one shall be detained for debt. This principle shall not limit the orders of a competent judicial authority issued for nonfulfillment of duties of support.

Article 8. Right to a Fair Trial

1. Every person has the right to a hearing, with due guarantees and within a reasonable time, by a competent, independent, and impartial tribunal, previously established by law, in the substantiation of any accusation of a criminal nature made against him or for the determination of his rights and obligations of a civil, labor, fiscal, or any other nature.

2. Every person accused of a criminal offense has the right to be presumed innocent so long as his guilt has not been proven according to law. During the proceedings, every person is entitled, with full equality, to the following minimum guarantees:

   a. the right of the accused to be assisted without charge by a translator or interpreter, if he does not understand or does not speak the language of the tribunal or court;

   b. prior notification in detail to the accused of the charges against him;

   c. adequate time and means for the preparation of his defense;

   d. the right of the accused to defend himself personally or to be assisted by legal counsel of his own choosing, and to communicate freely and privately with his counsel;

   e. the inalienable right to be assisted by counsel provided by the state, paid or not as the domestic law provides, if the accused does not defend himself personally or engage his own counsel within the time period established by law;

   f. the right of the defense to examine witnesses present in the court and to obtain the appearance, as witnesses, of experts or other persons who may throw light on the facts;

   g. the right not to be compelled to be a witness against himself or to plead guilty; and

   h. the right to appeal the judgment to a higher court.

3. A confession of guilt by the accused shall be valid only if it is made without coercion of any kind.

4. An accused person acquitted by a nonappealable judgment shall not be subjected to a new trial for the same cause.

5. Criminal proceedings shall be public, except insofar as may be necessary to protect the interests of justice.

Article 9. Freedom from Ex Post Facto Laws

No one shall be convicted of any act or omission that did not constitute a criminal offense, under the applicable law, at the time it was committed. A heavier penalty shall not be imposed than the one that was applicable at the time the criminal offense was committed. If subsequent to the commission of the offense the law provides for the imposition of a lighter punishment, the guilty person shall benefit therefrom.

Article 10. Right to Compensation

Every person has the right to be compensated in accordance with the law in the event he has been sentenced by a final judgment through a miscarriage of justice.

Article 11. Right to Privacy

1. Everyone has the right to have his honor respected and his dignity recognized.

2. No one may be the object of arbitrary or abusive interference with his private life, his family, his home, or his correspondence, or of unlawful attacks on his honor or reputation.

3. Everyone has the right to the protection of the law against such interference or attacks.

Article 12. Freedom of Conscience and Religion

1. Everyone has the right to freedom of conscience and of religion. This right includes freedom to maintain or to change one's religion or beliefs, and freedom to profess or disseminate one's religion or beliefs, either individually or together with others, in public or in private.

2. No one shall be subject to restrictions that might impair his freedom to maintain or to change his religion or beliefs.

3. Freedom to manifest one's religion and beliefs may be subject only to the limitations prescribed by law that are necessary to protect public safety, order, health, or morals, or the rights or freedoms of others.

4. Parents or guardians, as the case may be, have the right to provide

for the religious and moral education of their children or wards that is in accord with their own convictions.

Article 13. Freedom of Thought and Expression

1. Everyone has the right to freedom of thought and expression. This right includes freedom to seek, receive, and impart information and ideas of all kinds, regardless of frontiers, either orally, in writing, in print, in the form of art, or through any other medium of one's choice.

2. The exercise of the right provided for in the foregoing paragraph shall not be subject to prior censorship but shall be subject to subsequent imposition of liability, which shall be expressly established by law to the extent necessary to ensure:

    a. respect for the rights or reputations of others; or

    b. the protection of national security, public order, or public health or morals.

3. The right of expression may not be restricted by indirect methods or means, such as the abuse of government or private controls over newsprint, radio broadcasting frequencies, or equipment used in the dissemination of information, or by any other means tending to impede the communication and circulation of ideas and opinions.

4. Notwithstanding the provisions of paragraph 2 above, public entertainments may be subject by law to prior censorship for the sole purpose of regulating access to them for the moral protection of childhood and adolescence.

5. Any propaganda for war and any advocacy of national, racial, or religious hatred that constitute incitements to lawless violence or to any other similar action against any person or group of persons on any grounds including those of race, color, religion, language, or national origin shall be considered as offenses punishable by law.

Article 14. Right of Reply

1. Anyone injured by inaccurate or offensive statements or ideas disseminated to the public in general by a legally regulated medium of communication has the right to reply or to make a correction using the same communications outlet, under such conditions as the law may establish.

2. The correction or reply shall not in any case remit other legal liabilities that may have been incurred.

3. For the effective protection of honor and reputation, every publisher,

and every newspaper, motion picture, radio, and television company, shall have a person responsible who is not protected by immunities or special privileges.

Article 15. Right of Assembly

The right of peaceful assembly, without arms, is recognized. No restrictions may be placed on the exercise of this right other than those imposed in conformity with the law and necessary in a democratic society in the interest of national security, public safety or public order, or to protect public health or morals or the rights or freedom of others.

Article 16. Freedom of Association

1. Everyone has the right to associate freely for ideological, religious, political, economic, labor, social, cultural, sports, or other purposes.

2. The exercise of this right shall be subject only to such restrictions established by law as may be necessary in a democratic society, in the interest of national security, public safety or public order, or to protect public health or morals or the rights and freedoms of others.

3. The provisions of this article do not bar the imposition of legal restrictions, including even deprivation of the exercise of the right of association, on members of the armed forces and the police.

Article 17. Rights of the Family

1. The family is the natural and fundamental group unit of society and is entitled to protection by society and the state.

2. The right of men and women of marriageable age to marry and to raise a family shall be recognized, if they meet the conditions required by domestic laws, insofar as such conditions do not affect the principle of nondiscrimination established in this Convention.

3. No marriage shall be entered into without the free and full consent of the intending spouses.

4. The States Parties shall take appropriate steps to ensure the equality of rights and the adequate balancing of responsibilities of the spouses as to marriage, during marriage, and in the event of its dissolution. In case of dissolution, provision shall be made for the necessary protection of any children solely on the basis of their own best interests.

5. The law shall recognize equal rights for children born out of wedlock and those born in wedlock.

Article 18. Right to a Name

Every person has the right to a given name and to the surnames of his parents or that of one of them. The law shall regulate the manner in which this right shall be ensured for all, by the use of assumed names if necessary.

Article 19. Rights of the Child

Every minor child has the right to the measures of protection required by his condition as a minor on the part of his family, society, and the state.

Article 20. Right to Nationality

1. Every person has the right to a nationality.

2. Every person has the right to the nationality of the state in whose territory he was born if he does not have the right to any other nationality.

3. No one shall be arbitrarily deprived of his nationality or of the right to change it.

Article 21. Right to Property

1. Everyone has the right to the use and enjoyment of his property. The law may subordinate such use and enjoyment to the interest of society.

2. No one shall be deprived of his property except upon payment of just compensation, for reasons of public utility or social interest, and in the cases and according to the forms established by law.

3. Usury and any other form of exploitation of man by man shall be prohibited by law.

Article 22. Freedom of Movement and Residence

1. Every person lawfully in the territory of a State Party has the right to move about in it, and to reside in it subject to the provisions of the law.

2. Every person has the right lo leave any country freely, including his own.

3. The exercise of the foregoing rights may be restricted only pursuant to a law to the extent necessary in a democratic society to prevent crime or to protect national security, public safety, public order, public morals, public health, or the rights or freedoms of others.

4. The exercise of the rights recognized in paragraph 1 may also be restricted by law in designated zones for reasons of public interest.

5. No one can be expelled from the territory of the state of which he is a national or be deprived of the right to enter it.

6. An alien lawfully in the territory of a State Party to this Convention may be expelled from it only pursuant to a decision reached in accordance with law.

7. Every person has the right to seek and be granted asylum in a foreign territory, in accordance with the legislation of the state and international conventions, in the event he is being pursued for political offenses or related common crimes.

8. In no case may an alien be deported or returned to a country, regardless of whether or not it is his country of origin, if in that country his right to life or personal freedom is in danger of being violated because of his race, nationality, religion, social status, or political opinions.

9. The collective expulsion of aliens is prohibited.

Article 23. Right to Participate in Government

1. Every citizen shall enjoy the following rights and opportunities:

a. to take part in the conduct of public affairs, directly or through freely chosen representatives;

b. to vote and to be elected in genuine periodic elections, which shall be by universal and equal suffrage and by secret ballot that guarantees the free expression of the will of the voters; and

c. to have access, under general conditions of equality, to the public service of his country.

2. The law may regulate the exercise of the rights and opportunities referred to in the preceding paragraph only on the basis of age, nationality, residence, language, education, civil and mental capacity, or sentencing by a competent court in criminal proceedings.

Article 24. Right to Equal Protection

All persons are equal before the law. Consequently, they are entitled, without discrimination, to equal protection of the law.

Article 25. Right to Judicial Protection

1. Everyone has the right to simple and prompt recourse, or any other effective recourse, to a competent court or tribunal for protection against acts that violate his fundamental rights recognized by the constitution or laws of the state concerned or by this Convention, even though such violation may have been committed by persons acting in the course of their official duties.

2. The States Parties undertake:

a. to ensure that any person claiming such remedy shall have his rights determined by the competent authority provided for by the legal system of the state;

b. to develop the possibilities of judicial remedy; and

c. to ensure that the competent authorities shall enforce such remedies when granted.

CHAPTER III—ECONOMIC, SOCIAL, AND CULTURAL RIGHTS

Article 26. Progressive Development

The States Parties undertake to adopt measures, both internally and through international cooperation, especially those of an economic and technical nature, with a view to achieving progressively, by legislation or other appropriate means, the full realization of the rights implicit in the economic, social, educational, scientific, and cultural standards set forth in the Charter of the Organization of American States as amended by the Protocol of Buenos Aires.

CHAPTER IV—SUSPENSION OF GUARANTEES, INTERPRETATION, AND APPLICATION

Article 27. Suspension of Guarantees

1. In time of war, public danger, or other emergency that threatens the independence or security of a State Party, it may take measures derogating from its obligations under the present Convention to the extent and for the period of time strictly required by the exigencies of the situation, provided that such measures are not inconsistent with its other obligations under international law and do not involve discrimination on the ground of race, color, sex, language, religion, or social origin.

2. The foregoing provision does not authorize any suspension of the following articles: Article 3 (Right to Juridical Personality), Article 4 (Right to Life), Article 5 (Right to Humane Treatment), Article 6 (Freedom from Slavery), Article 9 (Freedom from *Ex Post Facto* Laws), Article 12 (Freedom of Conscience and Religion), Article 17 (Rights of the Family), Article 18 (Right to a Name), Article 19 (Rights of the Child), Article 20 (Right to Nationality), and Article 23 (Right to Participate in Government), or of the judicial guarantees essential for the protection of such rights.

3. Any State Party availing itself of the right of suspension shall immediately inform the other States Parties, through the Secretary General of the Organization of American States, of the provisions the application of which it has suspended, the reasons that gave rise to the suspension, and the date set for the termination of such suspension.

Article 28. Federal Clause

1. Where a State Party is constituted as a federal state, the national government of such State Party shall implement all the provisions of the Convention over whose subject matter it exercises legislative and judicial jurisdiction.

2. With respect to the provisions over whose subject matter the constituent units of the federal state have jurisdiction, the national government shall immediately take suitable measures, in accordance with its constitution and its laws, to the end that the competent authorities of the constituent units may adopt appropriate provisions for the fulfillment of this Convention.

3. Whenever two or more States Parties agree to form a federation or other type of association, they shall take care that the resulting federal or other compact contains the provisions necessary for continuing and rendering effective the standards of this Convention in the new state that is organized.

Article 29. Restrictions Regarding Interpretation

No provision of this Convention shall be interpreted as:

a. permitting any State Party, group, or person to suppress the enjoyment or exercise of the rights and freedoms recognized in this Convention or to restrict them to a greater extent than is provided for herein;

b. restricting the enjoyment or exercise of any right or freedom recognized by virtue of the laws of any State Party or by virtue of another convention to which one of the said states is a party;

c. precluding other rights or guarantees that are inherent in the human personality or derived from representative democracy as a form of government; or

d. excluding or limiting the effect that the American Declaration of the Rights and Duties of Man and other international acts of the same nature may have.

Article 30. Scope of Restrictions

The restrictions that, pursuant to this Convention, may be placed on the enjoyment or exercise of the rights or freedoms recognized herein may not be applied except in accordance with laws enacted for reasons of general interest and in accordance with the purpose for which such restrictions have been established.

Article 31. Recognition of Other Rights

Other rights and freedoms recognized in accordance with the procedures established in Articles 76 and 77 may be included in the system of protection of this Convention.

CHAPTER V—PERSONAL RESPONSIBILITIES

Article 32. Relationship Between Duties and Rights

1. Every person has responsibilities to his family, his community, and mankind.

2. The rights of each person are limited by the rights of others, by the security of all, and by the just demands of the general welfare, in a democratic society.

Appendix 2.
Human Rights Treaties: Regional Ratifiers

This table shows which countries in Latin America and the Caribbean have ratified each of six treaties. Years refer to dates of ratification; blank cells denote nonratification. Ratification imposes a legally binding obligation on states to comply with a treaty's requirements.

Country	American Convention on Human Rights (1969)	ICCPR[a] (1976)	ICESCR[b] (1976)	Convention Against Torture (1984)	Inter-American Convention on Forced Disappearance (1994)	International Criminal Court/Rome Statute (2002)
Antigua and Barbuda				1993		2001
Argentina	1984	1986	1986	1986	1995	2001
Bahamas						
Barbados	1982	1973	1973			2002
Belize		1996		1986		2000
Bolivia	1979	1982	1982	1999	1996	2002
Brazil	1992	1992	1992	1989		2002
Chile	1990	1972	1972	1988		
Colombia	1973	1969	1969	1987	2005	2002
Costa Rica	1970	1968	1968	1993	1996	2001
Cuba		2008[c]	2008[c]	1995		
Dominica	1993	1993	1993			2001
Dominican Republic	1978	1978	1978			2005
Ecuador	1977	1969	1969	1988	2006	2002
El Salvador	1978	1979	1979	1996		
Grenada	1978	1991	1991			
Guatemala	1978	1992	1988	1990	1999	
Guyana	1977	1977	1977	1988		2004

Country	American Convention on Human Rights (1969)	ICCPR[a] (1976)	ICESCR[b] (1976)	Convention Against Torture (1984)	Inter-American Convention on Forced Disappearance (1994)	International Criminal Court/ Rome Statute (2002)
Haiti	1977	1991				
Honduras	1977	1997	1981	1996	2005	2002
Jamaica	1978	1975	1975			
Mexico	1981	1981	1981	1986	2002	2005
Nicaragua	1979	1980	1980	1980		
Panama	1978	1977	1977	1987	1995	2002
Paraguay	1989	1992	1992	1990	1996	2001
Peru	1978	1978	1978	1988	2002	2001
Saint Lucia						
St. Vincent and the Grenadines		1981	1981	2001		2002
St. Kitts and Nevis						2006
Suriname	1987	1976	1976			2008
Trinidad and Tobago	1991 (suspended 1999)	1978	1978			1999
Uruguay	1985	1970	1970	1986	1996	2002
Venezuela	1977	1978	1978	1991	1998	2000

[a] International Covenant on Civil and Political Rights
[b] International Covenant on Economic, Social and Cultural Rights
[c] Signed only

Appendix 3.
Human Development Indicators

A country's human rights practices may reflect the broader economic and social context. The following tables provide key comparative data about select Latin American countries.

Table 1. Basic Country Indicators in Latin America, I

Country	Population (million)	Income level (GNI/capita)	Trade dependence (exports as % of GDP)	Level of debt	Inequality measure
Argentina	39.1	Upper middle ($5,150)	23.3	Severely indebted	40.9
Bolivia	9.3	Lower middle ($1,100)	35.1	Moderately indebted	168.1
Brazil	188.7	Lower middle ($4,730)	14.7	Severely indebted	51.3
Chile	16.5	Upper middle ($6,980)	41.0 (2005)	Moderately indebted	33.0
Colombia	45.6	Lower middle ($2,740)	20.8	Moderately indebted	63.8
Costa Rica	4.4	Upper middle ($4,980)	48.6 (2005)	Less indebted	37.8
Cuba	11.3	Lower middle	---	n/a	---
Dominican Republic	9.6	Lower middle ($2,850)	35.4	Less indebted	28.5
Ecuador	13.4	Lower middle ($2,840)	34.6	Severely indebted	44.9
El Salvador	7.0	Lower middle ($2,540)	26.9	Moderately indebted	57.5

Country	Population (million)	Income level (GNI/capita)	Trade dependence (exports as % of GDP)	Level of debt	Inequality measure
Guatemala	12.9	Lower middle ($2,640)	16.3	Less indebted	48.2
Haiti	8.6	Lower ($480)	12.1 (2004)	Less indebted	71.7
Honduras	7.4	Lower middle (1,200)	41.0	Moderately indebted	34.2
Mexico	104.2	Upper middle ($7,870)	31.9	Less indebted	24.6
Nicaragua	5.2	Lower middle ($1,000)	40.8	Less indebted	15.5
Panama	3.3	Upper middle ($4,890)	73.4	Severely indebted	57.5
Paraguay	6.0	Lower middle ($1,400)	50.1	Moderately indebted	65.4
Peru	28.4	Lower middle ($2,920)	26.1	Severely indebted	30.4
United States	299.0	High ($44,970)	11.2 (2004)	Moderately indebted	15.9
Uruguay	3.3	Upper middle ($5,310)	29.2	Severely indebted	17.9
Venezuela	27.0	Upper middle ($6,070)	38.5	Less indebted	48.3

Population figures, income levels (gross national income per capita), trade dependence, and level of debt are for 2006. World Bank data, http://www.worldbank.org. The inequality measure refers to the ratio of the wealthiest 10 percent of the population to the poorest 10 percent; the larger the measure, the greater the inequality. Inequality figures are for 2005. UN *Human Development Report* 2007/2008 (2008).

Table 2. Basic Country Indicators in Latin America, II

Country	Adult literacy (%)	Urban population (%)	Indigenous population (%)	Gender Empowerment Index	Corruption Perceptions Index	U.S. foreign assistance ($ million)
Argentina	97.2	90.1	3	.728	2.9	3.3
Bolivia	86.7	64.2	55	.500	2.9	223.6
Brazil	88.6	84.2	1	.490	3.5	38.6
Chile	95.7	87.6	5	.519	7.0	2.4
Colombia	92.8	72.7	1	.496	3.8	1,348.5
Costa Rica	94.9	61.7	1	.680	5.0	5.4
Cuba	99.8	75.5	0	.661	4.2	16.9
Dominican Republic	87	66.8	0	.559	3.0	45.7
Ecuador	91	62.8	25	.600	2.1	76.4
El Salvador	80.6	59.8	1	.529	4.0	66.4
Guatemala	69.1	47.2	41	---	2.8	102.2
Haiti	51.9 (2003)	38.8	0	---	1.6	242.8
Honduras	80	46.5	7	.589	2.5	87.1
Mexico	91.6	76.0	30	.589	3.5	238.0
Nicaragua	76.7	59.9	5	---	2.6	246.8
Panama	91.9	70.8	6	.574	3.2	31.2
Paraguay	91.6 (2003)	58.5	5	.428	2.4	53.0

Country	Adult literacy (%)	Urban population (%)	Indigenous population (%)	Gender Empowerment Index	Corruption Perceptions Index	U.S. foreign assistance ($ million)
Peru	87.7	72.6	45	.636	3.5	338.4
Uruguay	96.8	92.0	0	.525	6.7	.2
Venezuela	93	93.4	2 (2005)	.542	2.0	10.0
United States	99.0	80.8	---	.762	7.2	

Figures for adult literacy, urban population, and Gender Empowerment Index from UN Development Programme, *Human Development Report 2007/2008* (Geneva: United Nations, 2008); data for urban population from is 2005. Data for indigenous populations from CIA, *The World Factbook 2007* (Washington, D.C.: Government Printing Office, 2007). The Corruption Perceptions Index measures corruption in the public sector, based on survey data from Transparency International (www.transparency.org), 2007; lower scores indicate greater perceived corruption. Data on U.S. foreign assistance from 2006 and includs both military and economic assistance (economic assistance tends to constitute the bulk of most aid). See U.S. Agency for International Development, *U.S. Overseas Loans and Grants (Greenbook)*, 2008.

Appendix 4.
Select Internship Opportunities:
Human Rights in Latin America

1. Center for Human Rights Legal Action
Location: Washington, D.C., and Guatemala
Who May Apply: Students
Duration: Varies
Application Deadline: Rolling
Stipend: No
Further Information: http://www.caldh.org

2. Chiapas Media Project
Location: Chicago, Ill.
Who May Apply: Students
Duration: Varies
Application Deadline: Rolling
Stipend: No
Further Information: http://www.chiapasmediaproject.org

3. Comisión Mexicana de Defensa y Promoción de los Derechos Humanos
Location: Mexico City, Mexico
Who May Apply: Students
Duration: Varies
Application Deadline: Rolling
Stipend: No
Further Information: http://comisionmexicana.blogspot.com/

4. Council in International Education Exchange (CIEE)
Location: Cities throughout Latin America (human rights certificate and internship in Santiago, Chile)
Who May Apply: Advanced Spanish-language students
Duration: Varies
Application Deadline: Varies
Stipend: No
Further Information: http://ciee.org

5. Foundation for Sustainable Development
Location: Argentina, Bolivia, Ecuador, Nicaragua, Peru
Who May Apply: Undergraduates, graduate students, and young professionals
Duration: Part- or full-time
Application Deadline: Multiple Deadlines
Paid: No
Further Information: http://www.fsdinternational.org/?q=info/applications

6. Guatemala Human Rights Commission-USA
Location: Washington, D.C.
Who May Apply: Students
Duration: Minimum 20 hours/week
Application Deadline: Rolling
Stipend: No
Further Information: www.ghrc-usa.org

7. Human Strategies for Human Rights
Location: Online
Who May Apply: University students
Duration: 6 Months
Application Deadline: Rolling
Stipend: Depends
Further Information: http://web.archive.org/web/20030710030747/www.hshr.org/researchintern.htm

8. Inter-American Commission on Human Rights
Location: Washington, D.C.
Who May Apply: Juniors, seniors, graduate students, and young professionals
Duration: Minimum of two months

Application Deadline: 4 times a year
Paid: No
Further Information: http://www.cidh.org/intership.eng.htm

9. Latin America Working Group
Location: Washington, D.C.
Who May Apply: Students
Duration: No minimum specified
Application Deadline: Rolling
Paid: No
Further Information: http://www.lawg.org/about/Internships.htm

10. MADRE
Location: New York, N.Y.
Who May Apply: Students
Duration: Minimum 15 hours/week, 2-3 months
Application Deadline: 3 times a year
Stipend: Yes
Further Information: http://www.madre.org/programs/pe/intern.html

11. Nicaragua Network
Location: Washington, D.C.
Who May Apply: Students
Duration: Varies
Application Deadline: Rolling
Stipend: No
Further Information: http://www.nicanet.org

12. Peace and Justice Service (Servicio Paz y Justicia, SERPAJ)
Location: Montevideo, Uruguay
Who May Apply: Students
Duration: Varies
Application Deadline: Rolling
Stipend: No
Further Information: http://www.serpaj.org.uy/

13. Rigoberta Menchú Tum Foundation
Location: Mexico City, Mexico

Who May Apply: Students
Duration: Varies
Application Deadline: Rolling
Stipend: No
Further Information: http://www.rigobertamenchu.org

14. Trickle Up
Location: Guatemala and Nicaragua
Who May Apply: Students
Duration: 8-12 weeks, summer
Application Deadline: Beginning in December
Stipend: $500
Further Information: http://www.trickleup.org

15. Trinity-in-Trinidad (Trinity College Study Abroad)
Location: Trinidad and Tobago (human rights organizations)
Who May Apply: Undergraduate students
Duration: 1-2 semesters
Application Deadline: Mid-October for spring; early March for fall
Stipend: Academic credit
Further Information: http://www.trincoll.edu/Academics/StudyAway/
programs-new/trinidad/

16. Washington Office on Latin America—Sally Yudelman Internship
Location: Washington, D.C.
Who May Apply: Undergraduates
Duration: Minimum of 24-32 hours per week
Application Deadline: 3 times a year
Paid: No
Further Information: http://www.wola.org/internships.htm

For a listing of human rights internships in general, see University of
Minnesota Human Rights Program Website (http://hrp.cla.umn.edu/
internships.html) and the Trinity College Human Rights Program Website (http://www.trincoll.edu/depts/humanrights).

Appendix 5.
Suggested Assignments for Instructors

Some version of the following assignments can be used in conjunction with the text. In most cases, students can draw on the resources listed at the end of each chapter to complete the assignment. Instructors interested in further details should contact the author.

1. **Human Rights Conditions**. Early in the semester, groups of students are assigned a country or small subset of countries. After reviewing the relevant entries from an annual human rights report (e.g., Amnesty International), student groups summarize existing conditions for their assigned countries and identify what they find most striking. The objective of this in-class exercise is to demonstrate the contemporary relevance of human rights violations, illustrating the real-world conditions at stake when studying human rights.

2. **Testimonial Literature**. Students select a first-person human rights account to read. Chapters 2 and 5, in particular, offer numerous examples. In a concise paper or presentation, they summarize the work; discuss how issues raised in the course (theoretical and case-specific) help to place the work in its proper context; and identify the book's lessons for the study of human rights while revealing their own reactions to the text.

3. **Newspaper Journal**. For part of the semester, students read newspapers from around the world. They summarize an article per week and, drawing on course material, discuss the major human rights implications. Events surveyed do not have to be explicitly related to human rights, since

a partial goal of the exercise is for students to draw connections between otherwise disparate issues. Chapter 1 provides relevant databases for accessing the region's newspapers. If possible, students should be encouraged to read foreign-language newspapers.

4. **Surveying Organizations**. Students choose one or more human rights organizations, either NGOs (international or domestic) or regional human rights bodies. Part II identifies possible organizations. Students visit the organization's website and prepare an overview: its purpose, history, activities, as well as apparent strengths and weaknesses. Ideally, in technologically equipped classrooms, students show images from the organization's website.

5. **Film Critique**. After viewing at least two films listed in the book, students write a short comparative essay. The emphasis should be on identifying the key human rights themes raised in the film and discussing the student's reactions. (Note that in-class film clips can be shown very effectively throughout this course.)

6. **Analytical Review**. Students select an analytical reading addressing either human rights violations or reforms. They summarize the argument and assess critically its substantive strengths and weaknesses. The assignment can be part of a take-home essay exam. Chapters 3 and 6, in particular, offer several relevant readings.

7. **Research Paper**. Topics can focus on the sources of human rights violations, the causes of human rights reform, and the challenges of truth and justice. Students are encouraged to undertake comparative analysis—of countries, time periods, or human rights issues.

8. **Research Design**. Rather than write a full research paper, students prepare a brief research proposal. They provide a central research question, a brief statement of its significance, a strategy for answering the question (e.g., cases, time periods), a tentative outline, and a working bibliography. Students are given an in-class opportunity to peer review research designs.

9. **In-Class Debates**. Student groups are assigned different sides of controversial questions and asked to defend their assigned position. A gen-

eral, "out-of-character" discussion follows the debate. The exercise works especially well with debates about the origins of human rights abuse (e.g., human nature versus structural conditions) or the desirability of truth commissions versus prosecution.

10. **Role Playing**. Students are assigned different roles, such as perpetrator, victim, human rights activist, prosecutor, etc. They are presented with a brief, hypothetical scenario and asked to respond according to their assigned actor's putative interests. Following role playing, students discuss any lessons learned, identifying the complex motives and strategic dilemmas facing actors. Role playing complements especially well the issues raised in Chapter 7.

11. **Foreign Policy Essays**. Students write an "op-ed" short essay, taking a foreign policy position on a contemporary human rights issue of their choice in Latin America. The goal is to make a clear and succinct argument about what a foreign government or international organization *should* do in response to a human rights problem. Topics can be general or specific depending on a student's interests. Students are encouraged to read op-ed pieces in major newspapers to replicate tone and style.

12. **Exploring Data Sources**. Students are asked to visit a human rights database or truth commission report listed in the book. They present their reactions, including what they found interesting or problematic and how the data could be used to conduct human rights research. More specific exercises can be designed to probe the value and limits of human rights data.

Index

Note: Page numbers in *italics* indicate figures; those with a *t* indicate tables.

abortion laws, 64, 79n9
Abuelas de Plaza de Mayo (Grandmothers of the Plaza de Mayo), 112–13, 166
accountability, 159–83, 203
Acteal massacre (Mexico), 41
AIDS, 64, 86
Alfonsín, Raúl, 138
Alianza Anticomunista Argentina (AAA), 32
Alien Tort Claims Act (U.S.), 178–79
Allende, Salvador, 29, 66, 174
Amazon, indigenous peoples of, 117–19
American Convention on Human Rights (Pact of San José), 6, 83, 89t, 93, 209–21, 224–25t
American Declaration on the Rights and Duties of Man, 10, 89t
Amnesty International, 3, 12, 123, 140, 204; Berenson trial and, 96; femicide and, 121; Nobel Peace Prize for, 106; Pinochet trial and, 173, 174; transnational networks and, 103
amnesty laws, 172–73, 176, 178–80, 182
Andean Commission of Jurists. *See* Comisión Andina de Juristas
animosity assumption, 53
anticommunism, 53, 60–62, 69; School of the Americas and, 70–71. *See also* Cold War
anti-Semitism, 114

antiterrorism, 62–63, 69, 71. *See also* terrorism
Arbenz, Jacobo, 35
Arellano Stark, Sergio, 29–30
Arendt, Hannah, 55
Argentina, 27, 28t, 44t, 71; amnesty laws of, 172, 180; anti-Semitism in, 114; Catholic Church in, 114–15; compensation of victims in, 166; demographics of, 227t, 229t; dirty war of, 32–34, 46, 69, 85, 105, 172; human rights groups in, *111*, 114, 161; human rights reforms in, 136–38, *138*; human rights treaties of, 224t; Madres de Plaza de Mayo and, 105, *112*; memoral to victims in, 169–70; Operation Condor in, 67–68; organized labor in, 63; paramilitary groups in, 58; sexual-orientation laws of, 109; trials in, 171–72; truth commission of, 162t, 165–66; U.S. sanctions against, 125t. *See also* disappearances
Aristide, Jean-Bertrand, 42–44, 150
arpilleras (fabric artwork), 140
art, protest and, 139–40
Atlacatl Battalion, 37
Autodefensas Unidas de Colombia (AUC), 40
Aylwin, Patricio, 176

Bachelet, Michelle, 140, 199–201
Barrios Altos massacre, Peru, 92, 176
Belize, 119–20, 224t
Ben and Jerry's (corporation), 118
Benetech Website, 145

Berenson, Lori, 96

Body Shop (corporation), 118

Bolívar, Simón, 8

Bolivia, 59, 71, 119; demographics of, 227t, 229t; femicide in, 41; human rights treaties of, 224t; incidence of human rights violations in, 28t; Morales and, 65, 146–47, 199, 201; Operation Condor in, 67–68; sexual-orientation laws of, 109; truth commission of, 162t; U.S. sanctions against, 125t

boomerang effect, 104

Bordaberry, Juan María, 181

Brazil, 27, 28t, 32, 44t, 110, 189–91; Catholic Church in, 115; compensation of victims in, 167; Da Silva and, 199; death squads of, 38, *39*; demographics of, 227t, 229t; human rights groups in, *111*, 161; human rights reforms in, 139, 189; human rights treaties of, 224t; Operation Condor in, 67–68; sexual-orientation laws of, 109; street children of, 34, 38, *39*; U.S. sanctions against, 125t

Brodsky, Marcelo, 1, 170

Buergenthal, Thomas, 94, 95

Bureau of Democracy, Human Rights and Labor. *See* Bureau of Human Rights

Bureau of Human Rights and Humanitarian Affairs, U.S. State Department, 123

Bush, George H. W., 71

Bush, George W., 146, 199, 200

Cabello, Winston, 179

Cambodia, 35

Canada, 122, 150

capital punishment, 89t, 210–11. *See also* executions

Carandiru massacre, Brazil, 38

"caravan of death," 30

Cardoso, Fernando Henrique, 203–4

CARE (organization), 108

Caribbean School, United States, 70

Cartagena Declaration on Refugees, 89t

Carter, Jimmy, 136–37

Castro, Fidel, 53, 70, 149, 198–200

Castro, Raúl, 198

Center for Human Rights Legal Action, 231

Center for the Promotion of Human Rights and Frontier Studies (Centro de Estudios Fronterizos y de Promoción de los Derechos Humanos, CEFPRODHAC), 144

Central Intelligence Agency (CIA), 35; Operation Condor and, 68; torture manuals of, 72–73, 76

Chamorro, Violeta, 141

Chávez, Hugo, 66, 147–48, 199, 200

Chiapas Media Project, 145, 231

Chiapas, Mexico, 145, 196; Zapatistas of, 8, 40–41, 58, 116–17, *117*, 152–53

Chihuahua, Mexico, 121

children, 34, 38, *39*, 86; Argentina's dirty war and, 33–34; in prison, 38; rights of, 108, 216–17; sexual abuse of, 34, 87, 125

Chile, 27, 28t, 44t, 53, 58, 107, 161; abortion laws of, 64; amnesty laws of, 173, 176, 179, 182; Bachelet and, 140, 199–201; Catholic Church in, 114; compensation of victims in, 166, 167; demographics of, 227t, 229t; disappearances in, 21; Haiti and, 150; human rights groups in, *111*, 113–14; human rights reforms in, 136–38, *138*, 189; human rights treaties of, 224t; memorials to victims in, 168–69; Operation Condor in, 67–68; School of the Americas and, 71; truth commission of, 162t, 165; U.S. intervention in, 66; U.S. sanctions against, 125t; Villa Grimaldi in, 168–69, 177, 178t, 200. *See also* Pinochet, Augusto

Chile Documentation Project, 68

Clinton, Bill, 123, 146, 193

Cold War, 61–62, 69, 103, 123, 141, 192. *See also* anticommunism

Colina Group, Peru, 93

Colombia, 56, 124, 145–46, 153; antiterrorism laws in, 197–98; demographics of, 227t, 229t; displaced people in, 86, 193; femicide in, 41; human rights groups in, *111*; human rights treaties of, 224t; human rights violations in, 27, 28t, 44t, 110; indigenous groups in, 119;

paramilitary groups in, 39–40, 75, 193; street children of, 34; U.S. sanctions against, 125t
colonialism, 24–25, 64
Comisión Andina de Juristas (CAJ), 107
Comisión Mexicana de Defensa y Promoción de los Derechos Humanos, 231
Committee of Relatives of the Detained-Disappeared, 113
communism. See anticommunism
compensation, victim, 166–69, 181–82, 214
Constitution: Chilean, 137, 176; Mexican, 8–9; United States, 8
Convention against Torture and Other Forms of Cruel, Inhuman or Degrading Treatment or Punishment (UN), 22–23
Convention on the Rights of Persons with Disabilities (UN), 135
Correa, Rafael, 199
Corruption Perceptions Index (Transparency International), 229–30t
Costa Rica, 71, 93; demographics of, 227t, 229t; human rights treaties of, 224t; Pact of San José and, 209–21
Council in International Education Exchange (CIEE), 232
crimes against humanity, 96, 172–73, 176–79, 181
cross-national dynamics, 26, 26–28, 28t
Cuba, 53, 70, 110, 148–50, 153; during Cold War, 61; demographics of, 227t, 229t; Guantánamo Naval Base in, 196; human rights groups in, 111; human rights treaties of, 224t; incidence of human rights violations in, 28t; U.S. sanctions against, 124, 125t, 149–50
"cyberprotests," 41, 116–17. See also technology

Damas de Blanco (Cuba), 149
Darfur, 44, 146
Da Silva, Luiz Inácio "Lula," 199
death penalty, 89t, 210–11
death squads: Argentine, 32; Brazilian, 38, 39; Guatemalan, 34–36, 35, 64;

Haitian, 43; Honduran, 69; Peruvian, 92–93
Declaration for the Protection of All Persons from Enforced Disappearance (UN), 113
Declaration in Defense of Human Rights (Inter-American Conference), 10
Declaration on the Rights of Indigenous Peoples (UN), 119–20
Declaration on the Rights of Man and Citizen (France), 8
democratization, 57–58, 160–61, 170, 198–205; human rights reforms and, 136–39; human rights trials and, 179–80; police reforms and, 190–91
Díaz, Ricardo, 59
disabilities, persons with, 89t, 135, 144–45
disappearances (desaparecidos), 21–24, 137; amnesty laws for, 172–73, 176; in Argentina's dirty war, 32–34, 46, 85; of artists, 139–40; definitions of, 23; of human rights activists, 110–11; incidence of, 26, 26–28, 28t; levels of, 28t; memorials to, 168–70, 177; organizations for, 105, 112, 112–14; truth commissions on, 162–63t, 164–65
discrimination. See ideologies, exclusionary
domestic violence, 65
Dominican Republic, 64; abortion laws in, 79n9; demographics of, 227t, 229t; human rights treaties of, 224t; sexual trafficking in, 121–22; UN peacekeepers in, 87
Dorfman, Ariel, 192
drug trafficking, 27, 39–40, 59, 121, 192–93; aerial herbicides and, 66, 146–47, 193; Shining Path and, 37; war on terror and, 193–95
Due Obedience Law. See Ley de Obediencia Debida
Duvalier, François, 42, 150
Duvalier, Jean-Claude, 42, 150

Ecuador, 199; demographics of, 227t, 229t; human rights treaties of, 224t; indigenous groups in, 119; sexual-orientation

Ecuador (continued)
laws of, 109; truth commissions of, 163t;
U.S. foreign aid to, 97, 229t
Ejército de Liberación Nacional (ELN),
39–40
Ejército Revolucionario del Pueblo (ERP),
58
Ejército Zapatista de Liberación Nacional
(EZLN). *See* Zapatistas
El Mozote massacre (El Salvador), 37, 69
El Salvador, 27, 28t, 37, 44t, 56, 69, 189–
90; abortion laws in, 64; demographics
of, 227t, 229t; femicide in, 41; human
rights groups in, *111*, 114; human rights
treaties of, 224t; protest singers in,
140; Protocol of San Salvador and, 89t;
School of the Americas and, 71; street
children of, 34; truth commission of,
162t, 165; UN peacekeepers in, 141; UN
Truth Commission for, 95; U.S. sanctions against, 125t
environmentalism, 117–19
ethnicity, 23, 53–54, 64. *See also* race
European Union, 122, 149, 180
events-based approach, 24
exclusionary ideologies. *See* ideologies
executions, extrajudicial, 22–24, *26*,
26–28, 28t, 44, 87. *See also* capital
punishment

Falkland Islands, 138
Farabundo Martí National Liberation Front
(Frente Farabundo Martí para la Liber-
ación Nacional, FMLN), 141
FARC. *See* Fuerzas Armadas Revolucionar-
ias de Colombia
Federal Bureau of Investigation (FBI), 68
Federation of Associations for Rela-
tives of the Detained-Disappeared
(FEDEFAM), 113
Federation of Women with Different Ca-
pacities, 135
femicide, 41–43, *43*, 65, 91, 107, 110,
120–21, 203; documentation of, 144
feminism. *See* women's rights
Fernández Larios, Armando, 179

Filártiga v. Peña-Irala (U.S. federal court), 179
Final Stop Law. *See* Ley de Punto Final
FMLN (Frente Farabundo Martí para la
Liberación Nacional). *See* Farabundo
Martí National Liberation Front
Fonda, Jane, 121
foreign aid programs (U.S.), 97, 196–98,
197, 229–30t
forensic science, 165–66
Foundation for Sustainable Development, 232
Fox, Vicente, 116
France, 122; Operation Condor and, 67, 180
Fraser Subcommittee, U.S. House of Repre-
sentatives, 123
Fray Bartolomé de las Casas Center for
Human Rights, 8
Fuentes Alarcón, Jorge Isaac, 68
Fuerzas Armadas Revolucionarias de Co-
lombia (FARC), 39–40, 146, 193
Fujimori, Alberto, 36–37, 181
Fundación Solidez (Nicaragua), 135

gangs, 87, 107, 121, 146
Garcés, Joan, 174
Garzón, Baltasar, 174
Gender Empowerment Index (UN), 229–30t
Geneva Conventions, 56
globalization, 41, 63, 153; resistance to,
115–22; transnational advocacy networks and, 106. *See also* neoliberalism
Global Response (organization), 119
global system of human rights governance,
83–99
Guantánamo Naval Base (Cuba), 196
Guatemala, 27, 28t, 44t, 56–58, 109–10, 142;
death squads of, 34–36, *35*, 64; demographics of, 228t, 229t; femicide in, 41,
121; human rights groups in, *111*; human
rights reforms in, 132, 188–90; human
rights treaties of, 224t; police files of, 171;
prostitution in, 34; reparations for victims
in, 169, 181–82; truth commission of,
162t, 165, 170; U.S. intervention in, 66;
U.S. sanctions against, 125t, 197
Guatemala Human Rights Commission,
232

Guervera, Ernesto "Che," 41
Guzmán, Juan, 175–76

Haiti, 42–44, 56–57, 150–51, 153;
    demographics of, 228t, 229t; human
    rights groups in, *111*, 151; human rights
    treaties of, 225t; human rights viola-
    tions in, 27, 28t, 44t, 189–90; refugees
    from, 124; riots in, *59*, 59–60, 63; truth
    commission of, 163t; UN peacekeep-
    ers in, 87; U.S. sanctions against, 125t;
    vigilante justice in, 160, 181
Harkin Amendment to Foreign Assistance
    Act (U.S.), 123
Hayak, Salma, 121
health issues in workplace, 120. *See also*
    public health services
HIV disease. *See* AIDS
Holocaust, 24, 55
homosexuality. *See* sexual orientation
Honduras, 27, 28t, 44t, 57; abortion laws
    in, 64; compensation of victims in,
    168; death squads in, 69; demographics
    of, 228t, 229t; femicide in, 41; human
    rights activists in, 113; human rights
    treaties of, 225t; military coup in, 142,
    204; street children of, 34; truth com-
    mission of, 162t, 165; U.S. policies to,
    142; Velásquez Rodríguez case and,
    94–95, 113, 179–80
human development indicators, 227t–230t
Fray Bartolomé de las Casas Human Rights
    Center, 8
Human Rights Commission, 85
Human Rights Council, 85
Human Rights Data Analysis Group, 171
Human Rights Dataset (Cingranelli-Rich-
    ards), *26*
Human Rights First, 107
human rights reforms, 132–54, 188–91;
    models of, 133–34; technology for,
    41, 112, 115–17, 143–45, 171; treaties
    on, 224t–225t; war on terror and,
    196–98
human rights treaties, 89t, 195, 224t–25t.
    See also specific treaties

human rights violations, 55–65; causes of,
    52–76, *74*; compensation for, 166–68,
    181–82, 214; crimes against humanity
    and, 96, 172–73, 176–79, 181; decision-
    making process in, 55–60; global gover-
    nance of, 83–99; impunity for, 65, 159,
    180–83, 186n1; Kirkpatrick Doctrine
    and, 69; level of, 24, *26*, 26–28, 28t;
    perceived security threats and, 58–63,
    59; types of, 22–24
Human Rights Watch, 107, 174
Human Strategies for Human Rights, 232

IACHR. *See* Inter-American Commission
    on Human Rights
ideologies, 124; economic, 63; exclusionary,
    53, 55, 60–65, 73–74, *74*, 202; national
    security and, 61–62, 69, 203; School of
    the Americas and, 69–71, *70*. *See also*
    neoliberalism
immunity from prosecution, 176, 186n1
impunity, 65, 159, 180–83, 186n1
indigenous peoples, 59, 89t, 117–20; demo-
    graphics of, 229–30t; health care among,
    64; political groups of, 119, 146–47, *147*,
    205; U.S. policies and, 66, 193
inequality measure, 227–28t
Inter-American Commission on Human
    Rights (IACHR), 83, 88–93, 98, 110,
    121, 168; internships with, 232–33
Inter-American Conference, 10
Inter-American Convention on Forced Dis-
    appearance, 23, 89t, 224t–225t
Inter-American Convention on Terrorism, 195
Inter-American Convention on the Elimina-
    tion of All Forms of Discrimination
    against Persons with Disabilities, 89t
Inter-American Convention on the Preven-
    tion, Punishment, and Eradication of
    Violence against Women, 89t
Inter-American Convention to Prevent and
    Punish Torture, 89t, 224t–225t
Inter-American Court of Human Rights,
    83, 93–96, 98, *164*, 167, 182
Inter-American Defense College, 70
Inter-American Democratic Charter, 12

Inter-American Treaty of Reciprocal Assistance, 195
International Commission of Jurists, 107
International Committee of the Red Cross, 56, 190
International Court of Justice, 96
International Covenant on Civil and Political Rights, 4–6, 84, 224t–225t
International Covenant on Economic, Social and Cultural Rights, 4–6, 224t–225t
International Criminal Court (ICC), 84, 88, 96–98, 181, 224t–225t
International Federation for Human Rights, 108
international law, 94–96, 119, 172–73, 176–80, 219
International Monetary Fund (IMF), 63, 66, 116
international nongovernmental organizations. *See* nongovernmental organizations
Internet technology, 41, 112, 115–17, 143–44
internships, 231–34
Islamists, 195. *See also* September 11 attacks
Italy, Operation Condor and, 67, 180

Jackson-Vanik Amendment to Trade Act (U.S.), 123
Jamaica, 44t, 189–90; human rights treaties of, 225t
Jara, Victor, 139
Juárez, Mexico, 140; human rights groups in, 91, 103, 107, 113; murdered women of, 41–43, *43*, 110, 120–21

kidnapping, 87, 195. *See also* disappearances
Kirchner, Néstor, 105
Kirkpatrick Doctrine, 68–69, 141
Kissinger, Henry, 67
Klein, Naomi, 205

La Cantuta massacre, Peru, 93
Lagos, Ricardo, 199–200
Las Casas, Bartolomé de, 6–9
Latin America Ground School, 70

Latin America Working Group, 233
Lawyers Committee for Human Rights, 107
Leahy, Patrick, 146, 197
Lennon, John, 140
Ley de Obediencia Debida (Due Obedience Law, Argentina), 172
Ley de Punto Final (Final Stop Law, Argentina), 172
life imprisonment, 172, 180
literacy levels, 229–30t
local activists, 108–15; globalization protests by, 115–22
López Grijalba, Juan Evangelista, 179–80
Lopez, Jennifer, 103, 121

machismo, 54, 109
Mack, Myrna, 167
MADRE (organization), 233
Madres de Plaza de Mayo (Mothers of the Plaza de Mayo, 105, *112*, 112–13, 149, 166
maquiladoras, 41–43, 120–21
Marcos, Subcomandante, 41, 116–17, *117*
Mead, Margaret, 153–54
memorials, public, 168–70, 177
Menchú, Rigoberta, 142, 233. *See also* Rigoberta Menchú Tum Foundation
Mendes, Chico, 38
Menem, Carlos, 172
mental illness, 144–45
Merida Initiative, 194
mestizos, 64
Mexico, 91, 145, 161, 180, 196; demographics of, 228t, 229t; dirty war of, 40–43, *43*; human rights groups in, 103, 107, *111*; human rights treaties of, 225t; human rights violations in, 27, 28t, 44t, 109, 189–90; *maquiladoras* of, 41–43, 120–21; Merida Initiative in, 194; sexual-orientation laws of, 109; Tlatelolco massacre in, 40, 152, 182; Zapatistas of, 8, 40–41, 58, 116–17, *117*, 152–53
Military Commissions Act, 196
Montesa, Magdalena, 1
Montoneros, 32, 58
Morales, Evo, 65, 146–47, 199, 201
Moreno-Ocampo, Luis, 97

NAFTA. *See* North American Free Trade Agreement

National Liberation Army. *See* Ejército de Liberación Nacional (ELN)

national security doctrines, 61–62, 69, 203. *See also* security threats

neoliberalism, 60–63, 69, 74, *147*, 197; definitions of, 115–16; NAFTA and, 40–41, 116–17; poverty and, 66–67, 115, 202. *See also* globalization

Neruda, Pablo, 139

Netherlands, 121, 122

networking, politics of, 124–27

NGOs. *See* nongovernmental organizations

Nicaragua, 141–42; abortion laws in, 64; demographics of, 228t, 229t; disability rights in, 135; human rights treaties of, 225t; human rights violations in, 27, 28t, 44t; indigenous groups in, 119; Sandinista regime in, 61; U.S. sanctions against, 125t

Nicaragua Network, 233

"Night of the Pencils," 33–34

9/11. *See* September 11 attacks

nongovernmental organizations (NGOs), 45, 106–8, 135; documentation by, 164–65; environmentalism and, 119; internships with, 231–34; open source software of, 144. *See also specific groups*

Noriega, Manuel, 142–43

North American Free Trade Agreement (NAFTA), 40–41, 116–17

*Nuestras Hijas de Regreso a Casa (May Our Daughters Return Home), 113

Obama, Barack, 149, 200

Odio Benito, Elizabeth, 97

One World Action, 135

Operation Condor, 67–68, 180

Operation Rescue (Operación Rescate), 37

Organization of American States (OAS), 10, 150, 195; IACHR and, 89–92, *92*, 94

Pact of San José (Costa Rica). *See* American Convention on Human Rights

Palmer, Paula, 120

Panama, 228t, 229t; human rights treaties of, 225t; Operation Condor and, 68; School of the Americas and, 70–71; truth commission of, 163t; U.S. invasion of, 142–43; U.S. sanctions against, 125t

Paraguay, 177, 179, 182; Catholic Church in, 114; demographics of, 228t, 229t; disability rights in, 144–45; human rights treaties of, 225t; level of violations in, 27, 28t; Museum of Memory in, 177; Operation Condor in, 67–68; truth commission of, 163t; U.S. sanctions against, 125t

paramilitary groups, 23, 58; Colombian, 39–40, 75, 193; Mexican, 41; Peruvian, 37

Paterson, Kent, 43

Patriot Act, U.S., 62–63

Peace and Justice Service. *See* Servicio Paz y Justicia

Peréz Rojas, Carlos, 145

Perón, Isabel, 32

Perón, Juan, 32

personal integrity rights. *See* physical integrity rights

Peru, 56, 64; antiterrorism laws in, 197–98; demographics of, 228t, 230t; femicide in, 41; Fujimori extradition by, 181; human rights groups in, *111*; human rights treaties of, 225t; human rights violations in, 27, 28t, 44t, *164*, 176; sexual-orientation laws of, 109; Shining Path in, 36–37, 58, 92–93; truth commission of, 163t, 165; Túpac Amaru Revolutionary Movement in, 96; U.S. foreign aid to, 97, 230t; U.S. sanctions against, 125t

Phinney, Alison, 34

physical integrity rights, 22–24. *See also* human rights violations

Physicians for Human Rights, 108

Pinochet, Augusto, 53, 107, 113; constitutional reforms of, 137; coup by, *29*, 29–31, 174, 192; electoral defeat of, *138*; memorials to victims of, 168–69; trial of, 159, 173–78, 178t, 180–82

Plan Mexico, 194

police brutality, 59, 160, 189–91, 203

political prisoners, 22–24; incidence of, *26*, 26–28, 28t; overall trend in, 27, 28t; Uruguayan, 46, 132

Popular Revolutionary Army. *See* Ejército Revolucionario del Pueblo

Portugal, 67

poverty, 117; in Cuba, 149; democratization and, 198, 202–3; health issues and, 86; human rights violations and, 56–57; neoliberalism and, 66–67, 115, 202

prostitution, 121–22, 203, 211; children and, 34, 87, 125; femicide and, 41–43, *43*, 121

Protocol of San Salvador, 89t

Protocol to Abolish the Death Penalty, 89t

public health services, 64, 86, 108; psychiatric hospitals and, 145; in workplace, 120

Puerto Rico, 151–52, *152*

race, 23; colonialism and, 24–25, 64; cultural stereotypes and, 54; exclusionary ideologies and, 53, 55, 60–61, 63–64, 73–74, *74*, 202; immigrantion policies and, 54, 124; U.S. immigration policies and, 124

Reagan, Ronald, 138; Guatemala and, 142; Kirkpatrick Doctrine and, 69, 141; Sandinistas and, 61

Red Cross. *See* International Committee of the Red Cross

Reebok Human Rights Award, 145

Regional Disability Rights Program, 135

religion, 23, 214–15; anticommunism and, 61–62; human rights groups and, 114–15

rendition policies, 75

reparations, victim, 166–69, 181–82, 214

Revolutionary Armed Forces of Colombia. *See* Fuerzas Armadas Revolucionarias de Colombia (FARC)

Reynosa, Mexico, 144

Rigoberta Menchú Tum Foundation, 233–34

Ríos Montt, Efraín, 36, 58, 181–82

Rio Treaty (1947), 195

Romero, Oscar, 69, 114

Rome Statute. *See* International Criminal Court

Roosevelt, Eleanor, 10

Rwanda, 44

Santa Cruz, Hernán, *111*

Santayana, George, 187

Save the Children (organization), 108

School of the Americas (SOA), 69–71, *70*

Scilingo, Adolfo, 180

security threats, 58–63, *59*, 69, *74*, 74–75, 203

Sendero Luminoso. *See* Shining Path

September 11 attacks, 13–14, 192–96; U.S. Patriot Act and, 62–63. *See also* terrorism

Servicio Paz y Justicia (SERPAJ), 114, 233

sexism. *See* women's rights

sexual exploitation, 34

sexual orientation, 53; imprisonment for, 23; legislation on, 64, 109; local activists and, 108, 109; as threat to national identity, 64

sexual trafficking, 34, 121–22, 203, 211. *See also* prostitution

Shining Path (Sendero Luminoso), 36–37, 58, 92–93. *See also* Peru

Snow, Clyde, 166

software, documentation, 144, 171

solitary confinement, 23

South Africa, 162

Spain, 7–8, 180; human rights policies of, 122; Operation Condor and, 67; Pinochet trial in, 173–74

Straw, Jack, 174

Stroessner, Alfredo, 177, 182

Sudan, 44, 146

sweatshops, 120–22

Sweden, 122, 180

TANs. *See* transnational advocacy netorks

technology, for activists, 41, 112, 115–17, 143–45, 171

terrorism, 13, 61, 73–76, 192–98, *194*, *197*;

definitions of, 62; drug financing of, 193–94; social protest seen as, 59–60; U.S. Patriot Act and, 62–63. *See also* antiterrorism

Timerman, Jacobo, 114–15

Tlatelolco massacre, 40, 152, 182

torture, 85–86, 108; CIA manuals for, 72–73, 76; definitions of, 22–23; incidence of, *26*, 26–28, 28t; jargon for, 33; rendition policies for, 75; treaties on, 22–23, 89t, 224t–225t; types of, 23, 38

Torture Victims Protection Act (U.S.), 179

transnational advocacy netorks (TANs), 102–6, 124–27, 152–54; conferences of, 108; definition of, 103; for persons with disabilities, 135

Transparency International, 230n

Trickle Up (organization), 234

Trinidad and Tobago, 97, 225t, 234

Triple A. *See* Alianza Anticomunista Argentina

truth commissions, 161–68, 162t–163t, 182–83; public memorials and, 168–70, 177

Túpac Amaru Revolutionary Movement (Movimiento Revolucionario Túpac Amaru, MRTA, Peru), 96

Tupamaros, 36

Tutela Legal (organization), 114

UN High Commissioner for Human Rights, 85

UN High Commission for Refugees, 86–87

UNICEF, 86

United Nations, 9–12, *11*; on disability rights, 135; on disappeared persons, 113; Human Rights Committee of, 84–85; human rights governance by, 83–87; NGOs and, 106; peacekeeping missions of, 87, 141, 150; on rights of indigenous peoples, 119–20

United Self-Defense Forces of Colombia. *See* Autodefensas Unidas de Colombia

United States, 228t, 230t; Caribbean School of, 70; disability rights in, 135; foreign aid programs of, 196–98, *197*, 229–30t; human rights policies of, 122–24, 125t; human rights trials in, 178–80; Interna-

tional Criminal Court and, 97; Kirkpatrick Doctrine of, 68–69; Latin American policies of, 65–71; rendition policies of, 75; School of the Americas and, 69–71, *70*; U.S. Patriot Act of, 62–63

Universal Declaration of Human Rights, 4–6, 5t, 10, 11, 89

universal jurisdiction, 173

Uruguay, 33, 181; amnesty laws of, 182; demographics of, 228t, 230t; human rights groups in, *111*; human rights reforms in, 139, 189, *194*; human rights treaties of, 225t; level of violations in, 27, 28t; Memorial of Disappeared and Detained Citizens in, 168; Operation Condor in, 67–68; political prisoners of, 46, 132; sexual-orientation laws of, 109; truth commission of, 161, 163t; U.S. foreign aid to, 97, 230t; U.S. sanctions against, 125t

U.S. Patriot Act, 62–63

Velásquez Rodríguez, Angel Manfredo, 94, 95, 113, 179–80

Venezuela, 71, 110, 147–48, 199, 225t; demographics of, 228t, 230t; disability rights in, 135; human rights groups in, *111*; indigenous groups in, 119; level of violations in, 27, 28t; sexual-orientation laws of, 109; U.S. intervention in, 66

Vicaría de Solidaridad (organization), 114

Videla, Jorge, 172

video projects, 144–45

Vieques Naval Base (Puerto Rico), 151–52, *152*

Villa Grimaldi (Chile), 168–69, 177, 178t, 200

violations. *See* human rights violations

Washington Consensus, 198

Washington Office on Latin America (WOLA), 107, 234

Weber, Max, 58

Wernich, Christian von, 115

Western Hemisphere Institute for Security Cooperation, 71

Witness (organization), 144–45

women's rights, 60–61, 64–65; abortion
    laws and, 64, 79n9; in Colombia, 110;
    disabilities and, 135; domestic violence
    and, 65; Gender Empowerment Index
    and, 229–30t; sweatshops and, 120–22
World Bank, 63, 66, 116, 227–28t; indig-
    enous groups and, 118–19
World Council of Churches, 114
World Court. *See* International Court of
    Justice

World Health Organization (WHO), 86
World Organization Against Torture, 108

Yudelman Internship, 234

Zapatistas, 8, 40–41, 58, 116–17, *117*,
    152–53. *See also* Mexico